IFIP Advances in Information and Communication Technology

644

IFIP – The International Federation for Information Processing

IFIP was founded in 1960 under the auspices of UNESCO, following the first World Computer Congress held in Paris the previous year. A federation for societies working in information processing, IFIP's aim is two-fold: to support information processing in the countries of its members and to encourage technology transfer to developing nations. As its mission statement clearly states:

> IFIP is the global non-profit federation of societies of ICT professionals that aims at achieving a worldwide professional and socially responsible development and application of information and communication technologies.

IFIP is a non-profit-making organization, run almost solely by 2500 volunteers. It operates through a number of technical committees and working groups, which organize events and publications. IFIP's events range from large international open conferences to working conferences and local seminars.

The flagship event is the IFIP World Computer Congress, at which both invited and contributed papers are presented. Contributed papers are rigorously refereed and the rejection rate is high.

As with the Congress, participation in the open conferences is open to all and papers may be invited or submitted. Again, submitted papers are stringently refereed.

The working conferences are structured differently. They are usually run by a working group and attendance is generally smaller and occasionally by invitation only. Their purpose is to create an atmosphere conducive to innovation and development. Refereeing is also rigorous and papers are subjected to extensive group discussion.

Publications arising from IFIP events vary. The papers presented at the IFIP World Computer Congress and at open conferences are published as conference proceedings, while the results of the working conferences are often published as collections of selected and edited papers.

IFIP distinguishes three types of institutional membership: Country Representative Members, Members at Large, and Associate Members. The type of organization that can apply for membership is a wide variety and includes national or international societies of individual computer scientists/ICT professionals, associations or federations of such societies, government institutions/government related organizations, national or international research institutes or consortia, universities, academies of sciences, companies, national or international associations or federations of companies.

More information about this series at https://link.springer.com/bookseries/6102

Michael Friedewald · Stephan Krenn ·
Ina Schiering · Stefan Schiffner (Eds.)

Privacy and Identity Management

Between Data Protection and Security

16th IFIP WG 9.2, 9.6/11.7, 11.6/SIG 9.2.2
International Summer School, Privacy and Identity 2021
Virtual Event, August 16–20, 2021
Revised Selected Papers

 Springer

Editors
Michael Friedewald ⓘ
Fraunhofer ISI
Karlsruhe, Germany

Stephan Krenn ⓘ
AIT Austrian Institute of Technology
Vienna, Austria

Ina Schiering ⓘ
Ostfalia University of Applied Sciences
Wolfenbüttel, Germany

Stefan Schiffner ⓘ
University of Münster
Münster, Germany

ISSN 1868-4238   ISSN 1868-422X (electronic)
IFIP Advances in Information and Communication Technology
ISBN 978-3-030-99102-9   ISBN 978-3-030-99100-5 (eBook)
https://doi.org/10.1007/978-3-030-99100-5

This Springer imprint is published by the registered company Springer Nature Switzerland AG
The registered company address is: Gewerbestrasse 11, 6330 Cham, Switzerland

Preface

This volume contains the proceedings of the 16th IFIP Summer School on Privacy and Identity Management, which took place during August 16–20, 2021. While planned to be held in Esch-sur-Alzette, Luxembourg, the summer school finally had to be held as a fully virtual event, due to the ongoing COVID-19 pandemic and associated uncertainties.

The 16th IFIP Summer School was a joint effort among IFIP Working Groups 9.2, 9.6/11.7, 11.6, and Special Interest Group 9.2.2, in co-operation with the European Union's cybersecurity competence network pilot projects SPARTA[1], CyberSec4Europe[2], and CONCORDIA[3]. The summer school was also supported by Forum Privatheit[4] and the EnCaViBS project[5]. This IFIP Summer School brought together more than 40 junior and senior researchers and practitioners from different parts of the world from many disciplines, including many young entrants to the field. They met to share their ideas, build a network, gain experience in presenting their research, and have the opportunity to publish a paper through these proceedings.

As in previous years, one of the goals of the IFIP Summer School was to encourage the publication of thorough research papers by students and emerging scholars. To this end, it had a three-phase review process for submitted papers. In the first phase, authors were invited to submit short abstracts of their work. Abstracts within the scope of the call were selected for presentation at the school. After the school, authors were encouraged to submit full papers of their work, which received two to three reviews by members of the Program Committee. They were then given time to revise and resubmit their papers for inclusion in these post-proceedings, and were offered in-depth shepherding where necessary.

In total, 23 abstracts were submitted, out of which 20 were presented at the virtual conference, and nine were finally accepted for publication. Insightful keynote talks were given by Kai Kimppa ("Ethical social engineering penetration testing – can it be done?"), Sebastian Pape ("Serious Games for Security and Privacy Awareness"), François Thill ("Information Security Risk Management"), and Jakub Čegan ("Training Development in KYPO Cyber Range Platform"). Finally, a total of five workshops and tutorials on topics related to privacy and identity management complemented a diverse and educational program.

We are grateful to all contributors of the summer school and especially to the Program Committee for reviewing the abstracts and papers as well as advising the

---

[1] https://www.sparta.eu/.

[2] https://cybersec4europe.eu.

[3] https://www.concordia-h2020.eu/.

[4] https://www.forum-privatheit.de/.

[5] https://encavibs.uni.lu/.

authors on their revisions. Our thanks also go to all supporting projects, the Steering Committee for their guidance and support, and all participants and presenters.

February 2022

Michael Friedewald
Stephan Krenn
Ina Schiering
Stefan Schiffner

Organization

General Chair

Stefan Schiffner   University of Luxembourg, Luxembourg

Program Chairs

Michael Friedewald   Fraunhofer ISI, Germany
Stephan Krenn   AIT Austrian Institute of Technology, Austria
Ina Schiering   Ostfalia University of Applied Sciences, Germany

Program Committee

Florian Adamsky   Hof University of Applied Sciences, Germany
Rose-Mharie Åhlfeldt   University of Skövde, Sweden
Sébastien Canard   Orange Labs, France
José M. Del Álamo   Universidad Politécnica de Madrid, Spain
Jana Dittmann   Otto von Guericke University Magdeburg, Germany
Josep Domingo-Ferrer   Universitat Rovira i Virgili, Italy
Simone Fischer-Hübner   Karlstad University, Sweden
Jan Hajny   VUT Brno, Czech Republic
Marit Hansen   Unabhängiges Landeszentrum für Datenschutz
                                        Schleswig-Holstein, Germany
Paula Helm   University of Tuebingen, Germany
Dominik Herrmann   University of Bamberg, Germany
Demosthenes Ikonomou   ENISA, Greece
Galina Ivanova   University of Ruse, Bulgaria
Meiko Jensen   Kiel University of Applied Sciences, Germany
Stefan Katzenbeisser   University of Passau, Germany
Kai Kimppa   University of Turku, Finland
Jani Koskinen   University of Turku, Finland
Christiane Kuhn   Karlsruhe Institute of Technology, Germany
Bertrand Lathoud   Securitymadein.lu, Luxembourg
Joachim Meyer   Tel Aviv University, Israel
Sebastian Pape   Goethe University Frankfurt, Germany
Robin Pierce   Tilburg University, The Netherlands
Jo Pierson   Vrije Universiteit Brussel, Belgium
Henrich C. Pöhls   University of Passau, Germany
Maria Grazia Porcedda   Trinity College Dublin, Ireland
Tobias Pulls   Karlstad University, Sweden
Charles Raab   University of Edinburgh, UK
Delphine Reinhardt   University of Göttingen, Germany

Kjetil Rommetveit	University of Bergen, Norway
Arnold Roosendaal	Privacy Company, The Netherlands
Denis Royer	Ostfalia University of Applied Sciences, Germany
Sandra Schmitz	University of Luxembourg, Luxembourg
Stefan Strauss	Austrian Academy of Sciences, Austria
Regina Valutytė	Mykolas Romeris University, Lithuania
Simone van der Hof	Leiden University, The Netherlands

Contents

Keynote Papers

Challenges for Designing Serious Games on Security and Privacy Awareness

Sebastian Pape[1,2]([✉])[iD]

[1] Chair of Mobile Business and Multilateral Security, Goethe University Frankfurt,
Frankfurt, Germany
`sebastian.pape@m-chair.de`
[2] Social Engineering Academy GmbH, Frankfurt, Germany

Abstract. Serious games seem to be a good alternative to traditional trainings since they are supposed to be more entertaining and engaging. However, serious games also create specific challenges: The serious games should not only be adapted to specific target groups, but also be capable of addressing recent attacks. Furthermore, evaluation of the serious games turns out to be challenging. While this already holds for serious games in general, it is even more difficult for serious games on security and privacy awareness. On the one hand, because it is hard to measure security and privacy awareness. On the other hand, because both of these topics are currently often in the main stream media requiring to make sure that a measured change really results from the game session. This paper briefly introduces three serious games to counter social engineering attacks and one serious game to raise privacy awareness. Based on the introduced games the raised challenges are discussed and partially existing solutions are presented.

Keywords: Serious games · Security awareness · Privacy awareness · Social engineering

1 Introduction

Huizinga [28] discusses the importance of the play element in culture and points out that games have a long history, animals already played long before humanity arose: "Play is older than culture, for culture, however inadequately defined, always presupposes human society, and animals have not waited for man to teach them their playing." While one of the most significant aspects of play is that it is fun, it was only natural to explore the application of games for other purposes than entertainment. Abt [1] coined the term "serious games" in the 70s, although the idea was not new at that time. The "Landlord's game", a predecessor of Monopoly, was already created in 1902 to illustrate the dangers of capitalist approaches [39].

The main challenge of designing serious games is to keep the balance between entertainment and other purposes [20]. As the boundaries between playing and

M. Friedewald et al. (Eds.): Privacy and Identity 2021, IFIP AICT 644, pp. 3–16, 2022.
https://doi.org/10.1007/978-3-030-99100-5_1

not playing are fuzzy [47], whether the designer succeeds will also depend on the players' target group of the game. However, compared to traditional forms of learning serious games are more entertaining and engaging, and have demonstrated a potential in industrial education and training disciplines [45].

To foster the discussion, selected games to counter social engineering attacks and raise privacy awareness will be sketched in Sect. 2. Section 3 discusses the challenge of creating appropriate content for a specific target group and to cope with permanently changing attacks. Section 4 discusses different types of evaluating the game along with specific challenges for evaluating security and privacy awareness. Section 5 concludes the paper.

2   Sample Serious Games to Prevent Social Engineering and Raise Privacy Awareness

Social Engineering is defined as a technique that exploits human weaknesses and aims to manipulate people into breaking normal security procedures [33]. It is expected that machine learning techniques surface as new powerful tools in the social engineering area [8] while defenders still have a lack of tool support [6].

In general, companies have two main strategies to defend against social engineering attacks: social engineering penetration testing [55] or raising the security awareness via campaigns or trainings. For social engineering penetration testing, the penetration testers are supposed to attack the employees and find vulnerabilities. Unfortunately, experiments have shown that this approach can lead to employees becoming demotivated when confronted with the results of the test [16]. Furthermore, the social engineering penetration tests may interfere with the employees' right of personality, resulting in ethical [25] and legal [56] issues.

While traditional security awareness training may prove successful in particular against phishing, often the training is conducted in a way that it does not have a long lasting effect [52]. As already discussed in the previous section, serious games may be a viable alternative.

There is a number of serious board games targeting different aspects of security awareness, such as Collect it All [9,30,31], Control Alt Hack [12–15,23], d0x3d [22,23], Decisions and Disruptions [7], Elevation of Privileges [50,51], Operation Digitale Schlange [43,44], and the ISMS card game [54].

As a foundation for our discussion, we introduce the three serious games HATCH, PROTECT and the CyberSecurity Awareness Quiz in this section which all aim to counter social engineering attacks. Their relation is shown in Fig. 1 [34] and will be further elaborated in the next subsections. HATCH is a physical card game and PROTECT and the CyberSecurity Awareness Quiz are digital games which have also been integrated in the TREAT-ARREST project's cyber ranges platform [26]. Additionally to the serious security games, we also briefly introduce the serious game LEECH which is not connected to the previously described games and aims to increase the players' privacy awareness.

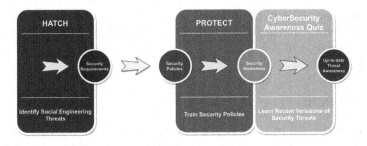

Fig. 1. Relation of HATCH, PROTECT and CyberSecurity Awareness Quiz [34]

2.1 HATCH

Schaab et al. [48] examined the psychological principles of social engineering and investigated which psychological techniques induce resistance to persuasion applicable for social engineering. Based on the identified gaps [49], the serious game HATCH [5] is proposed to foster the players' understanding of social engineering attacks. When playing HATCH, players attack personas in a virtual scenario based on cards with psychological principals and social engineering attacks. While personas are by definition imaginary, they provide a realistic descriptions of stakeholders or in this case employees, who have names, jobs, feelings, goals, and certain needs [18]. This way players can learn about the attackers' perspective, their vulnerabilities and get a better understanding of potential attack vectors. Figure 2a shows a scenario plan for small energy providers [11,38] and Fig. 2b describes one of the personas from the scenario.

(a) Scenario Plan   (b) Persona Card: Jonas, Accountant

Fig. 2. HATCH

However, HATCH can not only be used for training purposes but also to elicit security requirements to prevent social engineering [4]. Instead of the virtual personas, players describe social engineering attacks on their colleagues. Since players know their colleagues, no persona descriptions are necessary and players can exploit their knowledge about processes in their work environment, i.e., about how to cut through the red tape and informal ways of handling tasks. As a result, at the end of the game a list of potential attacks can be investigated by the IT department.

2.2   PROTECT

Based on the derived security requirements it is possible to adapt the organization's security policies. Since security policies are documents often unread by the users, the serious game PROTECT was developed to train users in behaving according to the organization's security policies [21]. PROTECT is the further development of PERSUADED [2] with the improvement of making the game more configurable and an improved graphical user interface as shown in Fig. 3a. Both games are digital card games where players have to defend against attacks with the correct defenses in a solitaire like game type. Special cards allow users to peak on the card pile and skip attack cards when they do not hold the corresponding defenses.

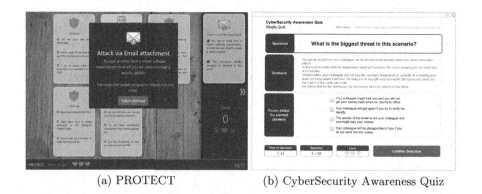

(a) PROTECT   (b) CyberSecurity Awareness Quiz

Fig. 3. Graphical user interfaces for serious games

2.3   CyberSecurity Awareness Quiz

Attackers adapt their attacks based on recent events, e.g., such as the COVID-19 pandemic [46], and naturally security policies can not be adapted too often and fast enough. Therefore, it is also important to raise the employees' awareness about recent attacks or attack variations. For that purpose, we propose the CyberSecurity Awareness Quiz [35] which allows to add new content with only little effort. Figure 3b shows the user interface for the players. We also propose a process for the timely development of new questions based on recent attacks. For that purpose, several relevant news feeds and websites are used as input. If adequate attacks are identified questions on the attack are derived along with correct and incorrect answers. The quiz content editor may then group selected questions to form a quiz or select all questions matching a certain keyword. In future work we intend to investigate by user studies if the implementation is also perceived as lightweight by the players and if players perceive the game suitable for occasional playing.

2.4 Leech

In contrast to the previous three games, Leech does not address security awareness, but privacy awareness. As a continuation to work on an assessment framework for privacy policies of Internet of Things Services [41] based on particular General Data Protection Regulation (GDPR) [42] requirements, the serious game Leech was developed. The aim of is Leech is to foster players' learning about the contents and structure of privacy policies so that they get a rough understanding what to expect in privacy policies. Leech is an adventure game (cf. Fig. 4a) and the player has to solve quests to complete the game. Two of the tasks are implemented as a mini game, i.e., sorting snippets of a privacy policy, (cf. Fig. 4b) to allow more complexity. Two pre-tests led to promising results and a quantitative evaluation of the game is planned as the next step by investigating players' online privacy literacy, demographics, values on privacy policies, actions within the game, and their in-game experience [37].

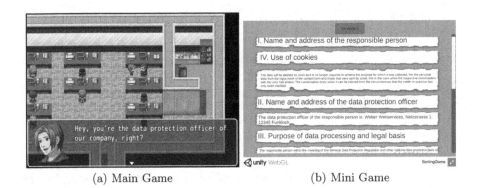

(a) Main Game   (b) Mini Game

Fig. 4. Leech

3   Game Content Creation and Adaption

Even if the main idea and game mechanics of a serious game are already finished, the content of the game needs to be designed or may need to be adapted later. In this section, we discuss two challenges regarding the content: Adapting it to the appropriate target group and adapting it to recent attacks.

3.1   Addressing Target Groups

Similar to awareness campaigns, the scope of serious games should be as specific as possible to the target audience [3]. One can already see from the different nature of the proposed games, that each of the games needs different content. For HATCH scenarios and persona descriptions need to be created. For PROTECT attack descriptions and matching defense pairs need to be created and for the CyberSecurity Awareness Quiz a catalog of questions along with correct and not so easy to determine wrong answers needs to be created. We will cover the creation of quiz questions in the next subsection and further elaborate on the most difficult task: Creating scenarios for HATCH.

We propose a systematic approach based on grounded theory as proposed by Faily and Flechais [18] (cf. Fig. 5). By conducting interviews with relevant stakeholders, systematically coding the answers, and grouping the codes different properties for the personas can be derived [27]. We have evaluated the approach by building a virtual scenario for consultant companies. The approach worked well and we obtained a reasonable scenario. However, the approach was quite time consuming, thus we propose further research in lightweight approaches which allow the creation of appropriate scenarios with less effort.

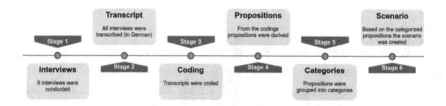

Fig. 5. Content creation process for HATCH [27]

3.2   Addressing Recent Attacks

Another challenge is to address the attackers' adaption of attacks. Naturally, the time span from discovering new types of attack, adapting the security policies and training the players in the new security policy is too long to be an effective tool. During the process of improving the security policies, the attacker might already have changed their attack theme.

In general, one would not want to wait until recent attacks start attacking the organization's employees, but rather try to prepare them beforehand. As a consequence, relying on public available information on attacks already observed in the wild seems to be a viable option. For that purpose appropriate web resources like news and security websites, feeds, blogs or even twitter accounts which publish content related to social engineering attacks need to be collected. Content which is presented in a structured manner is in general preferable, as it might allow an automation. Figure 6 shows an overview of the steps for a possible information procurement [35] for the CyberSecurity Awareness Quiz:

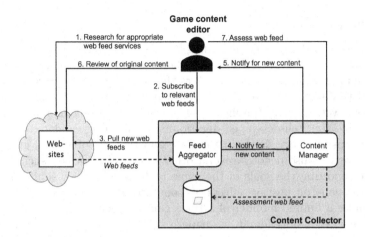

Fig. 6. Transforming news about attacks into questions [35]

In the initial step of the process, the game content editor will search for sources which publish content about social engineering attacks and implement a web feed service. This step will be repeated periodically to check if new appropriate web resources are available. The information from the feed will be aggregated automatically and if new content is found, the game content editor will get the new feeds to assess them manually and create new content for the game, when appropriate.

The CyberSecurity Awareness Quiz was specifically built, to allow the fast creation of new content. The generation of appropriate question and answer pairs can be done much faster than the creation of new scenarios for HATCH or the adaption of the security policies along with the creation of new attack/defense pairs for PROTECT. This also demonstrates that the serious game does not only need to be adapted to a specific target group, but also to a specific purpose: Here, the possibility to react to new attacks in the wild as fast as possible.

4 Evaluation of Serious Games

There are numerous dimensions to evaluate for serious games. The most obvious dimensions are the entertainment factor and the effectiveness of the serious game. However, there are several other dimensions which are worthwhile to investigate also. One of the aspects is to ensure no harm is done to the players respectively employees. While this might sound surprising on a first glance, it can easily be possible that players may be bullied during the game or that their personal data is exposed. We deal in the next subsection with the challenge of measuring the effectiveness of the serious game and in the following subsection, we briefly cover legal and ethical aspects.

4.1   Effectiveness

To the best of our knowledge, regarding the general evaluation of serious games, there is not much literature. However, there is a literature survey in a related area on gamification [24], which observes that many papers only report descriptive statistics and only papers are published with either all or at least a part of the tests were positive (publication bias). Further problems reported were a small sample size, self-developed questionnaires omitting validated psychometric measurements, very short time frames, and the lack of control groups. The literature review also denotes several other points of criticism, such as lack of clarity in reporting the goals of the game and the results. A similar literature review was done on positive effects on computer games in general [10], which also includes a limited number of serious games. Their result was comparable, in particular, they only found one paper explicitly making use of correlations. The only study specifically on serious games for CSA from Tioh et al. [53] also found that evaluations were done with small sample sizes and rather informally. However, the study also covers only a small set of games.

Although, we did not do a systematic analysis, from the papers on serious games, we have investigated, we found a similar pattern. In particular, the patterns of a low number of participants, not explicitly and measurable formulated goals, short time frames of the experiment, i.e., measuring directly after the game, and the lack of control groups were often seen. In particular long term measurements, e.g., several weeks after playing the game, would yield in more interesting insights as many effects might be measurable immediately after the game, but will vanish when time elapses. Furthermore, since many main stream media report also about security and privacy incidents, control groups for long term measurements are unavoidable. This dramatically increases the necessary effort for evaluating the effectiveness of serious games on security and privacy awareness. Since the duration of the games can be between a couple of minutes and several days and participants not only need to play the game, but also participate in the evaluation procedure, e.g., filling a questionnaire, the evaluation of serious games requires significant resources. As a further problem, this may also lead to a selection bias, as not all potential players might be willing to participate in such a time consuming evaluation.

Security and Privacy Awareness. One of the problems for security and privacy awareness is, that it they are hard to measure. Besides the idea of social engineering penetration testing of the employees, which we have already discussed, the best way of measuring security or privacy awareness are self-reported questionnaires such as human aspects of information security [40], security attitudes [19], security behaviour [17], and the online privacy literacy scale [32]. However, self-reported questionnaires might not be the most reliable measurement, as they might not only be influenced by the participants' mood, but participants also often get annoyed if they need to repeatedly answer the same questions, i.e., measuring before and after the game. As it is not well researched how repeatably answering the security and privacy awareness questionnaires might change the results, this might also effect the results.

4.2 Legal and Ethical Assessment

For the three introduced serious games countering social engineering threats, HATCH is the most obvious candidate for a legal assessment. On the one hand, because with real scenarios it may be used with the players as victims in the game putting their personal data at risk. On the other hand, because PROTECT and the CyberSecurity Awareness Quiz are both single player games, and therefore face less risks, e.g., of players bullying each other.

When playing HATCH with a realistic scenario, the employees' personal information might be at risk if players use it to describe their attacks. Legal requirements demand a careful consideration of conditions the game can be used in. Therefore, we provide a legal analysis of the requirements to use HATCH for threat elicitation [29]. The main outcome is that the virtual scenario may be used without hesitation since players are not as victims part of the game, and therefore other players do not attack them in the game. The realistic scenario should only be used for threat elicitation since the risk of players accidentally or intentionally exposing other players is real.

While the assessment was specifically investigating HATCH and one would need to do a legal assessment for each considered serious security game before playing it in an official context, some general conclusions can be drawn. The most important question arising is if employees' personal characteristics are subject to the game. If they are, the organization needs a justification why a more gentle type of training without considering the employees' personal characteristics is not appropriate. This could be the case if the organization wants to conduct a threat analysis, for example because there already have been some incidents or the organization is specifically exposed social engineering attacks and wants to mitigate that [36].

From an ethical perspective, one needs to also carefully consider other aspects, i.e., discrimination. This in particular concerns the virtual scenarios. While it might be natural to develop personas which realistically reflect the situation in most companies, this might also lead to stereotypes discriminating certain groups, e.g., females when the managing positions are all modeled with males and subordinate positions such as cleaning staff are modeled with female personas. One solution to this problem is to design gender inclusive personas (cf. Fig. 7). However, this can only be the first step as this version only addresses gender, but does not consider any minorities.

Fig. 7. Gender inclusive persona card for HATCH

5   Summary and Conclusion

We have briefly introduced serious games on security and privacy awareness. Based on the presented games, we have first discussed the challenged to create content which is appropriate for the players' target group and covers recent attacks. Furthermore, we have sketched, that the evaluation of serious games requires a lot of resources, such as long term experiments with a large sample size including control groups in order to be meaningful. Furthermore, in particular for security and privacy awareness, there is no automated measurement, resulting in self-reported questionnaires, which may cause problems if they are repeatedly answered. A systematic, standardized way to measure the outcomes of serious games may be desirable, although one of the remaining problems will probably still be to attract participants and in particular motivate them to participate in a long term study.

We have presented a legal assessment for HATCH. While some aspects can be transferred to other serious games, in order to use them in a broad manner in a professional context, individual assessments considering labor law might be necessary for each of the games. Further challenges of serious games include measuring dimensions which might not be expected at a first glance. This in particular refers to discrimination. While we have discussed gender inclusive persona cards for HATCH, gender was only addressed in a binary form. Future work could also try to cover further aspects of discrimination, e.g., consider minorities.

Acknowledgements. This work was supported by European Union's Horizon 2020 research and innovation program from the project CyberSec4Europe (grant agreement number: 830929) and from the project THREAT-ARREST (grant agreement number: 786890). We are also grateful to Kristina Femmer for designing plans and persona cards for HATCH.

References

1. Abt, C.C.: Serious Games. University Press of America (1987)
2. Aladawy, D., Beckers, K., Pape, S.: PERSUADED: fighting social engineering attacks with a serious game. In: Furnell, S., Mouratidis, H., Pernul, G. (eds.) TrustBus 2018. LNCS, vol. 11033, pp. 103–118. Springer, Cham (2018). https://doi.org/10.1007/978-3-319-98385-1_8
3. Bada, M., Sasse, A.M., Nurse, J.R.C.: Cyber security awareness campaigns: why do they fail to change behaviour? CoRR abs/1901.02672 (2019). http://arxiv.org/abs/1901.02672
4. Beckers, K., Pape, S.: A serious game for eliciting social engineering security requirements. In: Proceedings of the 24th IEEE International Conference on Requirements Engineering, RE 2016. IEEE Computer Society (2016). https://ieeexplore.ieee.org/document/7765507
5. Beckers, K., Pape, S., Fries, V.: HATCH: hack and trick capricious humans - a serious game on social engineering. In: Proceedings of the 2016 British HCI Conference, Bournemouth, United Kingdom, 11–15 July 2016 (2016). https://www.scienceopen.com/document?vid=ef4958b1-ff29-42e5-b58f-f66b8ef30a87
6. Beckers, K., Schosser, D., Pape, S., Schaab, P.: A structured comparison of social engineering intelligence gathering tools. In: Lopez, J., Fischer-Hübner, S., Lambrinoudakis, C. (eds.) TrustBus 2017. LNCS, vol. 10442, pp. 232–246. Springer, Cham (2017). https://doi.org/10.1007/978-3-319-64483-7_15
7. The Bristol Cyber Security Group University of Bristol: Decisions and disruptions homepage. http://www.decisions-disruptions.org/
8. Canavese, D., et al.: Cybersecurity outlook 1. Technical report, CyberSec4Europe, September 2020. https://cybersec4europe.eu/wp-content/uploads/2021/01/D3.10-Cybersecurity-outlook-1-Submitted.pdf
9. CIA: Cia: Collect it all - declassified training game. https://www.muckrock.com/foi/united-states-of-america-10/materials-for-the-game-collection-deck-35175/#file-162778
10. Connolly, T.M., Boyle, E.A., MacArthur, E., Hainey, T., Boyle, J.M.: A systematic literature review of empirical evidence on computer games and serious games. Comput. Educ. **59**(2), 661–686 (2012)

11. Dax, J., et al.: Sichere informationsnetze bei kleinen und mittleren energiever-sorgern (SIDATE). In: Rudel, S., Lechner, U. (eds.) State of the Art: IT-Sicherheit für Kritische Infrastrukturen, chap. Sichere Informationsnetze bei kleinen und mittleren Energieversorgern (SIDATE), p. 29. Universität der Bundeswehr, Neubiberg (2018)

12. Denning, T., Kohno, T., Shostack, A.: Control-alt-hack: a card game for computer security outreach, education, and fun. Technical report. UW-CSE-12-07-01, Department of Computer Science and Engineering University of Washington, July 2012

13. Denning, T., Kohno, T., Shostack, A.: Control-alt-hack^{TM}: a card game for computer security outreach and education (abstract only). In: Camp, T., Tymann, P.T., Dougherty, J.D., Nagel, K. (eds.) The 44th ACM Technical Symposium on Computer Science Education, SIGCSE 2013, Denver, CO, USA, 6–9 March 2013, p. 729. ACM (2013). http://doi.acm.org/10.1145/2445196.2445408

14. Denning, T., Lerner, A., Shostack, A., Kohno, T.: Control-alt-hack: the design and evaluation of a card game for computer security awareness and education. In: Sadeghi, A., Gligor, V.D., Yung, M. (eds.) 2013 ACM SIGSAC Conference on Computer and Communications Security, CCS 2013, Berlin, Germany, 4–8 November 2013, pp. 915–928. ACM (2013). http://doi.acm.org/10.1145/2508859.2516753

15. Denning, T., Shostack, A., Kohno, T.: Practical lessons from creating the control-alt-hack card game and research challenges for games in education and research. In: Peterson, Z.N.J. (ed.) 2014 USENIX Summit on Gaming, Games, and Gamification in Security Education, 3GSE 2014, San Diego, CA, USA, 18 August 2014. USENIX Association (2014). https://www.usenix.org/conference/3gse14/summit-program/presentation/denning

16. Dimkov, T., Van Cleeff, A., Pieters, W., Hartel, P.: Two methodologies for physical penetration testing using social engineering. In: Proceedings of the 26th Annual Computer Security Applications Conference, pp. 399–408 (2010)

17. Egelman, S., Peer, E.: Scaling the security wall: developing a security behavior intentions scale (SeBIS). In: Proceedings of the 33rd Annual ACM Conference on Human Factors in Computing Systems, pp. 2873–2882 (2015)

18. Faily, S., Flechais, I.: Persona cases: a technique for grounding personas. In: Proceedings of the SIGCHI Conference on Human Factors in Computing Systems, pp. 2267–2270 (2011)

19. Faklaris, C., Dabbish, L.A., Hong, J.I.: A self-report measure of end-user security attitudes (SA-6). In: Fifteenth Symposium on Usable Privacy and Security (SOUPS 2019), pp. 61–77 (2019)

20. Franzwa, C., Tang, Y., Johnson, A.: Serious game design: motivating students through a balance of fun and learning. In: 2013 5th International Conference on Games and Virtual Worlds for Serious Applications (VS-GAMES), pp. 1–7. IEEE (2013)

21. Goeke, L., Quintanar, A., Beckers, K., Pape, S.: PROTECT – an easy configurable serious game to train employees against social engineering attacks. In: Fournaris, A.P., et al. (eds.) IOSEC/MSTEC/FINSEC -2019. LNCS, vol. 11981, pp. 156–171. Springer, Cham (2020). https://doi.org/10.1007/978-3-030-42051-2_11

22. Gondree, M., Peterson, Z.N.J.: Valuing security by getting [d0x3d!]: experiences with a network security board game. In: Kanich, C., Sherr, M. (eds.) 6th Workshop on Cyber Security Experimentation and Test, CSET 2013, Washington, D.C., USA, 12 August 2013. USENIX Association (2013). https://www.usenix.org/conference/cset13/workshop-program/presentation/gondree

23. Gondree, M., Peterson, Z.N.J., Denning, T.: Security through play. IEEE Secur. Priv. **11**(3), 64–67 (2013). https://doi.org/10.1109/MSP.2013.69
24. Hamari, J., Koivisto, J., Sarsa, H.: Does gamification work?-a literature review of empirical studies on gamification. In: 2014 47th Hawaii International Conference on System Sciences, pp. 3025–3034. IEEE (2014)
25. Hatfield, J.M.: Virtuous human hacking: the ethics of social engineering in penetration-testing. Comput. Secur. **83**, 354–366 (2019)
26. Hatzivasilis, G., et al.: The threat-arrest cyber ranges platform. In: IEEE International Conference on Cyber Security and Resilience (CSR). IEEE, September 2021. https://ieeexplore.ieee.org/document/9527963
27. Hazilov, V., Pape, S.: Systematic scenario creation for serious security-awareness games. In: Boureanu, I., et al. (eds.) ESORICS 2020. LNCS, vol. 12580, pp. 294–311. Springer, Cham (2020). https://doi.org/10.1007/978-3-030-66504-3_18
28. Huizinga, J.: Homo Ludens: A Study on the Play Element in Culture, reprint 1971 (1938)
29. Kipker, D.K., Pape, S., Wojak, S., Beckers, K.: Juristische bewertung eines social-engineering-abwehr trainings. In: Rudel, S., Lechner, U. (eds.) State of the Art: IT-Sicherheit für Kritische Infrastrukturen, chap. Stand der IT-Sicherheit bei deutschen Stromnetzbetreibern, pp. 112–115. Universität der Bundeswehr, Neubiberg (2018)
30. Liao, S.: The CIA made a magic: the gathering-style card game for training agents, and we played it. The Verge, May 2018. https://www.theverge.com/2018/5/21/17374054/cia-collect-it-all-declassified-training-tabletop-card-game
31. Masnick, M.: Cia game kickstarter campaign (2019). https://www.kickstarter.com/projects/mmasnick/cia-collect-it-all?ref=2fbwg2
32. Masur, P.K., Teutsch, D., Trepte, S.: Entwicklung und validierung der online-privatheitskompetenzskala (oplis). Diagnostica (2017)
33. Papadaki, M., Furnell, S., Dodge, R.C.: Social engineering: exploiting the weakest links. European Network & Information Security Agency (ENISA), Heraklion, Crete (2008)
34. Pape, S.: Requirements engineering and tool-support for security and privacy, September 2020. http://publikationen.ub.uni-frankfurt.de/frontdoor/index/index/docId/59271
35. Pape, S., Goeke, L., Quintanar, A., Beckers, K.: Conceptualization of a CyberSecurity awareness quiz. In: Hatzivasilis, G., Ioannidis, S. (eds.) MSTEC 2020. LNCS, vol. 12512, pp. 61–76. Springer, Cham (2020). https://doi.org/10.1007/978-3-030-62433-0_4
36. Pape, S., Kipker, D.K.: Case study: checking a serious security-awareness game for its legal adequacy. Datenschutz und Datensicherheit **45**(5), 310–314 (2021). https://www.springerprofessional.de/en/case-study-checking-a-serious-security-awareness-game-for-its-le/19120160
37. Pape, S., Klauer, A., Rebler, M.: Leech: let's expose evidently bad data collecting habits - towards a serious game on understanding privacy policies (poster). In: 17th Symposium on Usable Privacy and Security (SOUPS 2021), June 2021. https://www.usenix.org/conference/soups2021/presentation/pape
38. Pape, S., Schmitz, C., Kipker, D.K., Sekula, A.: On the use of information security management systems by German energy providers. In: Presented at the Fourteenth IFIP Working Group 11.10 International Conference on Critical Infrastructure Protection, March 2020
39. Parlett, D.: The Oxford History of Board Games. Oxford University Press (1999)

40. Parsons, K., McCormac, A., Butavicius, M., Pattinson, M., Jerram, C.: Determining employee awareness using the human aspects of information security questionnaire (HAIS-Q). Comput. Secur. **42**, 165–176 (2014)
41. Paul, N., Tesfay, W.B., Kipker, D.-K., Stelter, M., Pape, S.: Assessing privacy policies of internet of things services. In: Janczewski, L.J., Kutyłowski, M. (eds.) SEC 2018. IAICT, vol. 529, pp. 156–169. Springer, Cham (2018). https://doi.org/10.1007/978-3-319-99828-2_12
42. Good Distribution Practice Regulation: Regulation EU 2016/679 of the European parliament and of the council of 27 April 2016. Official Journal of the European Union (2016)
43. Rieb, A., Lechner, U.: Operation digital chameleon - towards an open cybersecurity method. In: Proceedings of the 12th International Symposium on Open Collaboration (OpenSym 2016), Berlin, pp. 1–10 (2016). http://www.opensym.org/os2016/proceedings-files/p200-rieb.pdf
44. Rieb, A., Lechner, U.: Towards operation digital chameleon. In: Havârneanu, G., Setola, R., Nassopoulos, H., Wolthusen, S. (eds.) CRITIS 2016 - The 11th International Conference on Critical Information Infrastructures Security, pp. 1–6. Paris (2016, to appear)
45. Riedel, J.C., Hauge, J.B.: State of the art of serious games for business and industry. In: 2011 17th International Conference on Concurrent Enterprising, pp. 1–8. IEEE (2011)
46. Saleh, T.: Covidlock update: deeper analysis of coronavirus Android ransomware (2020). https://www.domaintools.com/resources/blog/covidlock-update-coronavirus-ransomware
47. Salen, K., Tekinbaş, K.S., Zimmerman, E.: Rules of Play: Game Design Fundamentals. MIT Press, Cambridge (2004)
48. Schaab, P., Beckers, K., Pape, S.: A systematic gap analysis of social engineering defence mechanisms considering social psychology. In: 10th International Symposium on Human Aspects of Information Security & Assurance, HAISA 2016, Frankfurt, Germany, 19–21 July 2016, Proceedings (2016). https://www.cscan.org/openaccess/?paperid=301
49. Schaab, P., Beckers, K., Pape, S.: Social engineering defence mechanisms and counteracting training strategies. Inf. Comput. Secur. **25**(2), 206–222 (2017). https://doi.org/10.1108/ICS-04-2017-0022
50. Shostack, A.: Elevation of privilege: drawing developers into threat modeling. Technical report, Microsoft, Redmond, U.S. (2012). http://download.microsoft.com/download/F/A/E/FAE1434F-6D22-4581-9804-8B60C04354E4/EoP_Whitepaper.pdf
51. Shostack, A.: Threat Modeling: Designing for Security, 1st edn. Wiley, Hoboken (2014)
52. Stahl, S.: Beyond information security awareness training: it's time to change the culture. Inf. Secur. Manag. Handb. **3**(3), 285 (2006)
53. Tioh, J.N., Mina, M., Jacobson, D.W.: Cyber security training a survey of serious games in cyber security. In: 2017 IEEE Frontiers in Education Conference (FIE), pp. 1–5. IEEE (2017)
54. IG UK: The ISMS card game homepage (2022). https://www.itgovernance.co.uk/shop/product/the-isms-card-game
55. Watson, G., Mason, A., Ackroyd, R.: Social engineering penetration testing: executing social engineering pen tests, assessments and defense. Syngress (2014)
56. Zimmer, M., Helle, A.: Tests mit Tücke- Arbeitsrechtliche Anforderungen an social engineering tests. Betriebs-Berater **21**(2016), 1269 (2016)

Information Security Risk Management

François Thill[✉]

Ministère de L'Économie, Luxembourg, Luxembourg
francois.thill@eco.etat.lu

Abstract. Behavioural security, technical security and organisational security are inter-related. Issues addressing security should therefore consider those three pillars in common not in silos.

This paper summarizes a keynote speech held on this topic at the 16th IFIP Summer School on Privacy and Identity Management.

Keywords: Information security · Risk management · Cybersecurity · Informed governance

1 Introduction

Behavioural security [1], technical security and organisational security are inter-related. Issues addressing security should therefore consider those three pillars in common, not in silos, as it is often the case.

In 2020, 84% of cyberattacks relied on social engineering [2], and studies show that implementing solely technical measures without involving and educating users is futile [1]. Organisational security is about increasing the efficiency of both behavioural and technical security by defining clear security targets, assessing risks, defining responsibilities and allocating resources effectively to treat these risks.

2 Technical Cybersecurity

Technical cybersecurity is the implementation, configuration, and maintenance of technical security measures, such as anti-virus, Intrusion Detection Systems (IDS), Intrusion Prevention Systems (IPS).

So-called *signature-based tools* rely heavily on the accuracy as well as on the timeliness of the data they use to recognize and stop threats. These technical security tools mostly implement proprietary standards. Customers using this type of technical security tools have to buy the appliance, the product license, and subscribe to costly information feeds updating the search patterns of these tools.

Skilled cyber criminals try to obfuscate [3] their attacks and adopt evasive measures to prevent automatic detection and mitigation of their attacks. This adaptive behaviour from the side of threat actors has decreased efficiency of proprietary cybersecurity tools and pushed companies to implement threat-hunting activities. This process is complex and

M. Friedewald et al. (Eds.): Privacy and Identity 2021, IFIP AICT 644, pp. 17–22, 2022.
https://doi.org/10.1007/978-3-030-99100-5_2

ties up many skilled cybersecurity resources (forensic and threat hunting). Especially if consumed as a service from an external Security Operations Centre (SOC), it can become very expensive [4]. Due to the scarcity of human resources[1], cybersecurity reveals as discriminatory in terms of costs and complexity.

3   Technical Cybersecurity is a Data Economy

Technical cybersecurity represents a data economy. Thanks to initiatives like the Malware Information Sharing Platform (MISP[2]), this data economy is slowly evolving from a data oligopoly to an open economy.

Data sets used in this data economy are for instance Indicators of Compromise also called "forensic artefacts of an intrusion that can be identified on a host or network" [5], their sightings, the sectors they are found in. There are of course many more data sets existing, including information about threat actors, vulnerabilities, efficiency of protective and reactive measures.

Standard commercial tools are no longer able to effectively and automatically counter threats (see previous chapter) pushing many companies to start threat hunting. This development, combined with the activities of the Computer Emergency Response Teams, is fostering a more open data economy in technical cybersecurity.

Some actors, especially governmental ones, continue to share their information only under the "need to know principle", providing vital cybersecurity information only to a few actors, thereby leaving others unprotected.

According to the ENISA study [6], threat intelligence is currently in the early adoption phase compared to incident response and security operations practices. Threat information, representing the raw material for threat intel, is data laboriously gathered by collecting, storing and analysing logs (network, end-point, firewall, Intrusion Detection Systems,...), as well as investigating low level security alerts to re-classify them if necessary and start an investigation to gather Indicators of Compromise (IOC). This redundant investigation done by company experts or third party experts (external Security Operations Centre SOC) into "low signals", potentially revealing malicious activities within their company or constituency networks, hide a huge synergy potential. Due to the scarcity of human resources in cybersecurity, these synergies should be capitalised through a more open data economy, allowing the continuous and timely exchange of threat indicators.

Especially in Europe, this has led to the creation of threat exchange platforms, where experts from SOC or Computer Emergency Response Teams share their findings such as indicators of compromise, forensic analysis, and context information.

One of the best-known initiatives is the Malware Information Sharing Platform (MISP). Like any data economy, this threat information economy needs to address data governance issues with regards to technical, semantical and legal interoperability of the

---

[1] https://go.globalknowledge.com/2020salaryreport.

[2] https://www.misp-project.org/.

data they share. It also has to comply with the European legislation on data exchange platforms[3] and most likely also on AI[4].

Technical and semantical interoperability issues are solved by defining cross-sectoral taxonomies. Legal interoperability is achieved by implementing legal requirements (secondary use, pseudonymisation, anonymization) coming for the General Data Protection Regulation[5] or from sectorial regulations such as banking[6] or health.

4 Organisational Security

Technical security is highly dependent on high quality data in terms of accuracy and timeliness. If technical security measures rely on biased, incomplete or outdated threat intelligence, their efficiency is directly affected and negative impacts may follow quickly.

This *direct causal link* between the accuracy of cybersecurity data and the effectiveness of measures is less obvious in organisational security. Erroneous decisions in organisational security might take some time to spread their harmful impact.

Risk assessment, "the overall process of risk identification, risk analysis and risk evaluation" [7] is required by both standards, such as the information security management standard ISO/IEC27001 and legal frameworks, such as Network and Information Security Directive[7] or the General Data Protection Regulation[8].

Many companies are required to implement a risk assessment process and feed the results into the internal governance process, as well as report its outcome to regulators. **Risk assessment is an integral part of governance, on company, corporate, national and European level**.

The Information Security Management Standard ISO/IEC 27001 requires that "repeated information security risk assessments produce **consistent**, **valid** and **comparable** **results"**. This general requirement applies not only to governance but also to **regulation**.

In organisational cybersecurity, the risk assessment process is most dependent on accurate data. **As mentioned above, the usage of biased, incorrect or incomplete data in organisational cybersecurity does not immediately create a visible impact. Reasons for incidents are most often sought after in the technical cybersecurity domain. The governance decisions that led to the configuration of these tools are rarely questioned.**

5 Organisational Cybersecurity Needs to Become a Data Economy

The breath-taking evolution of cybersecurity threats, especially due to the professionalization of threat actors [8], has dramatically changed the way to address organisational

---

[3] https://eur-lex.europa.eu/legal-content/EN/TXT/?uri=CELEX%3A52020PC0767.

[4] https://eur-lex.europa.eu/legal-content/EN/TXT/?uri=CELEX%3A52021PC0206.

[5] https://www.misp-project.org/compliance/gdpr/information_sharing_and_cooperation_gdpr.html.

[6] https://www.circl.lu/services/misp-financial-sector/.

[7] https://op.europa.eu/en/publication-detail/-/publication/d2912aca-4d75-11e6-89bd-01aa75 ed71a1/language-en.

[8] https://eur-lex.europa.eu/eli/reg/2016/679/oj.

cybersecurity as a company and as a country respectively within the European Single Market. Information about modus of operandi of threats, the appearance of catalysing technologies such as crypto currencies[9], or the discovery of new vulnerabilities[10] have to be collected to enrich the situational awareness of companies and the regulators. Obviously, this information also has to be cast into new risk scenarios during the risk identification phase.

Furthermore, threats and vulnerabilities have to be qualified respectively quantified. Their probabilities respectively ease of exploitation are changing over time and have to be adapted during the risk evaluation phase of the risk assessment process.

While the usage of this data is quite common in technical cybersecurity, **its valorisation in organization cybersecurity is not.** This data is however crucial for the realisation of a consistent and valid risk assessment process.

6   Creating the Data for Organisational Situational Awareness

As organisational cybersecurity will become an open data economy, data governance principles need to be developed to foster the creation of technically, semantically and legally interoperable datasets.

Contributors of these datasets are multiple:

- Computer Incident Response teams contributing with information about incidents (scenarios), threats, their probabilities, vulnerabilities, their ease of exploitations and effectiveness of risk treatment measures;
- Regulators with information about minimum scope of risk assessments, context information, impact thresholds, risk acceptance information, incidents (national and international);
- Security Operation Centres with information similar to threats;
- Security researchers;
- Research done with techniques known in finance [9].

The ISO/IEC 31000 standard [7] states "that risk assessment should be conducted systematically, iteratively and **collaboratively**, drawing on the knowledge and views of stakeholders[11]" fostering collaboration.

The Luxembourg government is conscious about the challenges this requirement of the ISO/IEC 31000 poses and is convinced about the importance of this approach. For this reason, the Luxembourg government will invest, in the context of the IPCEI-CIS[12], in the creation of a **cybersecurity data space** in the spirit of the European strategy on data[13], aligned with the Luxembourg Data-Driven Innovation Strategy [10] and the

---

[9] Some cyber-criminal business-cases could only materialize with the help of crypto-currencies.

[10] For instance, company networks opened to the Internet to allow for teleworking during the Covid-19 pandemic, leading to process and technical vulnerabilities.

[11] Stakeholder is defined in the standard ISO/IEC 31000 as "person or organization that can affect, be affected by, or perceive themselves to be affected by a decision or activity."

[12] https://www.bmwi.de/Redaktion/EN/Artikel/Industry/ipcei-cis.html.

[13] https://digital-strategy.ec.europa.eu/en/policies/strategy-data.

Strategy "Ons Wirtschaft vu Muer" [11]. It will be made available and accessible just like the other Common European Data Spaces[14].

Based on the cybersecurity data space, risk management information such as common and sectoral risk scenarios, risk estimation information such as threat probabilities, ease of exploitation of vulnerabilities will be made available broadly.

The Cybersecurity Competence Centre of SECURITYMADEIN.LU made very promising work in transforming technical cybersecurity information into risk information by mapping cybersecurity incidents via the Mitre Att@ck[15] to risk scenarios.

7 Towards an Informed Governance

Sharing risk information such as scenarios, threat probabilities, ease of exploitation of vulnerabilities is unproblematic from the point of view of the GDPR or other sectorial regulations. Sharing this information is of utmost importance [12], because risk managers generally have a hard time identifying relevant risk scenarios and even more problems qualifying respectively quantifying risks. Without accurate and objective information, risk management is futile and ends-up in a completely subjective exercise producing random results. This is especially true for small companies. They represent the vast majority of European companies, are often strategic actors in large' supply chains and play a key role in building inclusive and resilient societies [13]. For this reason, SMEs often handle highly critical data containing trade secrets, intellectual property rights or private data.

Regulators or cybersecurity agencies providing community-wide and objective risk information, based on factual information, will not only improve the quality of individual risk management. Thanks to the introduction of common risk taxonomies, risk management will become comparable, repeatable and reliable throughout the community. Only by achieving this level of collaboration and coordination, **risk management will become a governance tool instead of being a compliance exercise.**

Luxembourg has announced in its national cybersecurity strategy III[14] that the concepts of informed governance (risk management based on common taxonomies and collaborative situational awareness) will be developed. The creation of the cybersecurity data-space and the research done on the level of transforming technical cybersecurity information into organisational cybersecurity information brings Luxembourg a step closer to this goal. Sectorial regulation in cybersecurity (GDPR, Banking, NIS, Critical Infrastructure Protection, …) can be partially harmonised and the price of regulation can be reduced while increasing its efficiency dramatically.

References

1. ENISA: Cybersecurity Culture Guidelines: Behavioural Aspects of Cybersecurity (2019). https://www.enisa.europa.eu/publications/cybersecurity-culture-guidelines-behavioural-asp ects-of-cybersecurity

---

14 http://dataspaces.info/common-european-data-spaces/#page-content.
15 https://attack.mitre.org/.

2. ENISA: Threat Landscape 2020 – Main Incidents (2020). https://www.enisa.europa.eu/pub
   lications/enisa-threat-landscape-2020-main-incidents
3. ENISA: Threat Landscape 2015 (2016). https://www.enisa.europa.eu/publications/etl2015
4. ENISA: Proactive detection – Good practices gap analysis recommendations (2020).
   https://www.enisa.europa.eu/publications/proactive-detection-good-practices-gap-analysis-
   recommendations
5. OpenIOC: Sophisticated Indicators for the Modern Threat Landscape: An Introduction to
   OpenIOC (2017)
6. ENISA: Exploring the opportunities and limitations of current Threat Intelligence Platforms (2018). https://www.enisa.europa.eu/publications/exploring-the-opportunities-and-lim
   itations-of-current-threat-intelligence-platforms
7. ISO: ISO 31000:2018 Risk management — Guidelines (2018)
8. Europol: Internet Organised Crime Threat Assessment (IOCTA) (2020). https://www.europol.
   europa.eu/publications-events/main-reports/iocta-report
9. Verlaine, M.: On the extraction of cyber risks from structured products. Appl. Econ. **54**, 22
   (2021). https://doi.org/10.1080/00036846.2021.1998327
10. The Luxembourg Government – Ministry of the Economy: The Data-Driven Innova-
    tion Strategy for the Development of a Trusted and Sustainable Economy in Lux-
    embourg (2019). https://gouvernement.lu/en/publications/rapport-etude-analyse/minist-eco
    nomie/intelligence-artificielle/data-driven-innovation.html
11. The Luxembourg Government – Ministry of the Economy: Ons Wirtschaft vu muer –
    Roadmap for a competitive and sustainable economy 2025 (2021). https://meco.gouvernem
    ent.lu/en/publications/strategie/strategie-ons-wirtschaft.html
12. OECD: Digital Security Risk Management for Economic and Social Prosperity - OECD
    Recommendation and Companion Document (2015). https://www.oecd.org/sti/ieconomy/dig
    ital-security-risk-management.htm
13. OECD: OECD Studies on SMEs and Entrepreneurship: The Digital Transformation of SMEs
    (2021). https://www.oecd.org/publications/the-digital-transformation-of-smes-bdb9256a-en.
    htm
14. The Luxembourg Government – High Commission for National Protection: Stratégie
    nationale en matière de cybersécurité III (2018). https://hcpn.gouvernement.lu/en/publicati
    ons/strategie-nationale-cybersecurite-3/strategie-nationale-cybersecurite-3/strategie-nation
    ale-cybersecurite-3.html

Workshop and Tutorial Papers

Conceptualising the Legal Notion of 'State of the Art' in the Context of IT Security

Sandra Schmitz[✉] [iD]

Université du Luxembourg, 6, Avenue de la Fonte, 4264 Esch-sur-Alzette, Luxembourg
sandra.schmitz@uni.lu

Abstract. In the context of IT security, legal instruments commonly demand that IT security is brought up to the level of 'state of the art'.

As the first horizontal instrument on cybersecurity at EU level, the NIS Directive requires that Member States shall ensure that operators of essential services (OESs) and digital service providers (DSPs) take appropriate and proportionate technical and organisational measures to manage the risks posed to the security of network and information systems which they use in their operations, or in the context of offering specific services. Having regard to the 'state of the art', those measures shall ensure a level of security of NIS appropriate to the risk posed. Similarly, the GDPR requires data controllers, and to some extent processors, to take 'state of the art' into account when implementing appropriate technical and organisational measures to mitigate the risks caused by their data processing activities. The same applies to public electronic communications networks or services regarding the security of their networks and services under the EECC.

Although the notion is widely referred to in legal texts, there is no standard legal definition of the notion.

This paper, based on a workshop held at the 14th IFIP summer school, analyses the contexts in which the notion 'state of the art' is being used in legislation. Briefly, the reasons for abstaining from clear technical guidance are addressed. Following an introduction to the three-step theory developed by the German constitutional court, where 'state of the art' is located between the 'generally accepted rules of technology' and the 'state of science and technology', this paper argues that this approach can also be applied at EU level in the context of IT security.

Keywords: State of the art · NIS directive · GDPR

1 State of the Art in Legal Interventions

1.1 'State of the Art' as Protection Goal

In the context of IT security, EU legal instruments commonly demand that IT security is brought up to the level of 'state of the art'. Both, national and EU legislators, however, refrain from defining what 'state of the art' in IT security exactly means.

© IFIP International Federation for Information Processing 2022
Published by Springer Nature Switzerland AG 2022
M. Friedewald et al. (Eds.): Privacy and Identity 2021, IFIP AICT 644, pp. 25–32, 2022.
https://doi.org/10.1007/978-3-030-99100-5_3

Commonly, the notion refers to the highest level of general development achieved at a particular time. In law, the notion has some tradition in patent law[1] as well as in tort law[2]. As regards the latter, it may be used as a legal defence, meaning that for instance a manufacturer cannot be held liable if he can prove that the state of technical and scientific knowledge, at the time when the product was put in circulation, was not such as to enable the existence of a certain defect to be discovered. In patent law, state of the art is used in the process of assessing and asserting the novelty of an invention.

With increasing regulation of technology and in particular information technology, the notion of state of the art gained in importance.

As the first horizontal instrument on cybersecurity at EU level, the NIS Directive[3] requires that Member States shall ensure that operators of essential services (OESs) and digital service providers (DSPs) take appropriate and proportionate technical and organisational measures to manage the risks posed to the security of network and information systems which they use in their operations, or as regards DSPs in the context of offering services referred to in Annex III of the Directive.[4] Having regard to the 'state of the art', those measures shall ensure a level of security of NIS appropriate to the risk posed.[5] Similarly, Arts. 25 and 32 GDPR[6] require data controllers, and to some extent processors, to take the 'state of the art' into account when implementing appropriate technical and organisational measures to mitigate the risks caused by their data processing activities. According to Art. 40(1) EECC[7], the same applies to public electronic communications networks or services regarding the security of their networks and services. None of these legal interventions provides a binding legal definition of the concept of 'state of the art' in the context of IT security.

If one consults the vast body of EU legislation, the notion 'state of the art' is widely referred to in legal texts relating to environment and technology such as for instance

---

[1] Cf. for instance Art. 54 Convention on the Grant of European Patents (European Patent Convention).

[2] Cf. for instance Art. 7(e) Council Directive 85/374/EEC of 25 July 1985 on the approximation of the laws, regulations and administrative provisions of the Member States concerning liability for defective products (Product Liability Directive) [1985] OJ L 210/29.

[3] Directive (EU) 2016/1148 of the European Parliament and of the Council of 6 July 2016 concerning measures for a high common level of security of network and information systems across the Union [2016] *OJ L 194/1*.

[4] Arts. 14(1) and 16(1) NIS Directive.

[5] Ibid.

[6] Regulation (EU) 2016/679 of the European Parliament and of the Council of 27 April 2016 on the protection of natural persons with regard to the processing of personal data and on the free movement of such data,and repealing Directive 95/46/EC (General Data Protection Regulation) [2016] OJ L119/ 1.

[7] Directive (EU) 2018/1972 of the European Parliament and of the Council of 11 December 2018 establishing the European Electronic Communications Code [2018] OJ L 321/36 (EEEC).

the Medical Devices Regulation[8], the Radio Equipment Directive[9], or the Machinery Directive[10]. Similar as in the aforementioned acts, none of these acts provides a standard legal definition of 'state of the art'. Legal scholars thus refer to the notion as an indefinite, abstract general notion [1], or undetermined legal concept [2]. The objective behind using such a concept instead of referring to given standards is obvious: the legislator is keen on retaining options open to accommodate improvements over time. In particular in the field of technology, requiring a certain set level of technology would mean that a legal provision is likely to become outdated in no time.

1.2 State of the Art vs. Best Available Techniques

Besides 'state of the art', legal norms may require that the level of technology corresponds to the 'best available techniques'. In particular in environmental law, 'best available techniques' constitutes a substantial tool to regulate industrial emissions. At EU level, this notion was first introduced by the Integrated Pollution Prevention and Control Directive[11].

Art. 3(10) of Directive 2010/75/EU[12], which replaced the aforementioned Directive, provides a definition of 'best available techniques' in the context of emissions as meaning 'the most effective and advanced stage in the development of activities and their methods of operation which indicates the practical suitability of particular techniques for providing the basis for emission limit values and other permit conditions designed to prevent an, where that is not practicable, to reduce emissions and the impact on the environment as a whole: (a) 'techniques' includes both the technology used and the way in which the installation is designed, built, maintained, operated and decommissioned; (b) 'available techniques' means those developed on a scale which allows implementation in the relevant industrial sector, under economically and technically viable conditions, taking into consideration the costs and advantages, whether or not the techniques are used or produced inside the Member State in question, as long as they are reasonably accessible to the operator; (c) 'best' means most effective in achieving a high general level of protection of the environment as a whole.'

---

[8] Regulation (EU) 2017/745 of the European Parliament and of the Council of 5 April 2017 on medical devices, amending Directive 2001/83/EC, Regulation (EC) No 178/2002 and Regulation (EC) No 1223/2009 and repealing Council Directives 90/385/EEC and 93/42/EEC [2017] OJ L 117/1.

[9] Directive 2014/53/EU of the European Parliament and of the Council of 16 April 2014 on the harmonisation of the laws of the Member States relating to the making available on the market of radio equipment and repealing Directive 1999/5/EC [2014] OJ L 153/62.

[10] Directive 2006/42/EC of the European Parliament and of the Council of 17 May 2006 on machinery, and amending Directive 95/16/EC [2006] OJ L 157/24.

[11] Council Directive 96/61/EC of 24 September 1996 concerning integrated pollution prevention and control [1996] OJ L 257/26.

[12] Directive 2010/75/EU of the European Parliament and of the Council of 24 November 2010 on industrial emissions (integrated pollution prevention and control) [2010] OJ L 334/17.

The national implementation of Directive 2010/75/EU into German law, the Federal Immission Control Act (BImSchG[13]), uses the notions 'state of the art' ('Stand der Technik'[14]) and 'best available techniques' ('beste verfügbare Techniken'[15]) suggesting that they are not identical but closely connected. There seems to be consensus that in this context state of the art at least corresponds to best available techniques [3, 4, 5]. Accordingly, the minimum basis for state of the art in that context is the best available technique.

1.3 The Deployment of State of the Art in the Context of IT/Data Security Regulation

Although best available technique is almost equally vague as state of art, it clarifies that the technology must be 'available'. However, this leads to further questions, namely, whether the technology must be available in general on the market, and/or available to the individual operator.

The NIS Directive requires operators or essential services and digital service providers to ensure the security of the network and information systems which they use and 'having regard to the state of the art, those measures shall ensure a level of security' 'appropriate to the risk posed'. Recital 53, which may support the interpretation of the operative part, stipulates that disproportionate financial and administrative burdens on operators should be avoided by requiring measures proportionate to the risk presented. Arts. 25 and 32 GDPR require the data controller to take into account state of the art, the cost of implementation and the nature, scope, context and purpose of processing as well as the risks for rights and freedoms of data subjects posed by the processing, when implementing appropriate technical and organisational measures. GDPR and NIS Directive (and corresponding IT security regulation) follow a risk-based approach, meaning that the appropriateness of a security measure depends on the risk level. Since both instruments refer to the cost of implementation as a factor to be considered beside state of the art technology, this implies that 'availability' of a technology seems to be a mere objective criterion, meaning that the technology must be available in general on the market. Any further methodological guidance on how to comply with the state of the art requirement is lacking.

In order to respond to requests for guidance and to achieve an overall high level of security, some national legislators allow for ministerial orders to set security rules that

---

[13] Gesetz zum Schutz vor schädlichen Umwelteinwirkungen durch Luftverunreinigungen, Geräusche, Erschütterungen und ähnliche Vorgänge (BImSchG) (Act on the prevention of harmful effects on the environment caused by air pollution, noise, vibration and similar phenomena).

[14] § 3 s. 6 BIsmSchG: 'State of the art as used herein shall mean the state of development of advanced processes, facilities or modes of operation which is deemed to indicate the practical suitability of a particular technique for restricting emission levels. When determining the state of the art, special consideration shall be given to comparable processes, facilities or modes of operation that have been successfully proven in practical operation'. Translation provided by Inter Nationes, available at https://germanlawarchive.iuscomp.org/?p=315, last accessed 202/01/24.

[15] § 3 s. 6d BImschG.

should fulfill the state of the art criterion[16] or for the national competent NIS authority to approve security standards for specific sectors suggested by operators of critical infrastructures and their industry associations[17]. As regards the latter, in Germany, the national competent NIS authority further issued a guide to the contents and requirements of security standards for specific sectors [6]. Soft law instruments or ministerial orders allow for timely updates and thus greater flexibility as there is no lengthy legislative process. However, where industry associations set security standards for specific sectors, this does not necessarily mean that there is transparency as to which criteria have been used to determine the level of state of the art [cf. 7 p. 8]. Realistically speaking, industry associations have an interest to have approved what they consider to be best practice. Best practice in turn does not necessarily have to amount to state of the art.

2 A Three-Step-Test to Determine State of the Art Technology

2.1 The Development of the Three-Step-Test

The abstention from defining state of the art is not unique to EU law. As already mentioned, national legislation is equally reluctant to provide a definition of state of the art within the meaning of technology in general and IT security legislation in particular.

Against this background, it is not surprising that as early as 1978 the German Constitutional Court had been confronted with determining state of the art in context of atomic energy.

In its Kalkar decision[18], the German Constitutional Court approached the question irrespective from the particular context. The Court located state of the art between the 'generally accepted rules of technology' ('allgemein anerkannte Regeln der Technik') and the 'state of science and technology' ('Stand der Wissenschaft und Technik').

The generally accepted rules of technology can be identified by determining the prevailing opinion among practitioners.[19] Generally accepted rules of technology require that a certain technology has stood the test of practice and is generally accepted amongst the majority of experts, however, it does not have to be the best technology available [8]. This notion derives historically from building/construction law and the notion of generally accepted rules of architecture describing the dominating opinion of technical experts. There is a (rebuttable) presumption that technical standards such as DIN-norms amount to generally accepted rules [9]. In contrast, state of science and technology relates to a very high level of protection, that requires to take into account the latest scientific knowledge regardless of whether it is technically feasible and available [8, 10].[20]

---

[16] Cf. France: Art. 10 Décret no 2018-384 du 23 mai 2018 relatif à la sécurité des reseaux et sytèmes d'information des opérateurs de services essentiels et des fournisseurs de service numérique (Decree No. 1018-384 of 23 May 2018 on the security of the networks and information systems of critical service operators and digital service providers).

[17] Cf. Germany: § 8a Gesetz über das Bundesamt für Sicherheit in der Informationstechnik (BSIG) (Act on the Federal Office for information security).

[18] BVerGE 49, 89 (135 et seq.).

[19] Ibid.

[20] Cf. also BVerGE 49, 89 (135 et seq.).

Placing state of the art in between these two notions at normative level confirms the aforementioned finding that state of the art corresponds at least to the best technique available to the operator in question. The legal benchmark of what constitutes state of the art is thus shifted to the front of technical development, since general recognition and practical validation alone are not decisive for the state of the art of a technology.

2.2 The Dynamic Function of Technical Measures

What renders the determination of state of the art somehow 'tricky' is its dynamic function. Technical measures that today form part of the latest scientific knowledge may in no time become state of the art technology. State of the art state is regularly achieved when market maturity is reached and the technology is launched on the market. Equally the generally accepted rules may become outdated as their degree of innovation diminishes [7]. TeleTrust [7] summarises the innovative shift as follows:

'1. A measure will initially reach the "existing scientific knowledge and research" stage at its origin. 2. When introduced on the market, it will pass to the "state of the art" stage, 3. and as it is distributed and recognised more widely on the market, it will at some point be assigned to "generally accepted rules of technology." 4. if recognition is lost, this measure can no longer be used.'. Bearing in mind this product lifecycle, the border between state of the art and generally accepted rules of technology can be fluent and difficult to determine, meaning that a court or authority has to enter into technicians' controversies.

The dynamic nature also comes into play with regard to the aspect of when a technical measure has to amount to state of the art.

In the context of the GDPR, it has been argued [10] that data controllers are required to adapt their privacy measures regularly to advances in technology. The dynamic reference thus has the potential to enhance innovation, when data controllers are required to constantly adapt their protection measures [2]. In that regard Art. 25(1) GDPR requires that in the context of data protection by design or default, state of the art must be taken into account 'both at the time of the determination of the means for processing and at the time of processing itself'. Compliance with Art. 25 GDPR thus requires constant monitoring of the evolvement of state of the art which also needs to be taken into consideration by certification schemes. It has to be ensured that the certification body examines whether the data controller (or processor) keeps track with technological progress [2].

Although the NIS Directive lacks a determination of the time when state of the art must be taken into account, the ratio of the security provisions implies that the OESs or DSPS have to adapt the security measures to ensure a level of security of NIS appropriate to the risks posed.

2.3 The Objective Nature of the State of the Art Criterion and the Principle of Proportionality

As already indicated, the state of the art criterion is purely objective and does not take into account the individual means of the operator. State of the art can thus be described as 'the procedures, equipment or operating methods available in the trade in goods and services for which the application thereof is most effective in achieving the respective legal protection objectives' [11]. Accordingly, subjective elements such as high costs will justify a derivation from this. One may argue, that proprietary tools that are only offered by a single vendor to competitors under abusive conditions may not amount to methods that are 'available' in a strict sense. However, the state of the art criterion always has to be placed in context. Legal interventions commonly require that the technical measure that respects the state of the art is inter alia 'appropriate' (e.g. to the risks posed), 'proportionate to the cost of implementation', take into account the 'nature, scope, context and purpose of [data] processing' (GDPR) and/or risks. As regards for instance the NIS Directive, Recital 53 specifies that in order to avoid imposing a disproportionate financial and administrative burden on OESs and DSPs, the requirements should be proportionate to the risk presented by the NIS concerned. This is in line with the 'state of the art' requiring economically and technically feasible measures in corresponding legal interventions.

3 Conclusion

The determination of whether a particular technology amounts to state of the art can be a challenge for technicians and lawyers alike. The three-step-test introduced by the German Constitutional Court in the 1970s supports the translation from legal to technical requirements in that it clarifies the location of state of the art in between the highest innovative level of research and science and the generally accepted rules of technology which have stood the test of practice. This distinction takes into account the product lifecycle and the dynamic nature of technology. Due to the abstract nature of the three-step-test, i.e. that it is independent of the context, the test can be applied to all fields of technology. Further, the test is also feasible at the level of EU law.

Since the state of the art criterion in legal interventions is of an objective nature, the financial, administrative and technical means available to the individual operators are not to be considered in first place. Commonly the legal interventions will in that regard provide guidance as to what in terms of expenses, manpower etc. can be expected. Assessing state of the art in the context of a specific legal norm often also refers to appropriateness in terms of risk levels and thus has to be determined on a case-by-case basis. Data controllers (GDPR) and other addressees of the requirement of state of the art technology are advised to closely collaborate with regulators to determine appropriate measures.

Acknowledgements. The research for this article was funded by the Luxembourg National Research Fund (FNR) C18/IS/12639666/EnCaViBS/Cole (https://www.fnr.lu/projects/the-eu-nis-directive-enhancingcybersecurity-across-vital-business-sectors-encavibs/).

References

1. Martini, M.: Art. 25 DS-GVO, marginal no. 39a. In: Paal, B., Pauly, D. (eds.) DS-GVO BDSG, 3rd edn. Beck, München (2021)

2. Von Grafenstein, M.: Co-regulation and the competitive advantage in the GDPR: data protection certification mechanisms, codes of conduct and the 'state of the art' of data protection-by-design. In: González Fuster, G., van Brakel, R., de Hert, P.: Research Handbook on Privacy and Data Protection Law: Values, Norms and Global Politics, pp. 398–427. Edward Elgar Publishing (2022)
3. Schulte, M., Michalk, K.: § 3 BImSchG marginal no. 98. In: Giesberts, L., Reinhardt, M. (eds.): BeckOK Umweltrecht. 57th edn. Beck, München (2020)
4. Deutscher Bundestag, BT-Drs. 14/4599, p. 126
5. Deutscher Bundestag, BT-Drs. 17/8125, p. 3
6. BSI: Orientierungshilfe zu Inhalten und Anforderungen an branchenspezifische Sicherheitsstandards (B3S) gemäß § 8a Absatz 2 BSIG. https://www.bsi.bund.de/SharedDocs/Downloads/DE/BSI/KRITIS/b3s_orientierungshilfe.pdf?__blob=publicationFile&v=4. Accessed 24 Jan 2022
7. IT Security Association Germany (TeleTrust) in co-operation with ENISA: IT Security Act (Germany) and EU General Data Protection Regulation: Guideline "State of the art", Technical and organizational measures (2021). https://www.teletrust.de/fileadmin/user_upload/2021-09_TeleTrusT_Guideline_State_of_the_art_in_IT_security_EN.pdf. Accessed 26 Jan 2022
8. Jarass, H.: § 3 BImSchG, marginal no. 115. In: Jarasss, H. (ed.): BImSchG, Bundes-Immissionsschutzgesetz. 13th edn. Beck, München (2020)
9. Seibel, M.: Abgrenzung der "allgemein anerkannten Regeln der Technik" vom "Stand der Technik". In: NJW, pp. 3000–3004 (2013)
10. Martini, M.: Art. 25 DS-GVO, marginal no. 39d. In: Paal, B., Pauly, D. (eds.) DS-GVO BDSG, 3rd edn. Beck, München (2021)
11. Bartels, K., Backer, M.: Die Berücksichtigung des Stands der Technik in der DSGVO. In: DuD, p. 214 (2018)

Privacy-Preserving Identity Management and Applications to Academic Degree Verification

Jorge Bernal Bernabe[1], Jesús García-Rodríguez[1], Stephan Krenn[2(✉)],
Vasia Liagkou[3], Antonio Skarmeta[1], and Rafael Torres[1]

[1] University of Murcia, Murcia, Spain
{jorgebernal,jesus.garcia15,skarmeta,rtorres}@um.es
[2] AIT Austrian Institute of Technology, Vienna, Austria
stephan.krenn@ait.ac.at
[3] Computer Technology Institute and Press "Diophantus", Patras, Greece
liagkou@cti.gr

Abstract. This paper summarizes the contents and presentations held at a workshop at the IFIP Summer School on Privacy and Identity Management 2021, focusing on privacy-preserving identity management. In this document, we first introduce the necessary background on privacy-preserving identity management, including core cryptographic concepts. We then present a demonstrator scenario which benefits from the use of such technologies. Finally, we present a distributed privacy-preserving identity management framework offering an even higher level of security and privacy than previous work.

Keywords: Attributed-based credentials · Privacy-preserving identity management · Workshop

1 Introduction

Attribute-based credential systems, or *ABC-systems*, allow for strong yet privacy-preserving user authentication. In such a system, *users* can receive digital certificates (*credentials*) on pieces of the personal information (*attributes*) from an *issuer*. Such personal information may, for instance, include a user's first name, surname, nationality, or date of birth. A user can now use a credential to prove to a *verifier* that it possesses certain attributes, without the need to reveal more information than what is absolutely necessary. For instance, a verifier might require that a user has a specific age, e.g., in order to receive an age discount. The user can now selectively reveal only her date of birth to the verifier, while keeping all other identifying information private, in a way that guarantees

---

Authors are listed in alphabetical order, cf. https://www.ams.org/profession/leaders/CultureStatement04.pdf.

M. Friedewald et al. (Eds.): Privacy and Identity 2021, IFIP AICT 644, pp. 33–46, 2022.
https://doi.org/10.1007/978-3-030-99100-5_4

to the verifier that the revealed date of birth had indeed been certified by the issuer. Even more, certain schemes even allow a user to prove predicates over her attributes, e.g., allowing her to prove that she is older than 65 years, without revealing the precise birth date, thereby further increasing the privacy level.

Attribute-based credential systems have initially been envisioned by Chaum almost 40 years ago [12,13], and have received significant attention since then, resulting in a variety of different schemes, supporting different functionalities. The most widely known solutions are Microsoft's UProve [6,25] and IBM's Identity Mixer [7,9,10]. However, a large body of related work has been carried out over the last decades, including formal frameworks for ABCs [8], schemes allowing users to anonymously delegate parts of their rights to other users [2,3,11,14], issuer-hiding credential schemes allowing user to remain anonymous across multiple issuers [4], ABC systems with distributed issuers [18,32], ABCs bound to hardware tokens [1], cloud-based ABCs [21,23], or distance-bounding schemes [5].

Furthermore, ABC systems have been analyzed in the context of various application scenarios, including car rental [7], vehicular ad-hoc networks (VANETs) [17], ticketing systems [22], eHealth [26], or course evaluation in high schools [24,31].

Outline. The structure of this paper also follows the structure of the workshop held at the IFIP Summer School. In Sect. 2, we will introduce the fundamental concepts and cryptographic background of attribute-based credential systems to give an intuition on how such schemes work. In Sect. 3, we then introduce a demonstration scenario in the educational context, and present results from an initial user study carried out within the CyberSec4Europe project. Then, in Sect. 4, we introduce the OLYMPUS framework for distributed privacy-preserving identity management. We finally conclude in Sect. 5.

2   Concepts and Technologies

In this section, we will first introduce the basic processes and security and privacy properties of an ABC system, and then introduce the cryptographic building blocks from which such schemes can be built, and provide the basic intuition of the construction underlying most such schemes.

2.1   Entities and Processes

Figure 1 gives an overview of the different types of entities in an attribute-based credential system. The different processes in such a scheme can be described as follows:

Key generation. In a first step, all parties may generate local key material such as digital signature keys or encryption keys, depending on their role in the system. In most existing instantiations of ABC systems, in particular verifiers do not have a need for cryptographic keys.

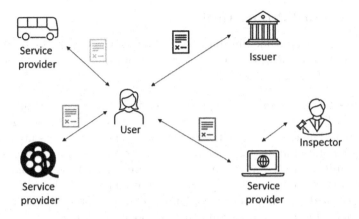

Fig. 1. Overview of entities in an ABC system.

Issuance. In the issuance phase, users may request certificates on personal attributes. Depending on the specific scenario, the issuer may certify arbitrary, self-claimed attributes, or perform rigorous validations, e.g., requiring in-person checks at an authority. After having agreed on the attributes to be certified, the user and the issuer engage in a potentially interactive protocol, at the end of which the user obtains a credential.

Presentation. In order to authenticate towards a service provider (also known as relying party or verifier), the user and the service provider agree on a so-called *presentation policy*, which, among others, defines the issuer accepted by the service provider, as well as the attributes to be revealed. The user then derives a *presentation-token* from her credential which she sends to the service provider, who may now decide to accept or reject the user's presentation.

While these processes exist in any ABC system, also the following steps are available in many schemes found in the literature:

Inspection. In order to prevent abuse of anonymous authentication, a predefined party, known as *inspector*, may open presentation tokens, thereby revoking the user's anonymity. The inspector can then compute a cryptographic proof that a given presentation token was issued by a specific user. The rules under which the inspector may be contacted by a service provider need to be agreed upfront with the user.

Revocation. Upon abuse, loss, or theft of a credential, different entities in the system may request revocation of a given credential, in which case any future attempt to authenticate using the given credential will let the service provider reject the presentation token.

Furthermore, additional processes and features can be found in the literature, including, e.g., advanced issuance, where attributes can be carried over from one credential to another without the issuer learning anything about the attribute, except for the fact that it was already including in a previous credential belonging to the same user.

2.2   Security and Privacy Goals

In the following, we provide informal descriptions of the security goals that need to be achieved by an ABC system. For formal definitions, we refer to the original literature, e.g., Camenisch et al. [8].

Correctness. This property requires that the ABC system functions as intended. That is, if all parties behave honestly during the key generation and issuance phases, a user will always be able to derive a presentation token for a given presentation policy, which will be accepted by the service provider.

Unforgeability. Intuitively, this property requires that no user is able to derive a valid presentation token for a given presentation policy, unless she has previously obtained a credential satisfying the presentation policy from the issuer. A bit more formally, we assume that an adversary may request arbitrary credentials on attributes of his choice, and also request arbitrary presentation tokens from other users, e.g., by taking the role of a corrupted service provider. Eventually, the adversary outputs a presentation token for a presentation policy of his choice. We now say that an ABC scheme is unforgeable, if the adversary is unable to generate a valid presentation token, if none of the obtained credentials satisfies the policy. Note that this notion of unforgeability implicitly also covers replay attacks.

In the case that the ABC system supports revocation, the adversary may decide which credentials to revoke, and also succeeds with a forgery if he only knows revoked credentials satisfying the given presentation policy.

Privacy. Privacy in an ABC system covers multiple flavours. Firstly, privacy guarantees that the service provider does not gain any information about undisclosed attributes. Secondly, it requires that even if the service provider and the issuer collude or are controlled by the same entity, they will not be able to re-identify the user, i.e., it is infeasible to link issuance and presentation sessions, except by the information explicitly disclosed during these phases. Finally, privacy guarantees unlinkability of different presentation sessions by the same user. That is, a service provider cannot distinguish two presentation tokens from the same user from two presentation tokens computed by different users, as long as the attributes revealed during presentation are the same for these two users.

Note that this latter property is not available in all ABC systems such as, e.g., UProve [6,25], where presentations of the same credentials can be linked and thus privacy is only guaranteed if credentials are only used once.

Besides these mandatory requirements, many ABC systems also give additional security guarantees. For instance in the case of inspection, non-frameability guarantees that no set of colluding users, issuers, and inspectors, are able to generate a presentation token which, when opened by the inspector, will link to a certain user outside this set. However, a detailed description of these advanced properties is beyond the scope of this workshop summary.

2.3   Cryptographic Building Blocks

In the following we briefly describe the two central cryptographic primitives that are typically being used when constructing ABC systems, and give some intuition how such systems are often constructed.

Digital signatures. A digital signature scheme [20] is a cryptographic mechanism for ensuring the integrity and authenticity of a message. To do so, a signer generates runs a key generation algorithm, obtaining a secret and a public key. Using the secret key, the signer can now compute signatures on arbitrary messages, which can then be validated by a verifier using the signer's public key.

The unforgeability property of a signature scheme ensures that no adversary, having seen arbitrarily many signatures on messages of his choice, may come up with a valid signature on a previously unsigned message. Sometimes, a stronger notion of unforgeability is needed, requiring that the adversary cannot generate generate fresh signatures on previously signed messages either.

Zero-knowledge proofs of knowledge. A zero-knowledge proof of knowledge [11,16,19,27] is a cryptographic protocol which allows a prover to convince a verifier that she knows a secret piece of information, without revealing anything more than what is already revealed by the statement itself. For instance, the prover may prove that she knows x such that $y = g^x$ in some cyclic group where the discrete logarithm problem is hard, without revealing any information about x. In the context of ABC systems, we usually consider non-interactive zero-knowledge proofs, where the prover locally computes a proof, and sends it to the verifier, without the need for additional communication rounds.

The intuition behind many ABC systems, including, e.g., [4,7,9,10], is now as follows. In the key generation phase, the issuer generates a key pair for a digital signature scheme. Upon issuance, the user and the issuer agree on a set of attributes $(a_1, \ldots, a_n)$, and the issuer computes a digital signature σ on $(a_1, \ldots, a_n)$. When computing a presentation token which discloses attributes $(a_i)_{i \in D}$, the user derives a zero-knowledge proof of knowledge π, proving that she knows a digital signature σ on $(a_1, \ldots, a_n)$, while keeping σ and $(a_i)_{i \notin D}$ private. The service provider then simply checks the validity of the zero-knowledge proof.

To add inspection, the inspector computes a key pair for a public key encryption scheme. Upon issuance, a unique user identifier is embedded as an additional attribute a_{n+1}, and the presentation token is enhanced as follows: the user computes a ciphertext c, and then generates a proof π showing that the user knows a signature σ on $(a_1, \ldots, a_n, a_{n+1})$, such that a_{n+1} is also contained in c; again, all information except for $(a_i)_{i \in D}$ are kept private.

Similarly, for revocation, on possibility is to embed a revocation handle as attribute a_{n+2}, and let the revocation authority publish a list of revoked attributes. The user can then extend the proof π to additionally show that the revocation handle embedded in her credential is not contained in the given list. For details on constructions, we refer to the original literature.

3   Demonstration Case and Piloting Results

In this section, we will now introduce the concrete use case which is currently under ongoing development within the H2020 CyberSec4Europe project[1], and present feedback from an initial user study which. While we only give a high-level summary here, we refer to the full reports for more details [28–30].

3.1   Demonstrator Background and Specification

In the early 2010s, a number of forged university degrees among civil servants was identified in Greece [15], where companies sold "degrees" on the Internet without requiring the buyer to do anything more than pay a fee. One way to combat this fraud could be the use of digital university certificates, which provide formal and tamper-proof proof of the courses taken and degrees obtained by a student. Motivated by the aforementioned incidents, the aim of this demonstrator within the H2020 CyberSec4Europe project is therefore to develop a platform that allows attribute-based credentials to be obtained from the university when passing an exam or obtaining a degree. These credentials can then be used in various scenarios, some of which are being developed as demonstrators within the project.

For example, when applicants apply for a PhD position at a university, they need to prove that they have certain degrees (e.g. a Bachelor's or Master's degree in a relevant field) and have taken certain courses to meet the formal requirements. To ensure the impartiality of the process at later stages, applicants may only want to prove that they meet the requirements, but not disclose any other sensitive information. For example, to avoid discrimination on the basis of age or gender, the applicant may wish to disclose their degree but not their full name, date of birth or the date on which the degree was issued; similarly, other forms of discrimination can be avoided by, for example, concealing the university that awarded the degree. Similar needs may arise when applying for a job where certain academic requirements must be met. Again, applicants may wish to withhold certain information, at least during the initial formal assessment of suitability, and only disclose it if invited. This also reduces the risk for the employer, as it never collects sensitive information about unsuccessful applicants, which could then be shared in the event of a data breach. Finally, anonymous credentials can also be useful, e.g., to prove to a public authority that courses have been taken with a sufficient number of ECTS credits to receive certain types of study allowance. However, again, it is not necessary to disclose the exact courses, grades, or number of ECTS credits taken.

3.2   The CyberSec4Europe Demonstrator

On a high level, the architecture chosen for the CyberSec4Europe demonstrator follows a natural approach, as can be seen in Fig. 2. The university serves as the

---

[1] https://cybersec4europe.eu.

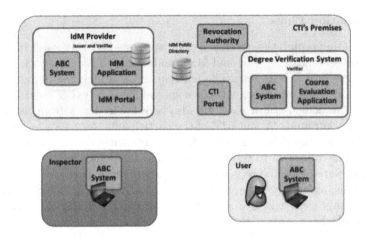

Fig. 2. High-level overview of the CyberSec4Europe architecture.

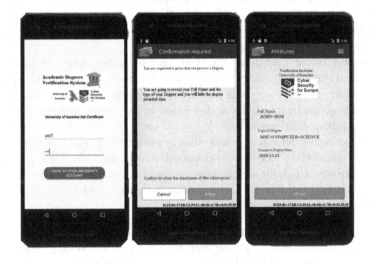

Fig. 3. Impressions of the graphical user interface.

identity provider, and employs all components necessary for issuing credentials to a user, who locally stores the received credentials. The Degree Verification System, as part of the job application portal, will later verify all presentation tokens received from a user during an application process. The inspector has currently not been implemented yet within our demonstrator, but will be located in a separate entity, which may or may not be controlled by the issuer.

On the user side, a mobile app was implemented, which allows the user to obtain and manage her credentials, and which can be used to derive presentation tokens when revealing sensitive information to a service provider. Some impressions of this application are given in Fig. 3.

3.3   Evaluation Phase

In a first piloting round, the developed pilot was tested with 42 participants with different backgrounds (i.e., BSc and MSc candidates) to give feedback regarding usability, perceived privacy, etc. The participants had mainly computer science related backgrounds, however, without a special focus on cyber security. Future versions of the demonstrator case will also seek for feedback from participants with other backgrounds. About 67% of the participants were male and 33% were female. The age ranged from 22 years to 35 years, with an average of 28 years.

After an introduction to the technology and the demonstrator scenario, the participants were requested to perform a variety of tasks, such as obtaining digital credentials, and applying for a PhD position at the university. Subsequently, the participants were asked to answer a questionnaire which was divided into three main blocks:

- The first set of questions aimed to understand whether the overall setup of the demonstrator was easy to understand, and whether the tasks where clearly communicated and explained to the students. Furthermore, we aimed at finding out whether from an efficiency and usability point of view, the developed solutions were acceptable.
- The second set of questions aimed at understanding whether participants understood the privacy guarantees of the developed solution. Furthermore, we tried to find out whether participants are willing to trust such solutions, and whether they understand the added value of the technology for the specific use case, but also in general.
- Finally, we asked whether it was clearly understood which attributes were actually revealed to the job application portal, and whether participants see the potential benefit in increasing compliance of service providers using privacy-enhancing identity management systems, in order to comply with legal regulations such as the GDPR.

On a high level, the feedback received from participants was positive, however showing slight biases, e.g., depending on the participants' background and age, which will be further addressed in the next revision of the demonstrator case. For detailed evaluation result, we refer to Sforzin and Bobba [30].

4   The OLYMPUS Framework

In this section, we give an overview on the identity management solution developed in the H2020 OLYMPUS project[2], and how it is applied to the use case that we are reviewing. This solution aims to offer advanced Single Sign (SSO) capabilities with special attention to privacy aspects. Concretely, the main focus is addressing the issues that traditional SSO solutions have in that respect, that mostly are caused by the fully trusted Identity Provider (IdP) that becomes a single point of failure:

---

[2] olympus-project.eu/.

- A compromised (or malicious) IdP can impersonate users, gaining full access to all their accounts and personal data. Also, the user's login credentials are jeopardized.
- A compromised (or malicious) IdP can forge identities, effectively bypassing access control mechanisms of service providers that trust the IdP for authentication.
- The IdP can track user behaviour, learning about which services the user interacts with and when they do it.

To tackle the root of the problem, the OLYMPUS identity management system distributes the task of the IdP among several partial identity providers. As the collaboration of all of them is necessary for performing their role, compromising one (or even all but one) identity provider is not enough to gain control over the system and carry out the aforementioned attacks. Apart from this, novel cryptographic mechanisms are applied to further mitigate the security risks and to boost user privacy and their control over their identity. As general and different scenarios as possible: minimizing hardware requirements, two complementary approaches, compatible (as much as possible) with standards and traditional technologies. Also, user-friendly (as it is a common issue of cryptographic approaches).

- Minimizing the requirements on user hardware, offering user-friendly authentication using passwords without requiring trusted hardware or software.
- A novel system compatible with traditional technologies that respects users' privacy while remaining user-friendly is obtained

The OLYMPUS solution is completely open-source, and can be found in the project's public repository[3]. There, you can find all the necessary code to deploy your own identity providers, as well as the library code for clients and verifiers. The project's documentation is linked within the repository, but you can also start to get used to the code base and its concepts through a guided use case demonstration available in a separate repository[4].

4.1   OLYMPUS Architecture and Roles

The ecosystem of the OLYMPUS identity management system (overview in Fig. 4, more details in [32]) involves three main participants: the virtual Identity Provider (vIdP), the user client and the relying party (RP).

Virtual IdP: It is a set of entities (partial IdPs) that collaborate to perform the role of identity provider. Each partial IdP has three modules for the main functionalities:
- Distributed authentication: account management and user login through password verification (and potentially multi-factor authentication). It is also a key component in the enrolment process, in which attributes from trusted external attribute providers are linked to the account.

---

[3] https://bitbucket.alexandra.dk/projects/OL/repos/olympus-identity/.
[4] https://bitbucket.alexandra.dk/projects/OL/repos/usecase-3/.

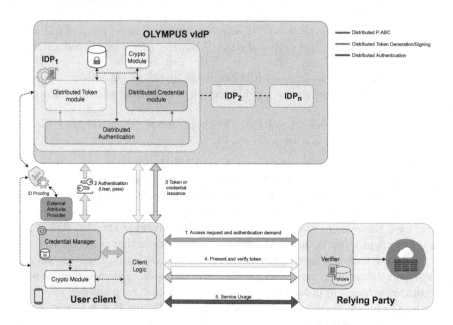

Fig. 4. Simplified version of the OLYMPUS architecture.

- Distributed credential module: Generates credential shares for the distributed p-ABC scheme. Each share is generated independently by each partial IdP (i.e., no communication or explicit collaboration is needed during the process).
- Distributed token module: Generates token shares (RSA-like signature shares), which are part of the OLYMPUS "online" approach, leveraging PESTO.

User client: Provides common identity functionalities (registration, authentication, managing attributes...), abstracting from the distributed nature of the IdP. Apart from application logic and flows, it is in charge of cryptographic operations (like combination of signature shares) and secure management of credentials.

Relying party: Accepts OLYMPUS tokens (PESTO or p-ABC) for user authentication in order to perform attribute-based access control. The relying party will define and communicate policies that must be fulfilled for granting access (e.g., being over 18 or revealing the user's name).

4.2 Application to the Use Case

The OLYMPUS virtual IdP is a great asset for ensuring privacy preservation for end users in the university use case. In particular, the p-ABC approach can be used to replace the Idemix [7] credentials used in the first-phase pilot, taking advantage of the improvements of OLYMPUS as an identity management system. More concretely, the p-ABC used in OLYMPUS is based on Pointcheval-Sanders multi-signatures (PS-MS), which are more efficient than the Camenisch-Lysyanskaya (CL) signatures used in Idemix. Additionally, PS-MS allow distributed issuance and the setup phase for the cryptography can be done independently by each partial identity provider. With the distribution of the IdP, we gain security against impersonation and forgery attacks. What is more, partial IdPs can be controlled by different legal entities, which leads to more beneficial conditions in terms of privacy and data control from the viewpoint of regulations like GDPR. However, it is true that deployment and management of the group of IdPs becomes more complex, especially in the case where multiple legal entities are involved, as agreements and contracts must be reached. Apart from the direct benefits of using the distributed scheme, the OLYMPUS infrastructure brings other technical advantages. First, it offers user-friendly account management and authentication, giving users familiar options like passwords and two-factor authentication. Also, the implementation is being integrated with W3C Verifiable Credentials specification, an emerging standard for representing digital credential, which encourages interoperability and adoption. However, Idemix has some functionalities that can be useful depending on the use case and are not supported by the current OLYMPUS implementation.

- Blind issuance, where the issuer does not learn user attributes but only commitments over them (blindly signs them).
- Other proof types, like (non)-membership.
- Credential revocation and inspection

Nevertheless, following a modular approach these functionalities are also technically possible (some theoretical work has already been done in this direction) using the OLYMPUS tools.

5   Conclusion and Future Work

In this workshop, we presented the conceptual foundations of privacy-preserving identity management solutions. We then presented a concrete application scenario in the educational domain which is currently under development within the H2020 CyberSec4Europe project. We presented first evaluation results, and ongoing developments based on the results of the H2020 OLYMPUS project, which can achieve additional security and privacy guarantees compared to the previous iteration.

Using the synergies of these two projects not only allows us to enhance the demonstration case within CyberSec4Europe, but also improves and evolves the OLYMPUS identity management system with new capabilities. First, we aim to establish a trusted public information framework for IdPs, users and relying parties based on Distributed Ledger Technologies (first approximation can be found in [33]). In addition, we are working on adding new functionalities to the framework, enabling fine-grained credential revocation and adding support for credential inspection.

Acknowledgements. The work leading to this workshop was funded by the European Union under the H2020 Programme Grant Agreement No. 830929 (CyberSec4Europe) and No. 786725 (OLYMPUS).

References

1. Baldimtsi, F., Camenisch, J., Hanzlik, L., Krenn, S., Lehmann, A., Neven, G.: Recovering lost device-bound credentials. In: Malkin, T., Kolesnikov, V., Lewko, A.B., Polychronakis, M. (eds.) ACNS 2015. LNCS, vol. 9092, pp. 307–327. Springer, Cham (2015). https://doi.org/10.1007/978-3-319-28166-7_15
2. Belenkiy, M., Camenisch, J., Chase, M., Kohlweiss, M., Lysyanskaya, A., Shacham, H.: Randomizable proofs and delegatable anonymous credentials. In: Halevi, S. (ed.) CRYPTO 2009. LNCS, vol. 5677, pp. 108–125. Springer, Heidelberg (2009). https://doi.org/10.1007/978-3-642-03356-8_7
3. Blömer, J., Bobolz, J.: Delegatable attribute-based anonymous credentials from dynamically malleable signatures. In: Preneel, B., Vercauteren, F. (eds.) ACNS 2018. LNCS, vol. 10892, pp. 221–239. Springer, Cham (2018). https://doi.org/10.1007/978-3-319-93387-0_12
4. Bobolz, J., Eidens, F., Krenn, S., Ramacher, S., Samelin, K.: Issuer-hiding attribute-based credentials. In: Conti, M., Stevens, M., Krenn, S. (eds.) CANS 2021. LNCS, vol. 13099, pp. 158–178. Springer, Heidelberg (2021). https://doi.org/10.1007/978-3-030-92548-2_9
5. Bosk, D., Bouget, S., Buchegger, S.: Distance-bounding, privacy-preserving attribute-based credentials. In: Krenn, S., Shulman, H., Vaudenay, S. (eds.) CANS 2020. LNCS, vol. 12579, pp. 147–166. Springer, Cham (2020). https://doi.org/10.1007/978-3-030-65411-5_8
6. Brands, S.: Rethinking public key infrastructure and digital certificates - buildingin privacy. Ph.D. thesis, Eindhoven Institute of Technology (1999)
7. Camenisch, J., Herreweghen, E.V.: Design and implementation of the idemix anonymous credential system. In: Atluri, V. (ed.) ACM Conference on Computer and Communications Security - CCS 2002, pp. 21–30. ACM (2002). https://doi.org/10.1145/586110.586114
8. Camenisch, J., Krenn, S., Lehmann, A., Mikkelsen, G.L., Neven, G., Pedersen, M.Ø.: Formal treatment of privacy-enhancing credential systems. In: Dunkelman, O., Keliher, L. (eds.) SAC 2015. LNCS, vol. 9566, pp. 3–24. Springer, Cham (2016). https://doi.org/10.1007/978-3-319-31301-6_1
9. Camenisch, J., Lysyanskaya, A.: A signature scheme with efficient protocols. In: Cimato, S., Persiano, G., Galdi, C. (eds.) SCN 2002. LNCS, vol. 2576, pp. 268–289. Springer, Heidelberg (2003). https://doi.org/10.1007/3-540-36413-7_20
10. Camenisch, J., Lysyanskaya, A.: Signature schemes and anonymous credentials from bilinear maps. In: Franklin, M. (ed.) CRYPTO 2004. LNCS, vol. 3152, pp. 56–72. Springer, Heidelberg (2004). https://doi.org/10.1007/978-3-540-28628-8_4
11. Chase, M., Lysyanskaya, A.: On signatures of knowledge. In: Dwork, C. (ed.) CRYPTO 2006. LNCS, vol. 4117, pp. 78–96. Springer, Heidelberg (2006). https://doi.org/10.1007/11818175_5
12. Chaum, D.: Untraceable electronic mail, return addresses, and digital pseudonyms. Commun. ACM **24**(2), 84–88 (1981). https://doi.org/10.1145/358549.358563
13. Chaum, D.: Security without identification: transaction systems to make big brother obsolete. Commun. ACM **28**(10), 1030–1044 (1985). https://doi.org/10.1145/4372.4373

14. Crites, E.C., Lysyanskaya, A.: Delegatable anonymous credentials from mercurial signatures. In: Matsui, M. (ed.) CT-RSA 2019. LNCS, vol. 11405, pp. 535–555. Springer, Cham (2019). https://doi.org/10.1007/978-3-030-12612-4_27
15. ekathimerini.com: Minister admits number of civil servants with forged degrees was exaggerated (2013). https://www.ekathimerini.com/news/154846/minister-admits-number-of-civil-servants-with-forged-degrees-was-exaggerated/
16. Fiat, A., Shamir, A.: How to prove yourself: practical solutions to identification and signature problems. In: Odlyzko, A.M. (ed.) CRYPTO 1986. LNCS, vol. 263, pp. 186–194. Springer, Heidelberg (1987). https://doi.org/10.1007/3-540-47721-7_12
17. de Fuentes, J.M., González-Manzano, L., Serna-Olvera, J., Veseli, F.: Assessment of attribute-based credentials for privacy-preserving road traffic services in smart cities. Pers. Ubiquit. Comput. 21(5), 869–891 (2017). https://doi.org/10.1007/s00779-017-1057-6
18. García-Rodríguez, J., Torres Moreno, R., Bernal Bernabe, J., Skarmeta, A.: Implementation and evaluation of a privacy-preserving distributed ABC scheme based on multi-signatures. J. Inf. Secur. Appl. 62, 102971 (2021). https://www.sciencedirect.com/science/article/pii/S2214212621001824
19. Goldwasser, S., Micali, S., Rackoff, C.: The knowledge complexity of interactive proof-systems (extended abstract). In: Sedgewick, R. (ed.) ACM Symposium on Theory of Computing - STOC 1985, pp. 291–304. ACM (1985). https://doi.org/10.1145/22145.22178
20. Goldwasser, S., Micali, S., Rivest, R.L.: A digital signature scheme secure against adaptive chosen-message attacks. SIAM J. Comput. 17(2), 281–308 (1988). https://doi.org/10.1137/0217017
21. Haböck, U., Krenn, S.: Breaking and fixing anonymous credentials for the cloud. In: Mu, Y., Deng, R.H., Huang, X. (eds.) CANS 2019. LNCS, vol. 11829, pp. 249–269. Springer, Cham (2019). https://doi.org/10.1007/978-3-030-31578-8_14
22. Han, J., Chen, L., Schneider, S., Treharne, H., Wesemeyer, S.: Privacy-preserving electronic ticket scheme with attribute-based credentials. IEEE Trans. Dependable Secur. Comput. 18(4), 1836–1849 (2021). https://doi.org/10.1109/TDSC.2019.2940946
23. Krenn, S., Lorünser, T., Salzer, A., Striecks, C.: Towards attribute-based credentials in the cloud. In: Capkun, S., Chow, S.S.M. (eds.) CANS 2017. LNCS, vol. 11261, pp. 179–202. Springer, Cham (2018). https://doi.org/10.1007/978-3-030-02641-7_9
24. Liagkou, V., Metakides, G., Pyrgelis, A., Raptopoulos, C., Spirakis, P., Stamatiou, Y.C.: Privacy preserving course evaluations in Greek higher education institutes: an e-participation case study with the empowerment of attribute based credentials. In: Preneel, B., Ikonomou, D. (eds.) APF 2012. LNCS, vol. 8319, pp. 140–156. Springer, Heidelberg (2014). https://doi.org/10.1007/978-3-642-54069-1_9
25. Paquin, C., Zaverucha, G.: U-prove cryptographic specification v1.1 (revision2). Technical report, Microsoft Corporation, April 2013
26. Pussewalage, H.S.G., Oleshchuk, V.A.: An anonymous delegatable attribute-based credential scheme for a collaborative e-health environment. ACM Trans. Internet Tech. 19(3), 41:1-41:22 (2019). https://doi.org/10.1145/3338854
27. Schnorr, C.P.: Efficient identification and signatures for smart cards. In: Brassard, G. (ed.) CRYPTO 1989. LNCS, vol. 435, pp. 239–252. Springer, New York (1990). https://doi.org/10.1007/0-387-34805-0_22
28. Sforzin, A.: D5.1 - Requirements analysis of demonstration cases phase 1. H2020 CyberSec4Europe project deliverable (2020). https://cybersec4europe.eu/

29. Sforzin, A.: D5.2 - Specification and set-up demonstration case phase 1. H2020 CyberSec4Europe project deliverable (2020). https://cybersec4europe.eu/
30. Sforzin, A., Bobba, R.: D5.3 - Validation of demonstration case phase 1. H2020 CyberSec4Europe project deliverable (2021). https://cybersec4europe.eu/
31. Stamatiou, Y., et al.: Course evaluation in higher education: the Patras pilot of ABC4Trust. In: Rannenberg, K., Camenisch, J., Sabouri, A. (eds.) Attribute-Based Credentials for Trust, pp. 197–239. Springer, Cham (2015). https://doi.org/10.1007/978-3-319-14439-9_7
32. Torres Moreno, R., et al.: The OLYMPUS architecture - oblivious identity management for private user-friendly services. Sensors 20(3), 945 (2020)
33. Torres Moreno, R., García-Rodríguez, J., Bernal Bernabe, J., Skarmeta, A.: A trusted approach for decentralised and privacy-preserving identity management. IEEE Access 9, 105788–105804 (2021)

The State of Surveillance – An Overall Account of Surveillance?

Felix Bieker[✉]

Unabhängiges Landeszentrum für Datenschutz (ULD, Office of the Data Protection Commissioner) Schleswig-Holstein, Kiel, Germany
fbieker@datenschutzzentrum.de

Abstract. The article argues that the extent of surveillance has reached a critical level for democratic societies. However, the jurisprudence of the ECtHR, ECJ and German constitutional court, which never question the extent of surveillance on the structural level, rather aims to legitimize even the most far-reaching measures and thus does not offer effective ex post protection. The introduction of legislative ex ante mechanisms also does not promise to counter the current issues surrounding surveillance measures. Instead, such a mechanism could further legitimize surveillance. The article concludes that while tools to assess the level of surveillance could be helpful when they depart from the premise that the extent of surveillance must be reduced, civil society is best suited to operate and advance these tools in the general discourse.

Keywords: Surveillance · Privacy · Data protection · Data retention · ECtHR · ECJ · Bundesverfassungsgericht · Big brother watch · Digital Rights Ireland · Surveillance calculus · Überwachungs-Gesamtrechnung

1 Introduction

As technology advances and is capable of processing ever more data, it brings new possibilities of surveillance. Whether it is location tracking via Wifi and Bluetooth or automated face or voice recognition, the new data produced by these technologies allow for further intrusions. And from this new data springs a "need" to process those data [1]. This "need" has meanwhile led to a steady stream of surveillance measures, which observers argue has already led to a surveillance society [2, 3].

This is exemplified by the myriad of new surveillance technologies introduced by various legislators: From the bulk retention of air passenger data [4], to DNA phenotyping [5], a technology falsely touted as "genetic composite sketch", the use of facial

I would like to thank all participants of the 2021 IFIP Summer School, who provided input at this tutorial. This work is funded by the German Ministry of Education and Research within the project "Privacy, Democracy and Self-Determination in the Age of Artifical Intelligence and Globalisation" (PRIDS), https://forum-privatheit.de.

M. Friedewald et al. (Eds.): Privacy and Identity 2021, IFIP AICT 644, pp. 47–53, 2022.
https://doi.org/10.1007/978-3-030-99100-5_5

recognition software [6] or the expanded monitoring of recipients of social welfare benefits [7], all of which often lead to the discrimination of already marginalized groups (generally cf. [8]).

All of these and the many other, already existing surveillance instruments impact the lives of large portions of the population. And they can create a feeling as well as a reality of being constantly monitored (also cf. [9]). In sum these surveillance pressures can have adverse effects on individuals as well as a democratic society as a whole [10].

Yet, these effects are only reluctantly being considered in the legal debate, where the focus, as is the nature of Western judiciary proceedings, lies on an individual complaint about a specific measure considered to violate specific rights. In the following, I will briefly introduce the relevant rights concerning data processing on the European and German national level and consider the jurisprudence of the European Court of Human Rights (ECtHR), the European Court of Justice (ECJ) and the German constitutional court (2). I will then consider whether and how an overall account of surveillance should and could be attained (3) and conclude with an outlook (4) for a way towards rescinding surveillance measures.

2 Rights, Courts and Surveillance

In Europe, there are several layers of rights protections, which aim, inter alia, to protect individuals from the State. On the regional level, there is the ECHR [11], which contains the right to privacy, while on the EU level, the Charter of Fundamental Rights (CFR) [12] additionally contains a right to data protection (in depth, cf. [10]). Both of these rights are concerned when personal data are processed and have been invoked against surveillance measures. On the national level, in Germany, there are especially the rights to informational self-determination as well as to the integrity and confidentiality of IT systems provided by the Basic Law [13], which also protect individuals from data processing and, inter alia, against surveillance measures.

These rights are enforced via judicial proceedings. However, courts will usually consider a specific measure and examine whether it violates any of the invoked rights. The courts will generally not move (much) beyond the scope of the claims and merely assess the case at hand, without considering the wider legal and societal implications of surveillance. Nevertheless, there have been judgments that (seem to) have referred to a broader scope of assessment.

In the recent ECtHR's Grand Chamber judgment in the case of Big Brother Watch [14], it appeared, prima facie, that the court had broadened its approach. It held that the UK's bulk data retention regime amounted to a fundamental rights violation. In its analysis, the ECtHR made reference to a 'global assessment' of the measure in question. Yet, when applying this standard, it found that there were several criteria, which, when they were all fulfilled, would provide sufficient safeguards to legitimize even one of the most far-reaching data retention schemes [14, paras. 360 et seqq.]. In that regard, the global assessment does the opposite of what it could be understood to mean: rather than consider the overall impact of surveillance or at least the wider implications of a surveillance measure, the Court effectively lowered the standard of protection [15] awarded by an earlier judgment by the chamber in the same case [16].

At the EU level, the ECJ, has repeatedly engaged with mass-surveillance instruments [17–20] and by now developed a steady jurisprudence on the requirements, which it finds to legitimize such measures (cf. most recently [21–23]). It has lately begun to acknowledge some of the risks of discrimination entailed in automated surveillance systems, especially those employing machine learning technology [19 para. 141; 21 paras. 180–182], which members of the affected marginalized groups have long pointed out [24–26]. However, the court has considered the wider effects of surveillance only fleetingly. In its seminal judgment on the data retention directive, *Digital Rights Ireland and Seitlinger*, the ECJ stated that such a mass retention was likely to create a feeling of constant surveillance [15, para. 37]. The Court has since reiterated this finding in subsequent judgments and found that certain measures would lead to 'virtually total' surveillance [20, paras. 71–72; 19, paras. 183–187]. However, the ECJ has only considered these effects with regard to the weight of an interference and, in all of these cases, found that the interferences with the right to privacy and the right to data protection were particularly serious. It has not taken the further implications of surveillance creating effects on democratic societies into consideration.

The passages from the ECJ judgments echo the case law of the German constitutional court: in a 2010 judgment concerning the German bulk data retention rules [27], the court found that the State could not completely register the populace's exercise of their constitutional freedoms. This argument was based on the court's most widely received ruling on data protection, the census judgment of 1983. There it had stated that it would not be in accordance with fundamental rights and the legal order, if modern information technology rendered the individual a mere object of automated processing [28]. It argued that individuals who are unsure whether their conduct is constantly monitored and permanently recorded, used or transferred to third parties, will try not to raise suspicion through deviant behaviour.

In its 2010 judgment, the court ruled that in the future, the legislator had to exercise greater restraint with regard to surveillance measures [27]. The State could not retain any data useful for law enforcement purposes. Rather, in a democracy under the rule of law, the retention of such data had to be an exception.

With this ruling, it may seem that the constitutional court reigned in the "needs" of surveillance. However, in the case of the bulk data retention at hand, it found the measure to still just be permissible with certain adjustments. The court only hinted that even further reaching surveillance could be struck down in an *orbiter dictum*, i.e. a non-operative part of the judgment, which has no direct legal effects. Consequently, the rules stayed in force until the ECJ found them incompatible with EU fundamental rights [17]. Furthermore, even though this issue has been raised by applicants in recent proceedings [29], the court has not engaged with its own arguments.

3   An Overall Account of Surveillance?

Nevertheless, the arguments of the constitutional court and the ECJ could be further pursued in order to broaden the scope of review for surveillance measures. There has long been a debate about the effects on and amount of surveillance in Western societies at least since these programmes were extended considerably in the wake of 9/11

[9, 30]. However, it has taken considerable time before these discussions reached the legal discourse.

In the German academic debate, the arguments of the constitutional court were used to argue that there was a limit of State surveillance which must not be exceeded, but which apparently had not yet been reached. With this so-called surveillance calculus (Überwachungs-Gesamtrechnung) [31], the court had stipulated a requirement of the legislator to maintain an overview of all State surveillance measures in effect and the gravity of the interferences entailed by these measures. Once a certain, but undefined, threshold was reached, the legislator would have to exchange one surveillance measure for another, rather than introducing additional ones.

However, such a compilation, in practice, encounters issues on several levels: On the micro level it is unclear, how the different surveillance measures of the various legislators on the EU, national and local level can be counted and, especially, weighed. Furthermore, it is unclear how the legislator would have to act, once the threshold was reached [32]. Would the oldest surveillance measure have to be repealed or would the latest never take effect?

Another difficult question is the qualification of interferences with rights. The gravity of an interference and whether it is justified is the result of a deliberative process, so different results may be reached via different argumentative avenues. Such results do not easily lend themselves to being quantified. Rather, it must be borne in mind that pseudo-mathematical calculations may seem to deliver objective results, but only serve to obscure the weighing that led to the result.

More importantly, on the macro level, such a calculus poses the question of the effects of such an evaluation by the legislator. After all, the legislator has demonstrated a great willingness to continually pass new legislation to introduce surveillance measures. If they are now asked to provide an evaluation of the existing surveillance regime, they might be tempted not to assess this question with the required rigor.

If the legislator, after carrying out such an in-depth assessment, concluded that the threshold of harmful surveillance has not been reached, such a calculus would ultimately serve to legitimize the present surveillance apparatus rather than challenge it. If the aggregate weight of all measures is to be examined, then a benchmark for an acceptable level of surveillance has to be defined in advance. Yet, it is doubtful that, if a benchmark were set at this point, the legislator itself or a court would find that the current level of surveillance is already unacceptable, as under the jurisprudence of the German constitutional court this would mean that the status quo is not in accordance with democratic principles [33].

An alternative approach to the surveillance calculus might be found in existing legislation: In Article 35(10) GDPR the legislator introduced the legislative data protection impact assessment (DPIA). With this instrument the legislator, as part of the general impact assessment of a new provision, can already perform a generalized DPIA. Under such a legislative DPIA the envisaged legislative measure would have to be vetted for adverse impacts on the rights of individuals. However, as any legal provision on a measure that still has to be realized in practice, it would only analyse the rules on an abstract level and would have to be accompanied by a specific DPIA once the rules have been implemented [34]. The scope of this assessment could include the effects of currently existing surveillance measures and how the proposed measure would impact on these.

However, the legislative DPIA, just as any instrument that obliges the legislator to consider whether a surveillance measure is justifiable, encounters the same issues with regard to the legitimization effect, described above. In deciding to introduce a new surveillance measure, the legislator has mostly already deemed that such a measure is indeed necessary to combat a perceived threat. This may indeed be the biggest obstacle to any ex ante control instrument.

According to the separation of power that is a facet of the rule of law, it is the responsibility of the administration to implement the measure in a way that complies to fundamental rights. Where this is not the case, individuals can challenge measures before the courts. Yet, from the case law of the German constitutional court, the ECJ and the ECtHR, it does not appear that the ex post control offered by the judiciary effectively limits the amount of surveillance on a structural level. Rather they inadvertently serve to further legitimize far-reaching surveillance measures. In that regard, the courts' jurisprudence could also be characterized as going two steps forward and one step back, as they will strike down particularly far-reaching provisions of surveillance measures, but not actually question the measures themselves. This could also be observed with the judgments on data retention, where all of the courts only prescribed several safeguards, but did not question the massive data collection itself.

4 Outlook: A Way Forward

With regard to the problematic legitimizing effect of legislative ex ante and judicial ex post control of mass surveillance, there may be other, more effective means of surveying surveillance for different actors. Certainly, an overview of the current state of surveillance can have a sobering effect for the public [35], who may not be aware of the extent of existing legal bases for such measures.

Perhaps such activities are better performed by independent advocacy groups and activists, rather than lawyers and courts. At a time, when the extent of surveillance is so expansive that, outside the constitutional law discourse, other disciplines argue that we have already been living in surveillance societies for a considerable time, we must seek these other avenues as more effective routes to organize against surveillance.

However, the lessons learnt from the legal discourse can be employed to develop tools that civil society can use in order to implement a useable way to monitor surveillance measures. In order to avoid the legitimizing effect, any such examination should be carried out independently from public bodies and start from the premise that the level of surveillance is already critical. The focus should be on rescinding surveillance measures rather than expanding them. Such a tool should further ensure that the deliberative nature of such an examination is not be expressed in pseudo-mathematical formulas. Rather, it should rely on providing an easily workable metric that allows for comprehensible illustration and comparison on a scale containing three or four tiers. Such a tool could provide an additional basis for discussions, organizing and protest in order to counter the effects of surveillance on our societies.

References

1. Rule, J.B.: "Needs" for surveillance and the movement to protect privacy. In: Ball, K., Haggerty, K.D., Lyon, D. (eds.) Routledge Handbook of Surveillance Studies, pp. 64–71. Routledge, London/New York (2014)
2. Lyon, D.: Surveillance society. In: Monitoring Everyday Life. Open University Press, Buckingham/Philadelphia (2001)
3. Zuboff, S.: Big other: surveillance capitalism and the prospects of an information civilization. J. Inf. Technol. **30**, 75–89 (2015). https://doi.org/10.1057/jit.2015.5
4. Orrù, E.: The European PNR framework and the changing landscape of EU-security. VerfBlog 21 December 2021. https://verfassungsblog.de/os3-pnr/
5. Bartram, I., Plümecke, T., Zur Nieden, A.: Extended DNA analyses: surveillance technology at the intersection of racism and sexism. Internet Policy Rev. **10**(4) (2021). https://doi.org/10.14763/2021.4.1603
6. Buolamwini, J., Gebru, T.: Gender shades: intersectional accuracy disparities in commercial gender classification. In: Proceedings of Machine Learning Research, vol. 81, pp. 1–15 (2018). http://proceedings.mlr.press/v81/buolamwini18a.html
7. Carter, L.: Prescripted living: gender stereotypes and data-based surveillance in the UK welfare state. Internet Policy Rev. **10**(4) (2021). https://doi.org/10.14763/2021.4.1593
8. Theilen, J.T., Baur, A., Bieker, F., Ammicht Quinn, R., Hansen, M., González Fuster, G.: Feminist data protection: an introduction. Internet Policy Rev. **10**(4) (2021). https://doi.org/10.14763/2021.4.1609
9. Fox Cahn, A., Enzer, E.: A hollow promise: 20 years of constitutional erosion in the name of counter-terrorism. VerfBlog 13 December 2021. https://verfassungsblog.de/os3-hollow-promise/
10. Bieker, F.: The Right to Data Protection – Individual and Structural Dimensions of Data Protection in EU Law. T.M.C. Asser Press/Springer, The Hague (2022)
11. Convention for the Protection of Human Rights and Fundamental Freedoms, ETS No. 005, 4 November 1950. https://www.coe.int/en/web/conventions/full-list?module=treaty-detail&treatynum=005
12. Charter of Fundamental Rights of the European Union, OJ C 326, 26.10.2012, pp. 391–407. https://eur-lex.europa.eu/legal-content/EN/TXT/?uri=celex%3A12012P%2FTXT
13. Grundgesetz für die Bundesrepublik Deutschland, BGBl III, 100-01. https://www.gesetze-im-internet.de/gg/BJNR000010949.html
14. ECtHR [GC]. Judgment of 25 May 2021, Big Brother Watch and Others v. the United Kingdom, App. nos. 58170/13, 62322/14 and 24960/15. ECLI:CE:ECHR:2021:0525JUD005817013. https://hudoc.echr.coe.int/eng?i=001-210077
15. Milanovic, M.: The grand normalization of mass surveillance: ECtHR grand chamber judgments in big brother watch and centrum för rättvisa. EJIL:Talk! 26 May 2021. https://www.ejiltalk.org/the-grand-normalization-of-mass-surveillance-ecthr-grand-chamber-judgments-in-big-brother-watch-and-centrum-for-rattvisa/
16. ECtHR. Judgment of 13 September 2018, Big Brother Watch and Others v. the United Kingdom, App. nos. 58170/13, 62322/14 and 24960/15. ECLI:CE:ECHR:2018:0913JUD005817013. https://hudoc.echr.coe.int/eng?i=001-186048
17. ECJ. Judgment of 8 April 2014, Case C-293/12 Digital Rights Ireland and Seitlinger and others. ECLI:EU:C:2014:238. https://curia.europa.eu/juris/document/document.jsf?text=&docid=150642&pageIndex=0&doclang=en&mode=req&dir=&occ=first&part=1&cid=5249759

18. ECJ. Judgment of 6 October 2015, Case C-362/14 Maximillian Schrems v Data Protection Commissioner. ECLI:EU:C:2015:650. https://curia.europa.eu/juris/document/document.jsf? text=&docid=169195&pageIndex=0&doclang=EN&mode=lst&dir=&occ=first&part=1& cid=6146191

19. ECJ. Opinion of 26 July 2017 Avis 1/15. ECLI:EU:C:2017:592. https://curia.europa.eu/ juris/document/document.jsf?text=&docid=194498&pageIndex=0&doclang=en&mode= lst&dir=&occ=first&part=1&cid=6146191

20. ECJ. Judgment of 21 December 2016, Joined Cases C-203/15 and C-698/15 Tele2 Sverige. ECLI:EU:C:2016:970. https://curia.europa.eu/juris/document/document.jsf?text=&docid= 186492&pageIndex=0&doclang=EN&mode=lst&dir=&occ=first&part=1&cid=6146191

21. ECJ. Judgment of 6 October 2020, Joined Cases C-511/18, C-512/18 and C-520/18 La Quadrature du Net. ECLI:EU:C:2020:791. https://curia.europa.eu/juris/document/document. jsf?text=&docid=232084&pageIndex=0&doclang=en&mode=lst&dir=&occ=first&part= 1&cid=6146191

22. ECJ. Judgment of 6 October 2020, Case C-623/17, Privacy International. ECLI:EU:C:2020:790. https://curia.europa.eu/juris/document/document.jsf?text=&docid= 232083&pageIndex=0&doclang=en&mode=lst&dir=&occ=first&part=1&cid=6146191

23. ECJ. Judgment of 2 March 2021, Case C-746/18, Prokuratuur. ECLI:EU:C:2021:152. https://curia.europa.eu/juris/document/document.jsf?text=&docid=238381&pageIndex=0& doclang=EN&mode=lst&dir=&occ=first&part=1&cid=6146191

24. Browne, S.: Dark Matters: On the Surveillance of Blackness. Duke University Press, Durham (2015). https://doi.org/10.1215/9780822375302

25. Kalluri, P.: Don't ask if artificial intelligence is good or fair, ask how it shifts power. Nature **583**, 169 (2020). https://doi.org/10.1038/d41586-020-02003-2

26. Costanza-Chock, S., Philip, N., Ahearn, C.: Design justice, A.I., and escape from the matrix of domination. J. Design Sci. (2018). https://doi.org/10.21428/96c8d426

27. Bundesverfassungsgericht. Judgment of 2 March 2010, BVerfGE 125, 260 – Vorratsdatenspeicherung. https://www.bundesverfassungsgericht.de/SharedDocs/Entscheidungen/DE/2010/ 03/rs20100302_1bvr025608.html

28. Bundesverfassungsgericht. Judgment of 15 December 1983, BVerfGE 65, 1 (43) – Volkszählung. https://openjur.de/u/268440.html

29. Bundesverfassungsgericht. Decision of 20 December 2018, - 2 BvR 2377/16 -. http://www. bverfg.de/e/rk20181220_2bvr237716.html

30. Naarttijärvi, M.: The 'Ketchup Effect': The development of public Surveillance in Sweden following 9/11. VerfBlog 15 December 2021. https://verfassungsblog.de/os3-ketchup-effect/

31. Roßnagel, A.: Die "Überwachungs-Gesamtrechnung" – Das BVerfG und die Vorratsdatenspeicherung, NJW 1238 (2010)

32. Hornung, G., Schnabel, C.: Verfassungsrechtlich nicht schlechthin verboten – Das Urteil des Bundesverfassungsgerichts in Sachen Vorratsdatenspeicherung, Deutsche Verwaltungsblätter, pp. 820–833 (2010)

33. Bieker, F., Bremert, B.: Rote Linien im Sand, bei Sturm: Die Überwachungs-Gesamtrechnung. FifF-Kommunikation (4), 34 (2019). https://www.fiff.de/publikationen/fiff-kommunikation/ fk-jhrg-2019/fk-2019-4/fk-4-19-p34.pdf

34. Bieker, F., Bremert, B., Hagendorff, T.: Die Überwachungs-Gesamtrechnung, oder. Es kann nicht sein, was nicht sein darf. In: Roßnagel et al. (eds) Die Fortentwicklung des Datenschutzes, vol. 139, Springer, Wiesbaden (2018)

35. Adensamer, A.: Aspekte einer Überwachungs-Gesamtrechnung, FifF-Kommunikation (4), 34 (2019). https://www.fiff.de/publikationen/fiff-kommunikation/fk-jhrg-2019/fk-2019-4/fk-4-19-p25.pdf

Selected Student Papers

Bringing Privacy, Security and Performance to the Internet of Things Through Usage Control and Blockchains

Nathanael Denis[1,2]([✉]), Sophie Chabridon[1,2], and Maryline Laurent[1,2]

[1] SAMOVAR, Télécom SudParis, Institut Polytechnique de Paris, Évry, France
{nathanael.denis,sophie.chabridon,maryline.laurent}@telecom-sudparis.eu
[2] Chair Values and Policies of Personal Information, Palaiseau, France

Abstract. The Internet of Things (IoT) is bringing new ways to collect and analyse data to develop applications answering or anticipating users' needs. These data may be privacy-sensitive, requiring efficient privacy-preserving mechanisms. The IoT is a distributed system of unprecedented scale, creating challenges for performance and security. Classic blockchains could be a solution by providing decentralisation and strong security guarantees. However they are not efficient and scalable enough for large scale IoT systems, and available tools designed for preserving privacy in blockchains, e.g. coin mixing, have a limited effect due to transaction cost and rate.

This article provides a framework based on several technologies to address the requirements of privacy, security and performance of the Internet of Things. The basis of the framework is the IOTA technology, a derivative of blockchains relying on a directed acyclic graph to create transactions instead of a linear chain. IOTA unlocks distributed ledgers performance by increasing throughput as more users join the network, making the network scalable. IOTA being not designed for privacy protection, we complement it by privacy-preserving mechanisms: merge avoidance and decentralised mixing. Finally, privacy is reinforced by introducing usage control mechanisms for users to monitor the use and the dissemination of their data.

Keywords: IoT · Privacy · Blockchain · IOTA · PET · Usage control

1 Introduction

The Internet of Things (IoT) is a ubiquitous network where connected devices exchange data between each other, as well as with users [6]. The devices collect data about their environment and usually transfer them to centralised cloud service providers, also known as CSPs. The CSPs process the data in order to provide a real-time and customised service to customers. Due to the amount of devices concerned, their heterogeneity and the personal nature of the data

© IFIP International Federation for Information Processing 2022
Published by Springer Nature Switzerland AG 2022
M. Friedewald et al. (Eds.): Privacy and Identity 2021, IFIP AICT 644, pp. 57–72, 2022.
https://doi.org/10.1007/978-3-030-99100-5_6

gathered, privacy and security are at risk in IoT systems, thus resulting in the need for new privacy-preserving solutions, well-tailored for the Internet of Things.

Currently, the most common model centralised around CSPs is troublesome for the IoT both for privacy and security reasons. Indeed, cloud service providers must not be automatically trusted and may snoop on users' data [17]. Besides, they can be vulnerable to internal attacks, from malicious employees, as well as accidental disclosures or external attackers [17]. Availability can be a matter of concern too, as physical infrastructure can be damaged, e.g. because of a fire [20]. Furthermore, centralisation hinders performance, specifically by increasing the cost of deployment and maintenance [23], which limits scalability.

Blockchain has been drawing attention as a solution to security issues, because of its properties regarding decentralisation and the removal of intermediate third-parties (cf. Sect. 2.1). However, conventional blockchains are not suitable for IoT systems, as they are computationally expensive, not scalable enough and introduce memory and bandwidth overhead [6]. Besides, while conventional blockchains address security issues, they provide no more than pseudonymity. Privacy in blockchains is a specific topic, different from security, that must be addressed using dedicated tools.

This article is structured as follows: Sect. 2 summarises the current state of the art about blockchains, usage control and privacy in the Internet of Things. Section 3 describes the car sharing use case over which both system and threat models are elaborated. Our framework for supporting privacy, security and performance in the IoT, is explained in Sect. 4. The security and privacy analysis is carried out in Sect. 5 before concluding in Sect. 6.

2   Related Work

Considering the need for decentralisation, security and privacy in the Internet of Things, this section identifies blockchain (Sect. 2.1) and usage control (Sect. 2.2) technologies as candidate solutions and discusses their current limitations and state of the art. We eventually discuss privacy of blockchain transactions in Sect. 2.3.

2.1   Blockchain

A blockchain is a "distributed and immutable ledger made out of unalterable sequence of blocks" [23]. This technology provides several properties of interest for the Internet of Things [4]: 1) decentralisation; 2) ability to audit the data; 3) disintermediation; and 4) transparency. Decentralisation and disintermediation are particularly relevant for large scale deployments and for security, as they limit the extent of data leaks and prevent potential misbehaviour from CSPs.

Blockchain Topology. Blockchains can be of three types: public, private or consortiums [23]. *Public blockchains* do not control access and are called permissionless, while private and consortiums do have a control layer and are called permissioned blockchains. Public blockchains are distributed and tamper-proof ledgers which are not controlled by a single entity and are open to anyone. New entries can be appended to the ledgers as long as the network participants agree. To this end, the participants use a consensus method in order to determine who can add a new block to the chain. Conversely, *private blockchains* restrict access to the public. Access to the network and involvement in the consensus protocol rely on authorisations, and require a third-party. Therefore, private blockchains are not completely decentralised, which has several consequences: 1) they are not as secured as public blockchains because they can not provide the same level of computational power; 2) being partly centralised, scalability and security are decreased; 3) private blockchains logically raise privacy levels as the data are restricted; 4) apart from large scale deployments, network response time is better and computational requirements are reduced. Private blockchains are consequently appropriate for some IoT use cases, in particular when high scalability is not needed. Finally, *consortium blockchains* are partially private blockchains, shared between several institutions instead of a single one. All these institutions are directly involved in the consensus protocol. The only concrete difference between consortium and private blockchains is the number of governing institutions. As a consequence, they will be considered as private blockchains in this paper.

Consensus Methods for the Internet of Things. Blockchains implement consensus methods to agree on which data can be appended to the ledger. Consensus methods are paramount in blockchains as they enable decentralisation. Moreover, the blockchain network is as secure as its consensus method is robust. Therefore, modifying the consensus method allows to trade security for performance, and the parameters of the blockchain network are deeply impacted by the selected consensus method. Performance of blockchains can be qualified as follows [23]:

- *throughput*, generally measured in transactions per second (TPS);
- *latency*, also referred to as block time, the time between the creation of two blocks on the blockchain;
- *network overhead*;
- *storage overhead*;
- *scalability*, to be understood as scalability in terms of the number of participants [28]. Scalability in terms of transaction processing capacity is directly linked to throughput.

Conventional blockchains heavily rely on *proof of work* (PoW) mechanisms, which are computationally expensive and not suitable for resource-constrained devices of the Internet of Things. The main alternative to proof of work in mainstream blockchains is the *proof of stake* (PoS), where the node responsible for block creation is chosen at random based on its proportional stake in the network. While this removes the resource-hungry computational race, it still introduces new issues. It is based on a monetary concept, the stake, which excludes

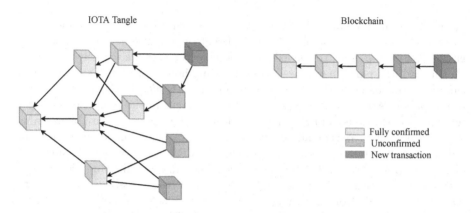

Fig. 1. Tangle transaction graph compared to traditional blockchains

many IoT use cases, including sensors, that do not require the use of currencies. Proof of stake gives the power to the most important holders, partially centralising the blockchain network. Finally, *Proof of Elapsed Time* (PoET) is another IoT-friendly consensus method. While miners still have to solve the computation puzzle, the winner is chosen based on a random wait time. The next block is created by the miner whose timer expires first, and miners are not competing. However, the verification of the right timer execution is done with a *Trusted Environment Execution* provided by Intel. Consequently, this consensus depends upon Intel which goes against the decentralisation property.

To make a blockchain network suitable for large scale IoT deployments, all these properties must be achieved simultaneously. To this end, the current literature is looking for specific consensus method for the Internet of Things. Raghav *et al.* [18] propose a lightweight consensus mechanism for blockchain in the IoT. This consensus method is called *Proof of Elapsed Work And Luck* (PoEWAL). Its performance, energy consumption and latency are compared to those of several consensus methods, including Proof of Work and Proof of Stake. It turns out its performance is overall better than Proof of Stake considering different parameters, without introducing monetary concepts, making it suitable for the IoT. Another line of research focuses on the use of artificial intelligence to integrate IoT with blockchains, especially to improve the consensus method. Salimitari *et al.* [22] propose a framework for consensus in blockchain-based IoT systems with the support of machine learning. Actually, their solution consists in a 2-step consensus protocol, first detecting anomalies with machine learning, then using the *Proof of Byzantine Fault Tolerance* (PBFT) consensus. PBFT consensus allows a distributed system to reach a consensus even though a small amount of nodes demonstrate malicious behaviour.

Directed Acyclic Graph is an Alternative to Blockchains. It is used by the IOTA technology [15] to build the Tangle, IOTA's graph of transactions. To issue a new transaction, a node of the IOTA network has to validate two pending transactions known as tips (cf. Fig. 1). In blockchains, blocks can be composed of several transactions. However, in the Tangle, each block is composed of only one transaction. A transaction is pending until confirmed by another transaction.

Then, the node processes a light proof of work to prevent spam. This unique system ensures scalability, as more users means faster tip validations, whereas common blockchains tend to saturate when the number of users increases. IOTA does not require a computationally expensive proof of work for strong security, but uses a proof of work affordable for IoT devices to protect from spam. Moreover, there are no rewards for the proof of work which implies the transactions are free, thus making micropayments possible, a boon for many IoT use cases. Storing a potentially huge ledger on devices is another issue to consider. For nodes with insufficient storage capacity, local snapshots can be created, removing old transactions and strongly reducing the size of the Tangle. Yet, the IOTA technology has a major flaw, because it is at the moment partly centralised. Indeed, IOTA relies on a *coordinator node* run by the IOTA Foundation, i.e. the foundation who created and has been developing IOTA, whose mission is to directly or indirectly validate transactions [26]. It does not completely centralise the network as all the nodes verify that the coordinator node does not break the consensus rules, yet it can freeze funds, ignore transactions and is a single point of failure, i.e. if the coordinator stops, after an attack or by purpose, transactions are no longer validated. In order to solve the coordinator issue, the IOTA Foundation is planning to release IOTA 2.0 by the end of 2021, after launching the test network in June 2021 [9]. The removal of the Coordinator is likely to be achieved by introducing new components, particularly a new consensus method called *Fast Probabilistic Consensus* (FPC) and a node accountability system to protect against basic attacks [16].

2.2   Usage Control

Usage control, as an extension of access control, monitors how the data can be used after initial access. It was first proposed by Sandhu and Park as the UCON model [14]. The UCON model extends traditional access control by introducing attribute mutability, as well as new decision factors, namely obligations and conditions. Obligations are requirements to be fulfilled by the subject to be granted access. Conditions are subject-independent environmental requirements for allowing access. Since attributes are mutable, authorisations and obligations can be done before or during the access. They are referred to as pre-authorisations and ongoing-authorisations, or respectively pre-obligations and on-going obligations. Improving user's control over the data is crucial to achieve privacy in IoT systems [3], and UCON provides the technical basis to enable this control.

Modern Usage Control Systems (UCS) Integrate Data Flow Control (DFC) to Complement UCON. To actually control the usage, another concept was introduced to complement UCON: Data Flow Control [7,13]. Data Flow Control (DFC) aims at controlling the flow of information, and ensuring the data are not disseminated to irrelevant actors. Therefore, DFC trackers are components of modern data usage control systems (UCS), whose purpose is to improve their behaviour, especially when multiple copies of the data are distributed over numerous devices.

The Integration of Usage Control with Blockchains is a Recent Topic of Research. Khan *et al.* [11] propose to integrate UCON in blockchains relying on the Hyperledger Fabric, a permissioned blockchain. For the authors, the purpose of introducing UCON is to monitor assets continuously to cover all possible access control models. Rizos *et al.* [19] suggest to extend UCON to distributed systems in order to strengthen the IoT security. More precisely, they adapt UCON to the MQTT and CoAP protocols. Finally, Kelbert and Pretschner [10] developed a fully decentralised usage control for distributed systems, including data flow tracking. In several situations, their decentralised policy enforcement outperforms a centralised one.

2.3   Transaction Privacy

While blockchain transactions are thought to be anonymous, the reality is more nuanced. Public blockchains do not require identifying information to make a transaction worldwide. Yet, transactions are publicly broadcast. The transaction content, as well as the operation itself disclose information about the individuals involved. Interested third parties automatically collect and analyse this information, for several purposes including law enforcement [12]. By default, public blockchains only provide pseudonymity, and anonymity provided the linkage between the pseudonym and the real identity is not possible. Yet, two behaviours facilitate significantly the re-identification analysis: address reuse and super-clusters with high centrality. Using address clustering, i.e. partitioning the addresses into subsets likely controlled by the same entity, combined with address tagging and graph analysis, it is possible to re-identify more than 69% of wallets stored by Bitcoin lightweight clients [12].

Privacy-Preserving Techniques Have Been Designed to Mitigate the Effectiveness of De-anonymisation. The most well-known tools for enforcing privacy in transactions are coin mixing and merge avoidance, which can theoretically be added on top of any blockchain [24]. Both aim at obfuscating the transactions by adding new fictional ones. In merge avoidance, a single transaction between two users is split into numerous transactions for both users, hiding the amount of the original transaction. Mixing relies on the same principle, but spurious transactions are created between all the mixing users, possibly multiple times before being sent to the actual target (cf. Fig. 2). Note that the service mixes the coins of several users to remove the linkage between the sender and the receiver of a transaction. Besides, some cryptocurrencies have been specifically designed to enforce privacy in their transactions, such as Zcash (ZEC) [2] and Monero (XMR) [21], obfuscating the transactions with several Privacy-Enhancing Technologies (PETs) and cryptographic tools.

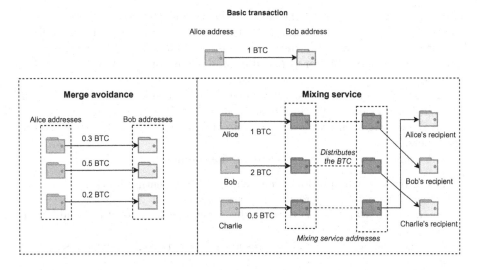

Fig. 2. Obfuscation with merge avoidance and mixing on the Bitcoin blockchain

Privacy in the IOTA Technology. Apart from using a directed acyclic graph instead of a blockchain, IOTA has several features that change the concerns related to privacy. Its main asset is the free transaction cost, making merge avoidance particularly relevant as transactions can be virtually split into infinite sub-transactions. Decentralised mixing is then relevant as the network does not rely on financial motivation. To this end, Sarfraz [24] designed a decentralised mixing service for the IOTA network, which requires no mixing fees. Mixing consists in joining coins from different senders before swapping their receivers, in order to remove linkage. Conversely, IOTA has some properties harmful to privacy. Indeed, the removal of the mining process prevents from creating tokens without taint. A token is considered as tainted if it belonged to at least one identifying address on the IOTA ledger. All IOTA tokens were created in the first *genesis* transaction. Only iotas that have never been linked to any identifiable address, i.e. an address belonging to someone who has been re-identified, can be considered as untainted [29].

3 System Model

To identify the needs in terms of performance, security and privacy for large scale deployments of IoT systems, a car club illustrating scenario is first proposed in Sect. 3.1. Section 3.2 then highlights the security and privacy threats based on this scenario.

3.1 Scenario

Car clubs (UK) or car sharing (US) is a model of car rental where people rent cars for a short period of time, often by the hour. They differ from classic rental models in that the owners of the cars are individuals themselves, instead of an agency. The context is highly dynamic, as many users may enter the car club or leave it on the same day. In order for the users to interact with the system, an application is responsible for registration and asking or granting access to the vehicles.

Mainly for security reasons, the car owners have the right to watch over their cars and know where they are, almost in real-time. The position of the cars as well as their navigation produce data about the car renters which are sent to the car owners.

The agents of the system can therefore be summarised as follows:

- the car owners, who propose their vehicles on the renting market;
- the car renters, who pay for renting the vehicles;
- the car itself, which sends data to the owners such as location, and whose access must be monitored;
- the Access Server (AS), which is responsible for managing the access to the cars;
- the Usage Control System (UCS), which monitors the data generated by other agents;
- the mixing server, responsible for obfuscating the transactions to preserve privacy.

Actually, both the Access Server and the Usage Control System control access, respectively to a physical object - the car - and to the data. The UCS also prevents the dissemination of the data to irrelevant actors.

3.2   Privacy and Security Threat Model

Depending on the data obtained by the attackers, and partially following the LINDDUN threat evaluation framework [5], the considered *risks to privacy* are:

- *linkability*: an attacker can link the sender and the receiver of a transaction, thus simplifying re-identification;
- *identification*: the attacker can link the pseudonym to the real identity of the car renter;
- *repudiation*: an attacker can exfiltrate information and deny it did.
- *inference*: "This category covers attacks where the attacker has used existing knowledge to aid the attack" [8]. An inference attack occurs when an attacker is able to infer valuable information from trivial information. For example, in our scenario, an attacker could infer working hours by gathering transactions timestamps.

Some threat categories from the LINDDUN framework have been excluded, either because they are not troublesome in our case or out of the scope of this paper. For instance, *unawareness* is ignored as the car renters are informed of the risk related to location data as they configure their own usage control policies. Furthermore, considering the system agents, the threat model identifies four attacker types:

1. the single car owner, who has legitimate access to some sensitive data of the car renters. The processing and dissemination of these data are restricted by the UCS;
2. several car owners colluding with each other to gather big sets of data;
3. the mixing server, who may keep for itself the addresses of senders and receivers, or put another way, secretly keep the links it is supposed to remove. It can use this information to carry out re-identification attacks;
4. external attackers, who wish to disable the UCS to help car owners disseminate data to other agents.

The car owners are considered honest-but-curious, which means they will fulfil their mission, but will snoop on the data of the users requesting their services. Honest-but-curious attackers are assumed to rely on transaction contents only, rather than network-level information, e.g. IP addresses, to re-identify users. External attackers are conversely malicious and may try actively to neutralise the UCS to enable car owners to disseminate their data. The main motivation of honest-but-curious attackers is to gather as much data as possible.

Concurrently, there are *risks to security* because a single agent of the system - namely the UCS - is responsible for the data protection. External attackers can be interested in neutralising the UCS, e.g. by disabling or modifying the UCS, to enable car owners to collude.

4   Proposed Framework

Regarding the different challenges for large scale deployments of IoT systems, as illustrated by the car sharing scenario (cf. Sect. 3.1), a set of complementary tools is needed to match privacy, security and performance requirements simultaneously. To this end, the originality of this article is to design a framework with the following features (cf. Fig. 3):

1. IOTA technology, as the most promising solution matching IoT performance requirements;
2. IOTA Access, an open-source framework used to control access to IoT devices. It is developed by the IOTA Foundation to complement the IOTA technology;
3. a Usage Control System, for car renters to monitor the usage of the data they produce;
4. a decentralised mixing service coupled with merge avoidance, to obfuscate the transactions and improve users' privacy.

IOTA and its Tangle are introduced along with IOTA Access, the framework developed by the IOTA Foundation to control the access to devices. IOTA Access is meant for any device, ranging from sensors to vehicles. The Usage Control System, which controls the data and how they are disseminated, is embedded into IOTA Access. The mixing service is external to the Tangle and they interact with one another. Merge avoidance can be programmed directly by the user, when sending the transactions to the mixing service.

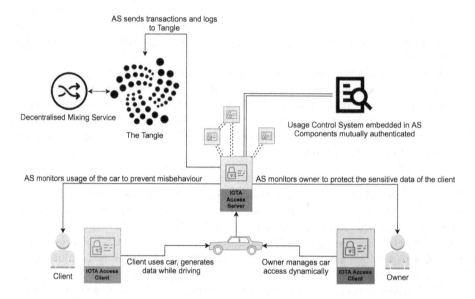

Fig. 3. Framework and relationships between agents

The IOTA Access framework is composed of three main components: a policy database to store the access control policies, a client so that the car owners can define their policies and can grant access to their cars, and finally a server monitoring the access and interacting with the Tangle. As the Access Server (AS) already controls the access to vehicles, the UCS is embedded into the AS even if the controlled objects differ. Indeed, the AS controls access to a physical device, the car, while the UCS monitors access to the data and prevents dissemination.

Decentralising the Framework. First, we emphasise that the IOTA Access server is already decentralised, as it can be deployed by anyone. In our use case, the most suitable solution is to pick one external trustworthy server to connect to, which is realistic as a list of trustworthy IOTA nodes is maintained by the community[1]. The same principle could be extended to IOTA Access servers, with a list of the top public ones.

Merge avoidance and mixing are used jointly to increase the effect of obfuscation. The effectiveness of merge avoidance is increased due to free transactions on the IOTA network. For the same reason, mixing is more efficient as the nodes involved in the mixing service do not have to pay for the transactions. Indeed, if IOTA nodes were encouraged to participate for money, decentralised mixing services would become vulnerable to edge insertion attacks [27] where nodes can claim undue rewards. Therefore, our framework uses a decentralised mixer to remove the threat of linkage and re-identification, and without introducing the edge insertion issue.

---

[1] https://trinity.iota.org/nodes.

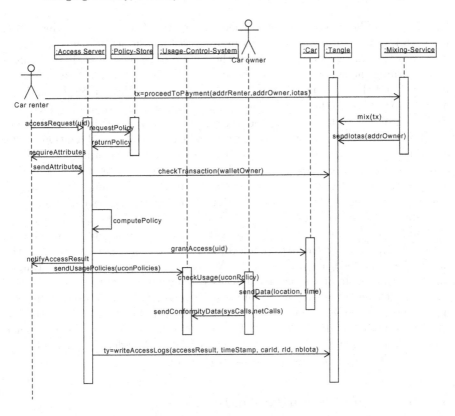

Fig. 4. The sequence diagram related to our framework

The Usage Control System must be decentralised as well in order to benefit from the IOTA 2.0 (without the coordinator) and to be resilient to some attacks like denial of service. Kelbert and Pretschner [10] implemented a decentralised usage control system. It is achieved by distributing the components of the UCS responsible for the policy enforcement, and it addresses both the UCON and the data flow tracking aspects. Additionally, decentralising the UCS reduces the communication and performance overhead compared to a centralised policy enforcement. In our framework, the Usage Control Systems are deployed along the IOTA Access servers which are decentralised as well, enabling the integration of Kelbert and Pretschner's solution.

Sequence of Interactions. Figure 4 details the sequence of interactions in our framework through the use case presented in Sect. 3.1.

These interactions unfold as follows. First, the car renter requires access to the vehicle. Before the access can be granted, the car renter must send iotas to the car owner's wallet. To avoid re-identification, the car renter sends the transaction to the mixing service, which removes the linkage between the car renter and owner while creating false intermediate transactions to obfuscate the transactions. The access request is then sent to the Access server, which then requests the car renter attributes to be able to take an access decision. Then, it fetches the car access policies from the policy store, before evaluating them and returning the access result to the car. If the evaluation is positive, the car is unlocked and the car renter can get inside. Afterwards, the car renter sends its data usage policies to the UCS, before using the car. These data usage policies are composed of the authorisations, the obligations to be fulfilled by the car owner and finally the conditions on the system. For example, a pre-obligation of the car owner is to accept to send the logs to the UCS, e.g. by reading instructions and ticking a box to actually agree. When driving, the car renter generates navigation data, relayed by the car to the car owners. To comply with the car renter policies, the UCS monitors the data usage of the car owner, who sends in return the mandatory data to enable the monitoring. These mandatory data are composed of system calls and some networks interactions, to ensure the car owner does not process the data in a forbidden way, e.g. store or disseminates the data. When the navigation is over, the Access server writes logs on the Tangle, detailing the result of the access policies evaluation, the timing information, the amount of iotas spent and finally a pseudonym for the car to simplify car management when a car owner has several vehicles. The addresses of the car renters i.e. their pseudonyms on the Tangle, are written in the logs as well when they request access to a car. Finally, we rely on the IOTA's default ledger, Trinity Ledger, to store the iotas as well as for transactions.

5   Privacy and Security Analysis

This section analyses the privacy and security risks in the system. It distinguishes the risks to privacy for the car renters, and the risks to security when the Usage Control System is neutralised.

5.1   Privacy Threats and Mitigations

Firstly, Table 1 describes, for the inference attacks, each combination of attackers, the data type they have access to, where data are stored in the system and an example of a privacy leakage associated to this risk. Secondly, Table 2 describes other threats to privacy and how they are mitigated.

Table 1. Inference attacks according to the attackers' profile

Attacker type	Data type	Data storage	Example
Honest-but-curious	Transaction	Tangle	Purpose of payment
Car owner (alone)	Location	Owner's device	Renter's job
Car owners (colluding)	Location	Owners' devices	Renter's job
Ext. attacker & car owners	Location	Owners' devices	Data sets on renters

Any user has access to the transactions on the Tangle, which are public and contain privacy-sensitive timestamps, users' addresses and values, i.e. how many iotas are sent to a car owner. Based on these elements, any honest-but-curious attacker can attempt to use the blockchain transactions for inference attack, e.g. use the amount of tokens in the transactions to infer for which purpose the payment is done. The merge avoidance mechanism integrated in our framework can help reduce the risk of inference by splitting the transactions into several smaller ones, thus making it harder to guess the purpose of the transactions.

Additionally, car owners may infer privacy-sensitive data from the car renters' location data. For instance, the location of the car renters might reveal the car renters driving habits, their jobs, their religion, their hobbies, or partially their social graph. Besides, when colluding, car owners can 1) merge their data about a given user to increase the quality of the inference; 2) increase the number of users in their databases thus improving their value. If a colluding external attacker successfully neutralises the UCS, as reported in Sect. 5.2, car owners can freely share user data through the system and can disseminate their data to a shared database for processing.

Table 2. Threats to privacy and their mitigation

Attacker type	Data type	Threat	Mitigation
Honest-but-curious	Transaction	Linkability	Mixing
Honest-but-curious	Transaction	Identification	No address reuse
Curious Mixer	Addresses	Linkability	Mixer decentralisation
Car owner	Renters' data	Repudiation	Data flow control, auditability

Table 2 summarises the privacy threats for the car renters at the exception of inference attacks, here above presented. By observing the transactions, a honest-but-curious attacker may attempt to make a link between the sender and the receiver. This risk can be mitigated by using the mixing server. Furthermore, when car renters use the same address multiple times for outward transactions, they are exposed to identification (cf. Sect. 2.3). This can be mitigated with IOTA's Trinity Ledger which automatically generates a new address for each outward transaction to forbid address reuse. Moreover, as the mixing service is decentralised, following Sarfraz [24] procedure, a node involved in the mixing process is not able to make links between any input or output addresses. Finally, the non-repudiation property is provided as the car owners are continuously monitored by the UCS.

5.2   UCS Neutralisation

The UCS is a paramount actor for controlling usage control and data flow transfers between the agents. It is consequently an attractive target, vulnerable to specific attacks which can be partially mitigated [10]:

- *denial of service*: the external attacker can disable temporarily the UCS, threatening the availability of the system and disabling the usage control mechanisms. Modern denial of service attacks are hard to mitigate, but the decentralisation of the UCS, as designed in our framework, alleviates the risk, as well as mutual authentication of all the infrastructure components, e.g. using certificates;
- *privilege escalation*: the external attackers can leverage vulnerabilities as illustrated in Babil *et al.* article [1] to bypass the UCS restrictions. These attacks are very diverse and implementation dependent, therefore out of the scope of this paper.

6   Conclusion

In this paper, we devise a framework to guarantee simultaneously the requirements in terms of scalability and security of large scale IoT systems, as well as the privacy of the users. To do so, we rely on several technologies. IOTA guarantees high transaction processing capacities and scalability with a balanced security fitting IoT needs. Usage control empowers the users with a tool to monitor how their data are used, while coin mixing and merge avoidance introduce obfuscation on the network to protect from re-identification and inference. Using a car sharing scenario, we highlight the threats faced by the agents in using the system, and we analyse the security of our solution.

As soon as the version of IOTA 2.0 without the coordinator is available and the framework feasible, other perspectives will be opened for privacy with cross-chain transactions [25]. As IOTA mixing brings two properties of interest - its free transactions and the support for decentralisation - there is a significant interest to integrate the IOTA mixing concept into other blockchains, to avoid payments of centralised mixing fees on their own networks.

Finally, our car rental use case focuses on access to physical objects. The concept could be taken further and applied to data-centric use cases, closer to the UCON philosophy of controlling access to data and not only objects. Besides, our framework can be applied to any IoT use cases involving large scale deployments, decentralisation and a demand for high processing capacities, all requirements taken together or separately. For instance, a widespread network of vending machines could benefit from this framework, especially for its zero fee transactions.

Acknowledgments. This paper is supported by the Future & Ruptures program of Foundation Mines-Télécom and the Institut Mines-Télécom VP-IP Chair on Values and Policies of Personal Information (https://cvpip.wp.imt.fr).

References

1. Babil, G.S., Mehani, O., Boreli, R., Kaafar, M.: On the effectiveness of dynamic taint analysis for protecting against private information leaks on Android-based devices. In: 2013 International Conference on Security and Cryptography (SECRYPT), pp. 1–8 (2013)

2. Bowe, H.S., Hornby, T., Wilcox, N.: Zcash Protocol Specification (2016). https://github.com/zcash/zips/blob/main/protocol/protocol.pdf
3. Cha, S., Hsu, T., Xiang, Y., Yeh, K.: Privacy enhancing technologies in the internet of things: perspectives and challenges. IEEE Internet Things J. **6**(2), 2159–2187 (2019)
4. Christidis, K., Devetsikiotis, M.: Blockchains and smart contracts for the internet of things. IEEE Access **4**, 2292–2303 (2016)
5. Deng, M., Wuyts, K., Scandariato, R., Preneel, B., Joosen, W.: A privacy threat analysis framework: supporting the elicitation and fulfillment of privacy requirements. Requirements Eng. **16**(1), 3–32 (2011)
6. Dorri, A.: A scalable lightweight blockchain-based framework for IoT security and anonymity. Ph.D. thesis, UNSW (2020). http://handle.unsw.edu.au/1959.4/65030
7. Harvan, M., Pretschner, A.: State-based usage control enforcement with data flow tracking using system call interposition. In: International Conference on Network and System Security, pp. 373–380 (2009)
8. Henriksen-Bulmer, J., Jeary, S.: Re-identification attacks-a systematic literature review. Int. J. Inf. Manag. **36**(6, Part B), 1184–1192 (2016)
9. IOTA Foundation: The Era of IOTA's Decentralization starts here (2021). https://blog.iota.org/iotav2devnet/
10. Kelbert, F., Pretschner, A.: Data usage control for distributed systems. ACM Trans. Priv. Secur. **21**(3), 1–32 (2018)
11. Khan, M., et al.: BlockU: extended usage control in and for blockchain. Expert Syst. **37**, e12507 (2020)
12. Martin, H., Christoph, F.: The unreasonable effectiveness of address clustering. IEEE UIC/ATC/ScalCom/CBDCom/IoP/SmartWorld (2016)
13. Myers, A.C., Liskov, B.: A decentralized model for information flow control. In: ACM Symposium on Operating Systems Principles, pp. 129–142 (1997)
14. Park, J., Sandhu, R.: The UCON ABC usage control model. ACM Trans. Inf. Syst. Secur. **7**(1), 128–174 (2004)
15. Popov, S.: The Tangle (2017). https://iotatoken.com/IOTA_Whitepaper.pdf
16. Popov, S.: The Coordicide (2020). https://files.iota.org/papers/Coordicide_WP.pdf
17. Qin, X., Huang, Y., Yang, Z., Li, X.: A blockchain-based access control scheme with multiple attribute authorities for secure cloud data sharing. J. Syst. Archit. **112**, 101854 (2020)
18. Raghav, Andola, N., Venkatesan, S., Verma, S.: PoEWAL: a lightweight consensus mechanism for blockchain in IoT. Pervasive Mob. Comput. **69**, 101291 (2020)
19. Rizos, A., Bastos, D., Saracino, A., Martinelli, F.: Distributed UCON in CoAP and MQTT protocols. In: Katsikas, S., et al. (eds.) CyberICPS/SECPRE/SPOSE/ADIoT -2019. LNCS, vol. 11980, pp. 35–52. Springer, Cham (2020). https://doi.org/10.1007/978-3-030-42048-2_3
20. Rosemain, M.: Millions of websites offline after fire at French cloud services firm (2021). https://www.reuters.com/article/us-france-ovh-fire-idUSKBN2B20NU
21. van Saberhagen, N.: Cryptonote Monero Whitepaper (2013). https://github.com/monero-project/research-lab/blob/master/whitepaper/whitepaper.pdf
22. Salimitari, M., Joneidi, M., Chatterjee, M.: AI-enabled blockchain: an outlier-aware consensus protocol for blockchain-based IoT networks. In: 2019 IEEE Global Communications Conference (GLOBECOM), pp. 1–6 (2019)
23. Salimitari, M., Chatterjee, M., Fallah, Y.P.: A survey on consensus methods in blockchain for resource-constrained IoT networks. Internet of Things **11**, 100212 (2020)

24. Sarfraz, U., Alam, M., Zeadally, S., Khan, A.: Privacy aware IOTA ledger: decentralized mixing and unlinkable IOTA transactions. Comput. Netw. **148**, 361–372 (2019)
25. Shadab, N., Houshmand, F., Lesani, M.: Cross-chain transactions. In: 2020 IEEE International Conference on Blockchain and Cryptocurrency (ICBC), pp. 1–9 (2020)
26. Silvano, W.F., Marcelino, R.: IOTA tangle: a cryptocurrency to communicate Internet-of-Things data. Futur. Gener. Comput. Syst. **112**, 307–319 (2020)
27. Simões, J.E., Ferreira, E., Menasché, D.S., Campos, C.A.V.: Blockchain privacy through merge avoidance and mixing services: a hardness and an impossibility result. SIGMETRICS Perform. Eval. Rev. **48**(4), 8–11 (2021)
28. Steen, M., Chien, A., Eugster, P.: The Difficulty in Scaling Blockchains: A Simple Explanation. arXiv:2103.01487, March 2021
29. Tennant, L.: Improving the Anonymity of the IOTA Cryptocurrency (2017). https://laurencetennant.com/papers/anonymity-iota.pdf

SynCare: An Innovative Remote Patient Monitoring System Secured by Cryptography and Blockchain

Claudio Pighini[1,3] ⬛, Alessio Vezzoni[2], Simone Mainini[2], Andrea G. Migliavacca[1],
Alessandro Montanari[2], Maria R. Guarneri[1,4], Enrico G. Caiani[3],
and Ambra Cesareo[1(✉)] ⬛

[1] LifeCharger Srl, Via Pico della Mirandola, 8/B, 20151 Milan, Italy
{cpighini,acesareo}@lifecharger.eu
[2] LiberActa Srl, Via Aurelio Saffi 21, 20123 Milan, Italy
{alessio.vezzoni,simone.mainini}@liberacta.com
[3] Dipartimento Di Elettronica, Informazione E Bioingegneria, Politecnico Di Milano,
20133 Milan, Italy
[4] Dipartimento Di Design, Politecnico Di Milano, 20133 Milan, Italy

Abstract. Remote patient monitoring involves the collection of patient-generated health data, using sensors/devices and mobile apps, to allow observation of patient's health status, also outside healthcare environments. The challenge in this field is to facilitate patient-centric data storing, sharing, and retrieving, with high attention to personal, sensitive data privacy and protection. This study presents SynCare, a patient-centered ecosystem developed by LifeCharger, for secure health-related data recording and remote patient monitoring. SynCare has been developed with the aim of making up a strong loop between patients, healthcare professionals and informal caregivers, building up secure channels for data sharing and supporting the patients in the management of their own health and related data. The system includes: 1) a mobile app for the patient, offering different features supporting the therapy and allowing the management of consents to share key data with the healthcare professionals and/or caregivers, 2) a database on Cloud, storing all the encrypted, sensitive health-data, 3) public Ethereum blockchain to validate the data sharing consents, 4) a clinical dashboard developed as a web application whose main purpose is to allow healthcare professional to display and analyze the data collected by the patient through the mobile app. The SynCare ecosystem implements a software developed by LiberActa srl to asynchronously load the anonymous consent data on the Ethereum public blockchain, decoupling the user experience from the blockchain interaction, which can be slow, without compromising the data security.

Keywords: Cyber security · Smart contract · Blockchain · Tele-monitoring

1 Introduction

Data is the new gold: it is continuously collected and analyzed, to derive information which companies and organization are willing to buy. Centralized organizations – both public and private, collect huge amount of personal and sensitive information and individuals have little or no control over the data that is stored about them and how it is used. There is, consequently, a growing public concern about user privacy. This also applies to health data and, even more, to patient-generated health data. In recent years there has been the multiplication and spread of health mobile apps and wearable devices capable of measuring vital and physiological parameters, leading to a powerful flood of data, which can be used for medical issues related research and to improve the care paths. Also, the present COVID-19 pandemic accelerated the rise of telemedicine, telehealth and health tele-monitoring services [1–3]. Healthcare professionals (HP) started or increased the use of ICT, such as email, text messages and video technology, to communicate with patients, sending prescriptions, monitoring symptoms, and giving medical consultations. In the name of the need to face the emergency, regulatory standard on ethics, privacy and data protection have been temporarily relaxed to allow this shift to socially distanced care [4, 5]. Nevertheless, attention to personal, sensible data privacy and protection must be re-established and, in this context, methods and application to favor secure exchange of data between parties (e.g., patient, general practitioners, medical specialists, hospitals, therapists, etc.) are urgently needed.

In this field Blockchain technology can play a key role. Since it was originally introduced and applied to the financial field [6], blockchain technology has gained substantial attention and the interest for its application in diverse fields has constantly increased. The working principle of the Blockchain can be explained using its original application field: Bitcoin transactions. Let's think to the Bitcoin Blockchain as an interconnected collection of digital wallets [7]. A hypothetic transaction of Bitcoins from wallet A to wallet B is simultaneously shared with all other wallets ('miners') in the underlying Bitcoin Blockchain, which use a cryptographic algorithm to validate the transaction. Once a transaction is validated by a certain number of miners, it is stored in a block, which contains the details of the transactions (e.g., transferred sum, ownership, etc.), and marked with a time stamp and a cryptographic hash (a mathematically generated alphanumeric string) of the data. This block is added to the end of the blockchain, which is followed by the transfer of assets (e.g., bitcoins) to the receiving party. The cryptographic hash plays a crucial role in the blockchain mechanism because it permits to create a distinct, digital signature that is unique to the current block of data and, at the same time is created starting from the hash of the previous block, defining a secure link between consecutive blocks (a chain). Thanks to this mechanism malicious changes are prevented from being made to the blockchain ledger and the information related to all previous transactions are completely transparent [7, 8]. Now, let's change the digital asset of the example and consider performing transaction of data. Blockchain offers various application possibilities, ranging from management of Electronic Medical Records (EMRs) to Remote Patient Monitoring (RPM) solutions.

This study presents SynCare, a user-centric, secure system for health-related data recording and remote patient monitoring, focusing on the methods and solutions we developed and applied to allows safe exchange of data between patients and healthcare professionals, and to manage data sharing consents by using smart contracts registered on blockchain. The paper is outlined as follows: "Related work" will discuss the existing literature related to this topic, considering the most common applications of blockchain in healthcare. Section "System design" describes the architecture of the whole healthcare ecosystem SynCare, while "Implementation" specifically focuses on methodological aspects of cybersecurity and privacy solutions implemented in SynCare. Section "Discussion" will contain a comprehensive analysis of our system, including a comparison to other previous solutions, advantages, and limitations. Section "Conclusion and future work" concludes the paper and discusses future work.

2 Related Work

Among the biomedical/health care applications of blockchain technology, one of the most popular is management of EMRs [9].

Healthcare in fact suffers from a data silo problem. Patients leave data scattered across various jurisdictions, moving from one provider's data silo to another. This has consequences not only for the patient, that lose easy access to past data and can interact with them in a broken manner, but also for organizations interested in using AI technology applied to large amount of labeled, clinical data from many sources to improve patient care and help clinicians.

The aim of applying blockchain-based technology in this case is to build a decentralized database management system where hospitals, providers, patients, and other relevant parties can store, share, exchange, and analyze data. One implementation example is Guardtime [10], a Netherland-based data security firm, which provided a blockchain-based system which links Electronic Health Record (EHR) data of patients with their blockchain-based identities. This system has been used in Estonia to secure 1 million health records.

Another known implementation is MedRec project [11]. Medication Reconciliation is a structured process in which Healthcare Providers partner with patients and their family/caregivers to obtain a complete and accurate, up-to-date list of the patient's medications which is then reconciled with admission, transfer and discharge orders. Blockchain implementation in MedRec project tried to facilitate this process moving from a slow access to fragmented medical data managed by healthcare providers to a system based on a decentralized approach to managing permissions, authorization, and data sharing between healthcare systems, based on patient agency.

Via smart contracts on an Ethereum blockchain, MedRec allows to log patient-provider relationships that associate a medical record with viewing permissions and data retrieval instructions for execution on external databases. Using this mechanism, providers can add a new record associated with a particular patient, and patients can authorize sharing of records between providers. This approach allows patients to know and decide who can access their healthcare data, acquire copies of their healthcare records or transferring them to another healthcare provider. Although it has been only tested as a proof of concept with medication data, MedRec demonstrated how biomedical and clinical research outcomes may significantly benefit from the application of blockchain to provide rapid, secure access to longitudinal research data.

Other examples of application of blockchain in the field of EMR management tried to address the limitations of this approach, namely lack of interoperability among different blockchain-based EMR solutions (lack of standard), scalability (high volume of clinical data), data security and privacy [12–25].

Another use case involves the application of blockchain technology to facilitate remote patient monitoring (RPM) [9]. RPM involves the collection of patient-generated health data, using sensors/devices and mobile apps, to allow remote monitoring of patient's health status, also outside healthcare environments. The aim in this field is to facilitate patient-centric data storing, sharing and retrieving, in agreement with the European General Data Protection Regulation (GDPR) which prohibits the processing of sensitive personal data of patients unless explicit consent is given by the patients. In a recent work Yue et al. [26] proposed an App architecture which allows patient to own, control and share their own data easily and securely by using blockchain technology. Healthbank is a Swiss digital health startup which offers its users a platform on which they can store and manage their health information in a secure environment [27, 28]. The data sovereignty lies fully in the hands of the user. As a next step, Healthbank plans to consistently apply and implement Blockchain technology for the underlying business model. Using a private blockchain based on the Ethereum protocol, Griggs et al. created a system where the sensors communicate with a smart device that calls smart contracts and writes records of all events on the blockchain [29]. In another work, Liang et al. [30] propose a mobile, patient-centered, blockchain-based system for personal health data sharing. This system is as a permissioned, private blockchain network developed on IBM Blockchain's Hyperledger Fabric. Similar solutions were applied for diabetic patients' monitoring [31] and cognitive behavioural therapy for insomnia [32]. Uddin et al. proposed a system for continuous RPM [33] and data sharing based on blockchain and end-to-end architecture.

3   System Design

SynCare is a patient-centered ecosystem for RPM developed by LifeCharger srl, born to 1) facilitate patient's self-monitoring and remote patient monitoring in chronic diseases, 2) support therapeutic alliance between patients and HPs and, 3) improve patients' engagement and therapeutic adherence for chronic patients or patients performing at-home therapies. To do this it is extremely important to maintain a loop between patients, healthcare professionals and informal caregivers. The main goals for such an ecosystem should be to:

1) build up secure channels for data sharing, in compliance with GDPR
2) support the patients in the management of their own health data
3) clearly define the digital health services, circumscribing the doctor-patient relationship. This is fundamental to guarantee to the healthcare professional the possibility to report the services provided, referring to specific tariffs, also defining the responsibilities connected to these services.
4) as LifeCharger srl, provide the above-mentioned services/ecosystem for the subscribed end-users, acting as a normal third party, without the need to view users' data without a user explicit consent.

Therefore, access to patients' data will be regulated, through the creation of informed digital consents, to clearly circumscribe a digital medical service. These informed digital consents must be traceable, transparent, and not tampered with, but must withdrawable, in compliance with GDPR.

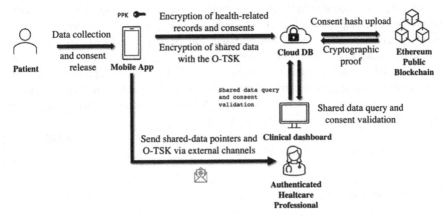

Fig. 1. Architecture and components of the SynCare ecosystem

The main components of the SynCare ecosystem are the following (Fig. 1):

- mobile app for the patient
- database on Cloud, storing all the encrypted, sensitive health-data
- public Ethereum blockchain to validate the data sharing consents
- dashboard for the healthcare professionals

The mobile app offers different features to patients; among others: 1) notifications to remind of drugs' intake or activities to perform, 2) a virtual diary to record and report symptoms, measurements of physiologic parameter, performed activities, visits and exams, 3) digital questionnaires, 4) medical reports manager, 5) management of online prescriptions, exams and visits reservation, drug ordering. All the data that are inserted and managed by the app are locally encrypted and then uploaded to a Cloud DB. Data can be subsequently decrypted and visualized only by the patient by using a private key saved on the smartphone. The patient can decide to share such data with third parties, such as a healthcare professional or an informal caregiver, signing a digital data sharing consent through the mobile app. This process can be applied to different use cases, ranging from remote patient monitoring and telemedicine to participation in research experimentations. To ensure that patients can be confident the signed consent is the one they agreed to use and hasn't been tampered with, our solution uses smart contracts as a ledger of the signed sharing consents. A smart contract is a transaction protocol stored in a blockchain, which is intended to automatically execute, control or document legally relevant events and actions according to the terms of a contract or an agreement, without any trusted intermediary's involvement or time loss. Because smart contracts are digital and automated, there's no paperwork to process and no time spent reconciling errors that often result from manually filling in documents. Moreover, considered that there's no third party involved, and the encrypted records of transactions are shared across participants, there's no need to question whether information has been altered for personal benefit. Finally, blockchain transaction records are encrypted, which makes them very hard to hack. Also, given that each record is connected to the previous and subsequent records on a distributed ledger, hackers would have to alter the entire chain to change a single record. The blockchain gives an objective proof of the timestamp at which the consent was released. Indeed, the blockchain reduces the risk that the timestamp associated to the consent could be manipulated during the signature by an eventual intruding attacker that could get hold of the mobile app's code source.

Once the consent is signed by the patient and uploaded on the blockchain, data can be shared, being encrypted and left securely "off-chain", validated and visualized by means of a clinical dashboard built as a web app.

This design ensures patients have the full control over their own health data and can decide who have access and how they are used.

4   Implementation

The present session will focus on the data-sharing methods implemented within SynCare ecosystem, describing how security and privacy issues have been handled using robust data-encryption, and smart contracts on blockchain.

4.1   Overall Flow

At the first run, the mobile app generates a Patient Private Key (PPK), saved inside the secure app local storage. The PPK is composed by an RSA-key pair used to sign the consents and to encrypt an AES secret key. When the patient inserts data within the app, these are encrypted using a One-Time Secret Key (O-TSK), which in turn, is encrypted with an AES encryption algorithm by using the local PPK. The encrypted data, together with the encrypted O-TSK, are then uploaded on the Cloud database, creating the secure health record. The data are saved on the Cloud and not on the smartphone for different reasons: 1) ensuring a light app memory, 2) saving space during data sharing (creating the shared data packet and sending procedure), 3) have a data backup in case the phone is lost by the user.

Through this mechanism, the patient is thus the only actor which can decrypt and visualize its own data using the PPK locally stored on his/her personal device. Whenever the patient signs a specific digital consent to share the data with a third party, the mobile app will automatically create the cryptographic hash of the signed consent, feeding the hash-generating function with the consent meta-data, and then upload it to the cloud DB. Subsequently, an asynchronous cloud server service will feed a Merkle Tree algorithm with the calculated consent hashes to generate the root hash and the cryptographic proof. This algorithm ascends the tree generating a path hash from each couple of leaves until the root is reached, creating the root hash. The hashes of each path are saved inside the cloud DB, associated with their consent hash, while the root hash is stored inside a smart contract deployed on the public Ethereum blockchain.

Once the consent is signed the data sharing can be triggered; specific functions of the mobile App will 1) query the Cloud DB to find the data specified by the consent, 2) decrypt them on the patient's device, 3) generate a O-TSK, 4) encrypt them again with the O-TSK, and finally 5) upload the new encrypted data (shared data) on the Cloud DB. The O-TSK is concatenated with the pointer to the shared data and sent through external channels (e.g., by email) to the third party. The O-TSK will be used by the third party to decrypt the patient's shared data.

Healthcare professionals are provided with a web app which acts as a clinical dashboard, allowing an intuitive and compact visualization and representation of the shared data, and more importantly, verifying their coherence with what has been specified in the sharing consent signed by the patient.

Every time the patients insert or update their health data inside the mobile app, the latter controls if the data are linked to a signed consent. In the positive case, the app automatically updates the shared data pointed by that consent, allowing the healthcare professional web app to query each time trustable and updated patient health-related data.

4.2 The Mobile App

Initial Setup

As anticipated in the previous paragraph, at the first run an initial setup procedure on the mobile app generates the PPK, thus, the RSA private (PvK)/public key (PbK) pair, and an AES 256-bit secret key. The PPK is stored in a secure location, corresponding to the KeyStore on the android operating system and the KeyChain for the iOS. These are two solutions offered by Google and Apple to memorize private information and lowering the risk of data breach in the case of smartphone hacking.

Once the user has been registered on the mobile app, the SynCare ecosystem associates the user's PBK to his/her public information, such as the email and the user ID. For this reason, every time the user logs in on the app the system checks if the PPK has changed, whether it is due to the change of the device or the deletion of the app. To avoid loss of data in the case of device change or app deletion, and to ensure continuity of use for the users, a backup function has been included, allowing the user to save the PPK encrypted into the cloud DB, and consequently allows its retrieval in case of loss.

The initial setup procedure also includes the signature of an umbrella consent to share data (see "sharing consent" paragraph).

Scheduling. Once the initialization is concluded, the user can start to schedule the activities that are prescribed into the therapy or, if the context provides for it, will receive a machine-readable, structured care plan which specific apps' functions will turn into scheduled activities.

The user can choose among different types of activity and schedule them following the guided procedure offered by the app (Fig. 2).

Every time an activity is scheduled, the app performs the following steps: 1) encodes the scheduling information following a JSON structure; 2) generates a 256-bit AES key for the symmetric encryption algorithm; 3) encrypts the JSON data structure with the AES key using AES-GCM, 4) encrypts in turn the AES key with the user PbK.

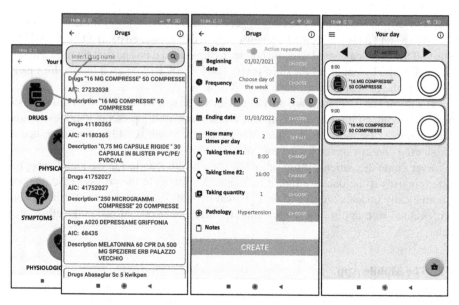

Fig. 2. Scheduling process of the mobile app

After these operations, a private packet is created with these two components: 1) the AES symmetric key encrypted with the RSA PbK, and 2) the JSON containing the information to be stored, encrypted with the AES symmetric key. This packet is securely saved inside the cloud DB. On the opposite, when the app needs to retrieve the user information to be visualized on the smartphone, the performed steps will be the following: 1) the app asks the LifeCharger cloud DB for the private packet ID; 2) the app uses the RSA PvK to decrypt the part of the packet containing the encrypted AES symmetric key, and 3) the AES symmetric key is used to decrypt the second part of the packet containing the encrypted JSON with the patient's scheduled activity information related to the therapy. This implementation for data encryption/decryption ensures that the patient is the only one who has access and can visualize his/her own data.

Digital Sharing Consents. The SynCare platform has been designed to allow the mobile app to share the patient's health-related data only through the signing of digital sharing consents. Digital sharing consents are smart contracts registered on blockchain which allow to clearly define the contract between the patient, the informal or professional caregiver or the generic third party with whom the patient wants to share the data. the contract defines:

- Contractors: who owns the data and who can access them
- Type of data shared: it is possible to share one or more datatypes (drugs, symptoms, physiological parameters) or select data with specific tags (e.g., classified per pathology)
- Temporal limits: continuous sharing (real time monitoring), one-shot sharing (visit-related sharing) or periodic sharing (monitoring)

- Finality for which the data are shared and linked data usage (this covers the definition of the legal responsibilities for the healthcare professional in case of medical services

Digital sharing consent can be classified into two main categories:

- **Umbrella sharing consents**: signed just once by the users, typically during the initial setup procedure. This kind of consents are mandatory; this means the user cannot use the app if he/she does not sign this kind of consent. One example of umbrella sharing consent is the one used for research projects, that authorizes LifeCharger srl or other partners of consortium research projects, to analyze the user data for statistical/research purposes or to share collected data with other companies/partners developing modules and components of the overall project platform. In this case the patient/subject who is enrolled in the research must give his/her consent for data sharing and processing, for the purposes and in the manner described in the consent, under penalty of non-participation in the project. Umbrella sharing consents are signed by the users by using the stored PvK.
- **Specific sharing consents**: these consents can be signed by the users, but the non-signature does not preclude the use of the app (see Fig. 3). The user has an active role in this case because he/she decides to share the data collected through the mobile app with a third party, and to do it will sign a specific consent, which describes the kind of data to be shared, the time of sharing (start and end date), the actors involved (sender and recipient) and the finality of use of the data. This kind of consent is typical of the patient-caregiver relationship

Once the patient has agreed to all consent policies, the app creates the signed consent record. Independently from the type of consent, this operation includes: 1) the calculation of a hash starting from the information described into the consent, thus the consent meta-data; 2) the creation of an unique ID that is assigned to the shared packet containing the shared data as UUID; 3) the calculation of the timestamp relative to the moment of consent signing; 4) application of a signature to the consent hash with the RSA PvK, in order to ensure that the data owner has done this operation. These data are added to the signed consent meta-data and saved encrypted into the cloud DB. As the user gave his consent for data sharing, the app will generate the packet that will contain the patient's data to be shared and described by the digital consent. This operation includes: 1) the encoding of the information inside a JSON structure; 2) the creation of a hash of the JSON data; 3) recovery of the PbK and to the package; 4) concatenate the hash with the timestamp; 5) the system signs with the PvK the concatenated string; 6) the generation of a 256-bit AES key, the O-TSK, which is used to encrypt the JSON part containing the health-related data; 7), finally, the packet of data to be shared is created by combining the encrypted JSON and other transparent anonymous data regarding general info of the consent, thus, the shared packet is saved on SynCare cloud DB.

Consent Withdrawal: In compliance with GDPR, our solution foresees the possibility for the patient to withdraw the consent at any time. To allow this, the system keeps track of all the shared data packet linked to each signed sharing consent. When a user decides to withdraw a previous consent, the linked shared data packets are delated from

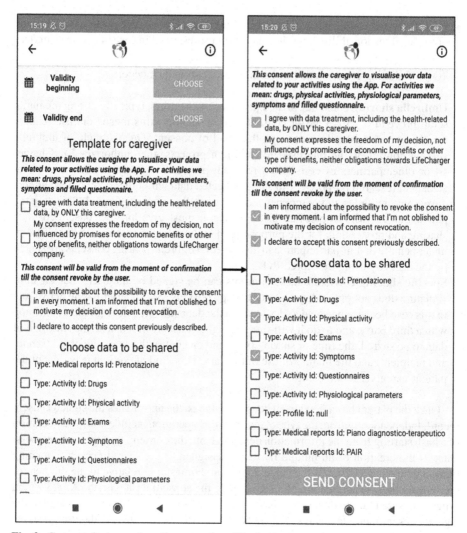

Fig. 3. Consent signing and sending procedure. The figure shows an example of a consent for an informal caregiver

the DB and the corresponding hash marked as "not valid", thus the mobile app will stop to share the data packets related to that consent. This means that the linked viewership permissions are modified and the third parties which previously received the link with the O-TSK to decrypt the shared data will not be no longer able to retrieve those data packets.

The data sharing between the app's user and the third parties inside the SynCare ecosystem starts from the assumption that the shared data can be opened only via browser. Indeed, at the end of the data packet creation that contains the patient's shared data, the app will generate a link that will be sent via a selected email client into the smartphone. The link il composed of the following parts:

1) the URL of LifeCharger srl https service that provides the clinical dashboard
2) the UUID that identifies the shared packet record, saved into the cloud DB, concatenated to the previous one (according to the syntax implemented by LifeCharger)
3) the "#" and a secret information (O-TSK) needed to recreate the symmetric key to decrypt the message.

This is an example of how the link looks like:
https://share.lifecharger.ey/(UUID)#(SECRET).

By inserting the O-TSK after the "#", the server will not be able to read the secret key that is used to decrypt the shared data. Thus, LifeCharger acts as clearinghouse during the data sharing process, without the possibility of seeing the shared data among the user and the third parties.

USE CASE: Mario suffers from Parkinson and during his last visit, his neurologist, Dr. Moore suggested that he joins the continuity care program using the SynCare platform. Thus, Mario downloaded the mobile app as suggested by Dr. Moore and registered on it. Subsequently Dr. Moore sent a sharing consent request via web Dashboard. In the request, Dr. Moore asks Mario to digitally sign an in-app consent that defines the relationship of the digital continuity care service: the consent defines that Dr. Moore will send a digital care plan that will be received and visualized by Mario through the mobile app as a structured agenda containing the assigned activities, and they will plan 5 video-visits in the next 12 months. Dr. Moore will monitor the trends and the care path of Mario to define the needed adjustments of the care plan; to do this, he needs to view data collected by Mario regarding the taken drugs, reported symptoms, vital signs, and questionnaires. The consent defines that these data will be accessible for Dr. Moore two days before and two days after the planned video-visits for a total period of 12 months. Mario agrees to all consent policies, signing the consent. From this moment, all data types described by the consent will be encrypted and included in the shared data packet by the mobile app. Two days before the next video visits with Dr. Moore, the app will generate and share with him via email a link containing the pointers to the shared data packet and the key to decrypt the data. He will use this link pointing to the web dashboard, and after authentication with his credentials, he will have access to the data of Mario. Dr. Moore, according to the signed consent, will be able to access and view the data for two days after the visit, then the sharing data packets will be deleted and will be available again and updated with new data at the next visit. Some weeks after starting using the mobile app, Mario decides to add his son Luca, as an informal caregiver, using the specific functionality of the app. To do this, he must sign another consent, specifying what types of data and how often to share with the child. He decides to share all data in a continuous way with Luca. So, this latter, using the reporting functionality of the app in caregiver mode can view all data regarding the health status and therapeutic path of the father, including pharmacological adherence and vital signs trends.

4.3 The Encrypted Cloud DB

The SynCare cloud DB relies on a non-relational database structure, where data are stored as simple key/value pairs. In particular, the structure of each record inside the SynCare cloud-based DB follows the typical structure of a JSON document.

In general, each record stored by the app is composed of a transparent unencrypted part, that represents the non-sensitive information (the user ID, a hexadecimal string that defines uniquely the patient inside the SynCare ecosystem, different timestamps, and reference keys linking to different collections) and an encrypted part, which encapsulates the obscured sensitive data.

From the previous paragraph, we can identify two types of data saved into the database by the app. The first one is represented by the information that only the user can read through the decryption procedure introduced in paragraph 4.2. The second one is the shared data packet that is stored on the cloud DB at the end of the data sharing procedure, waiting for the retrieval by a third party through the generated link, that is sent via email. In fact, the only way to open and visualize the patient's health-related sensitive data is to receive the mentioned link and, through the adopted web app (see paragraph 4.5), decrypt the patient's data. Consequently, neither the SynCare company owner, LifeCharger srl, nor a general third party, can access the sensitive part saved inside the records without the patient's authorization, given by signing a digital consent.

4.4 The Blockchain Consent Validation and Synchronization

The SynCare ecosystem implements a software developed by LiberActa srl (LA) to upload the anonymous consent data on the Ethereum public blockchain. This software is based upon a cloud backend that can interact through REST APIs and a smart contract deployed on the Ethereum blockchain.

This system aims to memorize on the Ethereum blockchain the past digital consent data signed through the mobile app. For this reason, the software was written to decouple the consent signing phase and the storage on the public blockchain. In particular, the consent data are passed to the LA backend every time a consent is signed by the mobile app. The consent data are initially saved only into the SynCare cloud DB. Consequently, the LA backend concatenates the received data inside a buffer. When the buffer maximum storage capacity or a certain established time are reached, a process is run to collect the unsaved consent data. This latter generates a Merkle Tree. The root of the generated Merkle Tree is then saved inside each record of the previously processed consents, together with the cryptographic proof that allows the consent validation. Therefore, the root of the Merkle Tree is stored inside the smart contract, allowing a light transaction into the public blockchain.

At regular intervals, SynCare downloads the cryptographic proofs saved into the LA database, associating them to the relative consents. Thus, to verify the existence of a certain consent on the blockchain, SynCare can simply 1) calculate the consent hash, 2) reconstruct the Merkle Tree root with the provided cryptographic proof, and 3) verify the presence of that root using the smart contract. This process is executed automatically by the SynCare clinical dashboard, without the need for an active user interaction.

4.5 The Clinical Dashboard

The clinical dashboard is a web application whose main purpose is to allow healthcare professionals to visualize the data collected by the patient through the mobile app, allowing to display and analyze the shared data. The Dashboard implements two key features that enforce the privacy and make the exchanges between the patient and the healthcare professional a sort of end-to-end encrypted channel. The first feature is the decryption performed on client side through Javascript code locally on the browser of the healthcare professional. The Dashboard retrieves the encrypted information from the Cloud DB. However, considered that the decryption key O-TSK is communicated by the patient by email or other means external to the SynCare platform and that the decryption is done on the browser, no sensitive information is exposed on the SynCare cloud infrastructure.

The other key feature provided by the Dashboard is a check, done on the client side through Javascript code, certifying that the information shared by the patient matches the consent previously signed. The encrypted shared data, in fact, contains a copy of the consent signed by the patient. It is worth noting that the consent is not just a pure text object but also contains a data structure, that is a formal description of the information that is going to be shared with the consent. It is a simple list of codes each one identifying a specific health information based on an agreed taxonomy.

The Dashboard performs the following checks: 1) the data shared by the patient must match with the data structure of the signed consent, 2) the consent must be signed by the same patient that encrypted the shared data, 3) the consent must have been registered in encrypted form by SynCare, and 4) the consent has been registered on the Blockchain. The SynCare Ethereum Smart Contract doesn't expose sensitive data, in fact only the cryptographic proof of existence of the consent is tracked on the Blockchain. The Dashboard can check if this cryptographic proof matches with the specific consent and provides the corresponding Ethereum transaction ID, so the check can be done externally to SynCare. Eventual failures in the checks described above produce an alert on the Dashboard.

A remarkable aspect of the Dashboard is that both the decryption and the compliance check between consent and shared data are done on client side, that is on the healthcare professional browser, so the users do not need to trust or rely on SynCare, and/or on the cloud application for these critical tasks. With this mechanism, the client can validate the consent data in automatic and transparent way.

As an additional safety measure the Dashboard needs the healthcare professional to be authenticated. This constraint does not invalidate the end-to-end encrypted channel described above but protects against malicious attempts to steal the decryption keys. In fact, intercepting the O-TSK sent to a healthcare professional without his/her credentials would be useless. Moreover, considered that the system works based on sharing packets (shared data packet) each packet linked to a specific consent, is encrypted with a different O-TSK, therefore having the credentials to access the client and a link with the O-TSK, will allow the decryption of only the data packet specified in that specific consent.

5   Discussion

Scalability of blockchain-based healthcare solutions is a major challenge especially in relation to the volume of data involved. It is not optimal, or even practicable in some cases, to store the high-volume biomedical data on blockchain as this is bound to cause serious performance degradation [9]. To solve this problem, our solution uses a smart contract registered on a public blockchain as a ledger of the sharing consents signed by the patient. All the patient's sensitive data are left "off-chain" and opportunely encrypted to be stored and shared. This solution allows fast and lightweight blockchain transactions, reducing the costs of each blockchain consent storage and simplifying the maintenance of the smart contract. Moreover, contrarily to the majority of the existing implementations in the same field that use private [11, 26, 30–33] or semi-private [29] blockchains, our solution exploits the advantages of the public Ethereum blockchain, namely robustness and stability, without affecting privacy and data security, having the sensitive data saved encrypted off-chain. Moreover, in most of the solutions using private blockchain data are saved not encrypted, this means that whoever has the access credentials can see private information of patients. As a final advantage of using a public Ethereum blockchain we mention the savings in maintenance costs.

For what concerns "off-chain" data security, our solution applies data encryption with AES using 256 bit one-time, disposable, secret key. This means that each time data is encrypted a new key is used; moreover, the private key saved on the user's smartphone is used to encrypt the secret key which has encrypted the data ensuring greater data security.

Considering the data sharing function, our solution puts the patient at the center of the process: in fact, the user decides which data to send by consent creation or acceptance of consent generated by a third party. The system has been designed in such a way that it is always the user that initializes the data sharing, in fact the data package created is linked to the consent for data sharing signed by the patient.

An important limitation of previous implementations is the limited speed of the blockchain-based transactions, which can introduce some significant latency. Our solution tries to reduce this problem allowing to create an asynchronous loading of consent data inside the public blockchain, decoupling the user experience from the blockchain interaction, which can be slow, without compromising the data security. Moreover, by collecting all the consent data into the LA buffer and memorizing them as a Merkle Tree root, the cost of every transaction inside the blockchain is drastically reduced.

The main limitation of the system regards the time of encryption/decryption of data, which in the current version of the system, is performed each time the user opens the calendar function. This means long charging times when shifting from a function to another of the mobile app. This problem worsens increasing the amount of data inserted by the user.

6   Conclusions and Future Work

To conclude, SynCare allows continuous and trustable patient remote monitoring, in compliance with privacy normative and leaving to patients the full control of data-access permissions. Data sharing consents managed as smart contracts allow to clearly define which data are shared with the healthcare professionals, the temporal characteristics of the data-sharing (e.g., continuous, one-shot, starting and ending dates), and how the data are used (which performance is expected). This is the first step for a clear definition of the medical performance in telemedicine, including responsibility and accountability, and could foster the spread of telemedicine and teleassistance services. Next steps of development will focus on speeding up and optimizing the processes of encryption/decryption of data to ameliorate the user experience avoiding long charging time when opening the app and switching between app's functionalities. As already mentioned in the discussion, the latency introduced by encryption/decryption process is currently the main limitation of the system that worsen the user experience. To ameliorate this aspect, we introduced a local Realm on the smartphone, where a subset of useful data is saved unencrypted. As a future work, we plan to make specific performance tests to quantify the latency introduced by the blockchain-based transactions, including encryption/decryption phases. On the other hand, we are working on additional features: the first one regards the refinement of the consent management, introducing the fundamental possibility to modify and/or withdraw the consent, with consequent change of viewership permissions. Another improvement wants to take advantage of the use of blockchain to provide to the patient/user a log of all data accesses to the shared data. This would add transparency to patient-provider relationships while keeping participants informed and engaged in the evolution/use of their records. Finally, we plan to further increase the security of our solution, trying to minimize the possibility of external attacks aimed at manipulating the source code of the app. To do this we will perform a security analysis with an attacker model.

References

1. Lin, C., et al.: Clinical informatics accelerates health system adaptation to the COVID-19 pandemic: examples from Colorado. J. Am. Med. Inform. Assoc. **27**, 1955–1963 (2020)
2. Perrone, G., Zerbo, S., Bilotta, C., Malta, G., Argo, A.: Telemedicine during Covid-19 pandemic: advantage or critical issue? Med. Leg. **88**, 76–77 (2020)
3. World Health Organization: Responding to community spread of COVID-19: interim guidance, 7 March 2020 (2020)
4. Bassan, S.: Data privacy considerations for telehealth consumers amid COVID-19. J. Law Biosci. **7**, Isaa075 (2020)
5. Martinez-Martin, N., et al.: Ethics of digital mental health during COVID-19: crisis and opportunities. JMIR Mental Health. **7**, e237-76 (2020)
6. Nakamoto, S.: Bitcoin: a peer-to-peer electronic cash system (2019)
7. Dwyer, G.P.: The economics of bitcoin and similar private digital currencies. J. Financ. Stab. **17**, 81–91 (2015)
8. Böhme, R., Christin, N., Edelman, B., Moore, T.: Bitcoin: economics, technology, and governance. J. Econ. Perspect. **29**, 213–238 (2015)
9. Agbo, C.C., Mahmoud, Q.H., Eklund, J.M.: Blockchain technology in healthcare: a systematic review. In: Healthcare, vol. 7. no. 2, Multidisciplinary Digital Publishing Institute (2019)
10. Mettler, M.: Blockchain technology in healthcare: the revolution starts here. In: 2016 IEEE 18th International Conference on e-health Networking, Applications and Services (Healthcom), pp. 1–3 (2016)

11. Azaria, A., Ekblaw, A., Vieira, T., Lippman, A.: MedRec: using blockchain for medical data access and permission management. In: 2016 2nd International Conference on Open and Big Data (OBD), pp. 25–30 (2016)
12. Esposito, C., De Santis, A., Tortora, G., Chang, H., Choo, K.R.: Blockchain: a panacea for healthcare cloud-based data security and privacy? IEEE Cloud Comput. **5**, 31–37 (2018)
13. Kaur, H., Alam, M.A., Jameel, R., Mourya, A.K., Chang, V.: A proposed solution and future direction for blockchain-based heterogeneous medicare data in cloud environment. J. Med. Syst. **42**(8), 1–11 (2018). https://doi.org/10.1007/s10916-018-1007-5
14. Xia, Q., Sifah, E.B., Smahi, A., Amofa, S., Zhang, X.: BBDS: blockchain-based data sharing for electronic medical records in cloud environments. Information **8**, 44 (2017)
15. Milojkovic, M.: Privacy-Preserving Framework for Access Control and Interoperability of Electronic Health Records using Blockchain Technology (2018)
16. Dagher, G.G., Mohler, J., Milojkovic, M., Marella, P.B.: Ancile: privacy-preserving framework for access control and interoperability of electronic health records using blockchain technology. Sustain. Cities Soc. **39**, 283–297 (2018)
17. Hussein, A.F., et al.: A medical records managing and securing blockchain based system supported by a genetic algorithm and discrete wavelet transform. Cogn. Syst. Res. **52**, 1–11 (2018)
18. Li, H., Zhu, L., Shen, M., Gao, F., Tao, X., Liu, S.: Blockchain-based data preservation system for medical data. J. Med. Syst. **42**(8), 1–13 (2018). https://doi.org/10.1007/s10916-018-0997-3
19. Allanson, J., Fairclough, S.H.: A research agenda for physiological computing. Interact Comput **16**, 857–878 (2004)
20. Wang, H., Song, Y.: Secure cloud-based EHR system using attribute-based cryptosystem and blockchain. J. Med. Syst. **42**, 1–9 (2018)
21. Zhao, H., Bai, P., Peng, Y., Xu, R.: Efficient key management scheme for health blockchain. CAAI Trans. Intell. Technol. **3**, 114–118 (2018)
22. Zhao, H., Zhang, Y., Peng, Y., Xu, R.: lightweight backup and efficient recovery scheme for health blockchain keys. In: 2017 IEEE 13th International Symposium on Autonomous Decentralized System (ISADS), pp. 229–234 (2017)
23. Zhang, X., Poslad, S.: Blockchain support for flexible queries with granular access control to electronic medical records (EMR). In: 2018 IEEE International Conference on Communications (ICC); pp. 1–6 (2018)
24. Zhang, A., Lin, X.: Towards secure and privacy-preserving data sharing in e-health systems via consortium blockchain. J. Med. Syst. **42**, 1–18 (2018)
25. Omar, A.A., Rahman, M.S., Basu, A., Kiyomoto, S.: Medibchain: a blockchain based privacy preserving platform for healthcare data. In: Wang, G., Atiquzzaman, M., Yan, Z., Choo, K.-K.R. (eds.) SpaCCS. LNCS, vol. 10658, pp. 534–543. Springer, Cham (2017). https://doi.org/10.1007/978-3-319-72395-2_49
26. Yue, X., Wang, H., Jin, D., Li, M., Jiang, W.: Healthcare data gateways: found healthcare intelligence on blockchain with novel privacy risk control. J. Med. Syst. **40**(10), 1–8 (2016). https://doi.org/10.1007/s10916-016-0574-6
27. Healthbank Homepage. https://www.healthbank.coop. Accessed 22 July 2021
28. Nicholm, P.B.: Blockchain Applications for Healthcare. https://www.cio.com/article/304 2603/blockchain-applications-for-healthcare.html. Accessed 22 July 2021
29. Griggs, K.N., Ossipova, O., Kohlios, C.P., Baccarini, A.N., Howson, E.A., Hayajneh, T.: Healthcare blockchain system using smart contracts for secure automated remote patient monitoring. J. Med. Syst. **42**, 1–7 (2018)
30. Liang, X., Zhao, J., Shetty, S., Liu, J., Li, D.: Integrating blockchain for data sharing and collaboration in mobile healthcare applications. In: 2017 IEEE 28th Annual International

Symposium on Personal, Indoor, and Mobile Radio Communications (PIMRC), pp. 1–5 (2017)

31. Saravanan, M., Shubha, R., Marks, A.M., Iyer, V.: SMEAD: a secured mobile enabled assisting device for diabetics monitoring. In: 2017 IEEE International Conference on Advanced Networks and Telecommunications Systems (ANTS), pp. 1–6 (2017)

32. Ichikawa, D., Kashiyama, M., Ueno, T.: Tamper-resistant mobile health using blockchain technology. JMIR mHealth uHealth. **5**, e111 (2017)

33. Uddin, M.A., Stranieri, A., Gondal, I., Balasubramanian, V.: Continuous patient monitoring with a patient centric agent: a block architecture. IEEE Access **6**, 32700–32726 (2018)

Taxpayers' Rights, the Right to Data Protection and Cybersecurity in the EU

Mylana Pfeiffer[(✉)]

University of Luxemburg, Esch-sur-Alzette, Luxemburg
mylana.pfeiffer.001@student.uni.lu

Abstract. This paper mainly questions whether taxpayers can claim certain cyber-security guarantees based on EU law. The author starts by introducing EU tax law, the notion of taxpayers' rights and why data protection and cybersecurity become more and more important in the field of EU tax law. Further, the author presents briefly what data protection and cybersecurity in a EU context mean and which impact it has on taxpayers. One main point of the study is to compare the data protection law and the cybersecurity law and the guarantees for taxpayers therein. Therefore, the paper outlines the intersections and divergences of EU data protection law and EU cybersecurity law. Another aspect of the paper is the question whether there is or even should be a taxpayers' right to cybersecurity.

Keywords: Taxpayers' rights · Cybersecurity · Data protection

1 Introduction

All modern tax administrations use digital means in their daily tasks. Digital tools can consist of basic services, such as an online platform or an email address for communication or more advanced digital technologies, such as a virtual assistant for value added tax (VAT) or an automatic profit tax return. On the one hand, the use of these tools assures a good administrative practice and increases efficiency of the tax administrations. On the other hand, these constantly evolving technologies bring new challenges to assure taxpayers' rights. The legislators of all EU countries are fully aware of these difficulties and address them in various manners, among other things through law. For example, the German legislator introduced in May 2021 a new IT security act (IT-Sicherheitsgesetz 2.0) amending the "BSI" Act (Gesetz über das Bundesamt für Sicherheit in der Informationstechnik). In France, the National Assembly's deputies fiercely discuss a new cybersecurity law in view of the increased risk. The EU reacted by issuing the Cybersecurity Act. Considering these legislative responses, it is time to ask whether taxpayers' rights keep pace with this development.

An important category of taxpayers' rights is the right to data protection. This right is of a strong public interest. Taxpayers share personal information with the tax administration trusting that their information will be held safe and confidential. This is only possible if high cybersecurity standards are assured. Does this mean, that taxpayers can

© IFIP International Federation for Information Processing 2022
Published by Springer Nature Switzerland AG 2022
M. Friedewald et al. (Eds.): Privacy and Identity 2021, IFIP AICT 644, pp. 90–104, 2022.
https://doi.org/10.1007/978-3-030-99100-5_8

legally claim cybersecurity protection from the tax administration in relation to their personal data? This is not clear. Cybersecurity and data protection go hand in hand and cybersecurity is a precondition to a successful data protection. However, the fact that cybersecurity and data protection are related notions, does not guarantee their enforcement to be equal. The legal differences can be found in the meaning and scope of the legal bases to data protection and cybersecurity law, as well as in the obligations they impose on the tax administrations if they apply to tax administrations at all. This paper is only limited to the analysis of the EU Data Protection Regulation and parts of the EU Cybersecurity law. For the sake of brevity and coherence, the EU cybersecurity certification framework and other European legislation that might cover some aspects of cybersecurity, such as the EU Machinery Directive are not discussed herein.

Cybersecurity and data protection issues can arise in multiple scenarios creating different implications on taxpayers' rights. In this research, the author addresses the cybersecurity threats coming from outside, such as cyberattacks, putting at risk the protection of taxpayers' data. The internal threats, coming from whistle-blowers or the practice of naming and shaming are not dealt with in this study.

In Sect. 1 the author introduces the reader to EU tax law and the notion of taxpayers' rights. In Sect. 2 the author delineates the content and the limits of the taxpayers' right to data protection. Section 3 presents how the data protection law and the cybersecurity law interact with each other and which impact this interaction has on taxpayers' rights.

2 EU Tax Law, Poor Soil for Taxpayers' Rights?

Tax law is often perceived as a traditionally national matter in the hands of the States. To some extent it is still true. There is no tax administration at the EU level, nor is there a tax law code. It is up to the national tax administrations to ensure the collection of taxes. However, this important subject is not entirely outside the scope of EU law. One main priority of the EU Member States and the EU itself is to realize an effective Internal Market, including tax law. As a result, tax law has been progressively incorporated into EU law, which resulted in a patchwork. In metaphoric terms, the EU tax law patchwork consists of a harmonized VAT patch, a non-harmonized direct taxation patch, and an EU operated customs duties patch. The reason behind this step-by-step regulation is the EU's limited competence delineated in its founding treaties and the EU's undisputable talent to make something big out of very little. Similar to the ancient patchwork quilts that our ancestors sewed out of the little fabric in their possession, the EU tax law was progressively formed out of the legal spheres that the Member States were willing to manage at the EU level.

The non-homogeneous EU tax law leads to multiple complexities regarding the application of EU taxpayers' rights to EU taxpayers. The question of whether EU law applies or not is a very important one and is always carefully analysed by the Court. But before reflecting upon this matter, what are taxpayers' rights?

The notion of taxpayers' rights is at once self-explanatory and extremely complex to define. It is self-explanatory because everyone has an idea of what it means or at least thinks to have an idea. It is complex because this idea does not provide for a general definition. In fact, there is no generally agreed definition of taxpayers' rights. For this reason, a literal interpretation seems to be a good start to interpret this notion. The English term "taxpayers' rights" and the French version of it "droits des contribuables" focus on the legal claims of persons who actually pay taxes. In German, there are two terms to describe a taxpayer, "Steuerzahler" and "Steuerschuldner". The latter is broader and englobes all persons who own taxes to the tax administration [1]. This understanding of the taxpayer notion focuses not on the moment of an actual payment of taxes, but on the moment when the claim to tax arises. In this case, even if an individual does not pay taxes, but should have paid them or will have to pay them, he is considered as a taxpayer. This broader personal scope of the term taxpayer seems to be the most suitable to interpret the notion of taxpayers' rights. Brzezinski also suggests such a broad definition and describes taxpayers' rights as rights "that belong to a taxpayer or other person in whom tax law is interested" [2]. This definition of taxpayers' rights would expand its scope to all persons finding themselves in a situation related to tax law. Also, this definition does not distinguish between fundamental rights and simple rights. One could suggest that the notion of taxpayers' rights englobes all rights, fundamental and regular ones. However, many publications on taxpayers' rights refer to taxpayers' fundamental rights or fundamental principles when talking about taxpayers' rights [3, 4, 5]. These are sometimes referred to as basic rights in hands of taxpayers or the minimum standard of protection of taxpayers [6]. This is especially true for discussions on the bill or the Charter of taxpayers' rights refer to fundamental rights [7]. Fundamental rights are certainly the most essential rights that need to be defended, especially if one seeks to achieve the minimum standard of protection at an international level. Here it is important to note that fundamental rights are most of the time implemented through regular rights, which contribute to their effectiveness. Therefore, it is important to consider all layers of law when studying taxpayers' fundamental rights.

As to the Court, it generally ignores this notion in its case law and refers to "the right for the taxpayer" [8] or "taxpayer has certain rights under the Charter" [9].[1] This can be explained by the fact that this notion does not appear in any primary or secondary law of the EU. This notion being absent from EU law and case law, it is not possible to define it with certainty.

However, several EU non-legislative and non-binding documents address taxpayers' rights. For instance, the Package for fair and simple taxation [10] including the Action Plan for fair and simple taxation in 2020 [11]. In addition, since at least a decade the Commission elaborates on a Taxpayer Charter at the EU level [12, 13]. In the end, it decided to publish the Taxpayer Charter in form of a Roadmap which aims at listing taxpayers' existing rights [14, 15]. It is called Communication on Taxpayers' Rights in the Single Market and is meant to englobe the whole relevant case law on this matter. It will apply to the direct and the indirect taxation and will probably list some fundamental rights as well as secondary rights [16]. At this moment, the document still needs to be adopted by the Commission but is announced to be published in the third quarter of 2021. Furthermore, the European Taxpayers' Code has been published in 2016 and specifies on its front page that it is a non-binding instrument meant to provide for a guideline and best practices of taxation, but only of a purely informative character [13]. Its major aim

---

[1] The Court mentions "taxpayer's right" once in the Sabou case, but not in the meaning of a general taxpayer's right, rather as an abbreviation for the right to the taxpayer.

is to contribute to easier tax compliance and therefore prevent tax fraud, evasion and avoidance. It contains a list with 9 general principles, such as data protection, privacy and respect of law [13]. The guidelines specify that the principles listed are not part of EU law but a compilation of principles that can be found in all Member States [13].

And again, none of these documents of the European Commission define the notion of taxpayers' rights. They provide a list of shared principles across the Member States and/or present rights that the taxpayers already have under EU law [17]. At least, the reference to taxpayers' rights in the political documents of the European Commission confirms that this notion exists at the EU level.

To conclude, the current EU tax law is certainly not the richest ground to yield strong taxpayers' rights and it is up to the Member States to assure that taxpayers' rights are guaranteed. The aforementioned non-binding instruments of the Commission will improve the awareness of the existing taxpayers' rights but will not expand or add new taxpayers' rights at the EU level. The legal problems of situations where taxpayers find themselves in a legal gap without protection will continue to subsist even after the publishing of the Communication [18].

3 The Taxpayers' Right to Data Protection

3.1 EU Data Protection

The early traces of the EU data protection law can be already found in a Communication of the Commission in 1973 [19]. Primary law refers to data protection in Art. 8 of the Charter and Art. 16 Treaty on the Functioning of the European Union (TFEU). The first piece of secondary legislation only appeared in 1995 in the form of the Directive 95/46/EC, which is now replaced by the General Data Protection Regulation (GDPR). In addition, the Directive 97/66/EC [20] aimed to fortify data protection specifically in the telecommunications sector and was revised with the Directive 2002/58/EC [21].

The two different layers of data protection at the EU level, primary and secondary, must be distinguished. Primary law is formed by the founding treaties, the Charter of fundamental rights and the general principles of the EU. It applies directly to the Member States and the EU organs [22]. Secondary law is made by the EU organs and implements primary law. The primary law rules over secondary law.

Art. 16 (1) TFEU simply states that everyone has the right to the protection of personal data without going into detail. Art. 16 (2) TFEU confers competence to the EU to foresee the details of this right into secondary legislation [23]. In the EU case law on the right to data protection, the Court does not use this legal basis but directly refers to the secondary legislation and the Charter. Before the Charter became binding, the Court referred to the general principles defending the fundamental rights. The Charter [24] is a constituent of primary law and has the same legal value as the Treaties (Art. 6 (1) TEU). In its Art. 8, the Charter grants protection of personal data. It reads:

"Article 8 - Protection of personal data.

1. *Everyone has the right to the protection of personal data concerning him or her.*
2. *Such data must be processed fairly for specified purposes and on the basis of the consent of the person concerned or some other legitimate basis laid down by law. Everyone has the right of access to data which has been collected concerning him or her, and the right to have it rectified.*
3. *Compliance with these rules shall be subject to control by an independent authority."*

Different elements of this provision need to be further commented.

First, the protection of this article is activated when personal data is processed. This is an important element, because in contrast to the right to private and family life protected in Art. 7 of the Charter, there is no need to prove an interference with privacy for this right to apply [25]. In Art. 8 of the Charter, there is no need to prove an interference and the simple fact of data processing offers the protection. The protection consists of a guideline setting minimum guarantees about how to lawfully process the data.

Second, the right to the protection of personal data is constituted by 5 underlying guarantees: The fair processing, the processing for specified purposes, the legitimate basis by law or by consent, the access to data, the right to rectification of data and an independent supervision. The Charter did not invent the fundamental right to data protection. It reaffirms what has already existed, be it in secondary law, the Convention 108 and a number of political documents. Therefore, the content of Art. 8 of the Charter can be explained with the help of the GDPR, the most important secondary legislation in the data protection field [26]. The GDPR implements the fundamental right of data protection anchored in the Charter and makes this right effective [27]. It also defines rather broad concepts. From the Recital 39 of the GDPR we can read that the concept of fairness is connected to the transparency principle. The principle of transparency in this context requires that the information shared with the individual on the processing of his personal data should be "easily accessible and easy to understand, and that clear and plain language be used".[2] The expression processing for specified purposes refers to the purpose limitation principle. It means that data collected for a specified purpose cannot be processed repeatedly for other purposes than the initial one. The legitimate basis by law or by consent requires for a legal or consensual basis prior to the data processing. The right to access information can be activated by the data subject on request and is relevant for the use of the right to rectification of personal information. The independent supervision is an independent public authority in every Member State that monitors the efficiency of data protection law. Finally, it needs to be noted that there is no mention or reference to cybersecurity. The fundamental right to data protection only focuses on the rights of a person concerning its data, ignoring the threats coming from outside and the obligations of the processor or controller to keep the data safe.[3] Therefore, it can be claimed that there is no fundamental right to data protection in the sense of a securitization of data. There is only a fundamental right to data protection in form of

---

[2] Recital 39 GDPR.

[3] This statement does not refer to the GDPR, which is secondary law. It only discusses the content of the fundamental right to data protection included in the Charter.

a code of conduct of how process personal data guaranteeing the minimum rights of a person when its data is processed.

Comparing the Charter to the GDPR, the GDPR has a much richer catalogue of rights and obligations. Of course, the Charter contains only one article of 3 paragraphs on data protection in contrast to the GDPR which consists out of 99 articles on 88 pages. Also, the Charter and the GDPR pursue different aims [27]. While the Charter is a fundamental right that protects a minimum the personal data of each one to whom EU law applies, the GDPR has a broader aim to ensure that this right is effectively protection in harmony with other fundamental rights and fundamental freedoms [27]. Thus, the act of comparison can only result in differences. The differences can also be found in the application of the different legal bases of data protection law to taxpayers.

3.2 The Application of the Data Protection Right to Taxpayers

The first question to ask before applying EU law is whether EU law governs a situation. Purely national scenarios or situations outside the scope of EU law are not regulated by EU law. There must be a linking event in a case connecting it to EU law. Art. 51 (1) of the Charter delineates its scope to situations that implement EU law. Also Art. 6 (1) TEU announces that the Charter shall not extend EU competences. The GDPR states explicitly in its Art. 2 (2) (a) that it does not apply "in the course of an activity which falls outside the scope of Union law".

This is a very serious criteria, especially when it comes to the application of fundamental rights. This question has been dealt by the Court decades before the existence of the Charter. Before the Charter, the fundamental rights were protected by the Court through general principles of EU law [28]. The most prominent cases prior to the Charter concerning the application of fundamental rights are the *ERT* case, the *Wachauf* case and the *Annibaldi* case. These three cases show the three possible situations of application and non-application of EU general principles of fundamental rights. The *ERT* case refers to a national law that constitutes an infringement to the freedom to provide service. The Court held that the justification to this infringement needed to be "interpreted in the light of the general principles of law and in particular of fundamental rights" [28]. The *Wachauf* case [29] concerns the application of fundamental rights to situations where national authorities implement EU secondary law, in this case a Regulation. The *Annibaldi* case gives an example of a situation where EU law does not apply and therefore the Court did not assess the fundamental rights [30]. The case law since the coming into force of the Charter in the field of taxation interprets more specifically what Art. 51 (1) of the Charter means by "implementing Union law". In 2013, the Court stated in the *Akerberg Fransson* case, with a reference to the *ERT* case, that "the fundamental rights guaranteed in the legal order of the European Union are applicable in all situations governed by European Union law, but not outside such situations" [31]. It explained further that such situations are when Member States "act in the scope of Union law" [31]. This case covers an active behaviour of a Member State. This is due to the specific facts of the case, where Mr. Fransson was accused of providing false information in his tax returns of income and VAT. He was pursued in administrative and criminal instances and claimed the ne bis in idem principle to apply protected by Art. 50 of the Charter and Art. 4 of the Protocol No. 7 to the ECHR. The Court revealed a link between Mr.

Fransson's VAT offences and the EU budget which must be protected according to Art. 325 TFEU. Also, it specified that as VAT is regulated at the EU level, the illegal activities of Mr. Fransson enter the scope of EU law. The Member State's active behaviour of penalizing such activities falls into the scope of the EU law, even if the VAT directive does not foresee penalization [31]. This argument was confirmed in the *Berlioz* case [8]. A couple of months later in 2013, the Court judged in the *Sabou* case that the Charter is applicable to cases where Member States apply EU law, in this particular case the mutual assistance procedure Directive 77/799, even if the EU law did not oblige the Member States to do so in the scenario of the case. The decision of a Member State to apply EU law is sufficient to open up the scope of application of the Charter [9]. The very recent *D. H. T* case demonstrates that the Charter does not apply to situations where national law expands the scope of a EU Regulation and applies the GDPR provisions also to legal persons, and not only to natural persons as initially foreseen by the GDPR [32]. Germany expanded the scope of the GDPR in order to grant the same data protection to natural and legal persons. In this case and in contrast to the *Akerberg Fransson* case, the national measures were not necessary for the implementation of the GDPR. Therefore, the situation had no connecting element to EU law to make the Charter applicable. In the *Belgische Staat* case, the Court judged the case as inadmissible regardless the fact that the facts were linked to VAT fraud. This is because the case grounded on the use of evidence from criminal proceedings linked to VAT fraud to reassess the income tax, which is not regulated by EU law and therefore falls out of its scope. The analysis of the recent tax case law in relation to the application of the Charter shows that there must be a connecting element linking a situation to EU law. In other words, if the situation is somehow ruled by EU law the Charter applies. This link does not have to be immediately perceptible like in the *Akerberg Fransson* case.

Regarding the material scope of application, neither the TFEU, nor the Charter exclude the application of data protection law to an EU tax law context. These are general provisions applying to all fields of EU law. The GDPR does not exclude tax administrations out of its scope, neither. The Court confirmed the application of the GDPR to tax administrations in the *Puskar* case. The questions of the case referred to the interpretation of the data protection directive but are also valid for the GDPR that replaced the directive. The Court stated that "the collection (of data) and their use by the various tax authorities at issue in the case in the main proceedings therefore constitute 'processing of personal data' within the meaning of Article 2(b) of that directive". It further reads that the objective of the tax administrations to collect and process information are linked to the objective of a controller. Therefore, the tax administrations have to respect the obligations in the GDPR.

As to the personal scope, Art. 16 (1) TFEU grants the data protection to everyone. The wording of the Charter as well does not distinguish between natural or legal persons. It could be argued that the way the Art. 8 of the Charter is formulated "everyone has protection… concerning him or her" indicates that it applies only to natural persons. The Court interpreted that Art. 8 of the Charter does not grant the same level of protection to legal persons as it does to natural persons [32]. By ruling this the Court refers to the ECHR case law in relation to Art. 8 ECHR. However, it does not say that there is no protection at all, and the ECHR has shown that legal persons also have rights protected by Art. 8 of the ECHR. The GDPR, however, explicitly limits its scope to natural persons.

If the Charter opens new opportunities for taxpayers, they are not unlimited, and the restricted scope of application has always to be considered [33]. Case law shows that the Charter covers all situations with a connection to EU law. It also shows that there are still situations falling entirely out of scope where taxpayers are only covered by national or international law. But even for situations falling into the scope of the EU data protection law, the right to data protection is not absolute. The data protection rights in the Charter as well as in the GDPR even if applicable can be restricted. Art. 52 of the Charter provides general conditions of restriction that apply to all fundamental rights of the Charter. For a restriction to be valid, it needs to have a legal basis. It further has to pass the proportionality test, testing the aptitude, the necessity, and the strict proportionality of the restrictive measure [34].

As to the GDPR, Art. 23 GDPR lists grounds of restrictions to some of the rights and obligations of the regulation in addition to its restricted scope.[4] Art. 23 (e) GDPR mentions "other important objectives of general public interest of the Union or of a Member State, in particular an important economic or financial interest of the Union or of a Member State, including monetary, budgetary and taxation matters, public health and social security".[5] This restriction serves in the interest of Member States and against the taxpayer's interests, but should not decrease taxpayers' rights excessively as Art. 23 (1) GDPR states that they must have a legal basis and respect "the essence of the fundamental rights and freedoms and is a necessary and proportionate measure in a democratic society".

To conclude, the taxpayers' fundamental right to data protection defends the taxpayers' data against unlawful processing and offers the taxpayers guarantees comparable to minimum standards about how data should be processed. Its scope is limited but generally applies to taxpayers.

4 Cybersecurity for All, Except for Taxpayers?

4.1 The Narrow Scope of Application of the EU Cybersecurity Law

The NIS directive [35] is presented by the European Commission as "the first piece of EU-wide legislation on cybersecurity" [36]. This might be true in the sense that the NIS directive is a specific legislation on cybersecurity, but not in the sense that no other instrument addressed cybersecurity before. Some aspects of cybersecurity have already been addressed in other legislation, among others in the GDPR.[6] The NIS also has a rather narrow scope of application [37] and does not apply to tax authorities. It follows

---

[4] Art. 2 (2) of the GDPR.

[5] Further described in Rec. 112 GDPR. This restriction has also been cited in (Art. 3 1. b) of the Decision of the Management Board of the European Union Agency for Cybersecurity of 21 November 2019 on internal rules concerning restrictions of certain rights of data subjects in relation to processing of personal data in the framework of the functioning of ENISA PUB/2020/96 OJ L 37, 10.2.2020.

[6] The GDPR came into force approximately two months before the NIS directive.

a different aim than the GDPR. While the NIS directive aims to secure the network and information security and the data therein, the GDPR targets the risks to personal data of individuals. This may devalue to some extend the NIS directive in the tax law context. It is still worth to present this directive as it explains what the current regulation on cybersecurity is.

Reading the NIS directive [35], the reader will disappointedly realise that the term of cybersecurity appears only once in its recital, and only when talking about "international cooperation on cybersecurity".[7] Instead, in its title and in all its articles it refers to "security of network and information systems".[8] In contrast, the proposal for a revised NIS directive includes the notion of cybersecurity 140 times, including in the title [38]. The proposal to revise the directive aims at overcoming the deficiencies of the NIS directive, by inter alia expanding the scope of application to all large and medium companies and providing for a standard of security measures to tackle cybersecurity challenges. The proposal refers to the EU Cybersecurity Act Regulation [39] which includes a definition of cybersecurity. The EU Cybersecurity Act gives a permanent mandate to the EU Agency for cybersecurity to manage the ICT certification in the EU, to increase cooperation between the Member States and to support them in case of cybersecurity related problems. This regulation is interesting because it introduces new notions and definitions at the EU level. It defines in its Art 2 (1) cybersecurity as "the activities necessary to protect network and information systems, the users of such systems, and other persons affected by cyber threats". It further reads that "'cyber threat' means any potential circumstance, event or action that could damage, disrupt or otherwise adversely impact network and information systems, the users of such systems and other persons".

With the constant digitalization and automation of the public sector, taxpayers' data also face cyber threats and only high standards of cybersecurity can guarantee their protection. But as already noted above, the NIS directive does not apply to tax administrations and taxpayers cannot claim cybersecurity rights based on this particular legislation. The larger scope of application of the proposal for a revised NIS directive includes public administrations, but only to a certain kind of public administrations.[9] It seems that there is no political will to include tax administrations into the scope of the revised directive.[10] First, because the Annex I to the proposal lists the administrations to whom the revised NIS directive would apply, and tax administrations are not mentioned in it. This list refers only to the public administration entities of central governments and some public administration entities of NUTS (territorial units for statistics) [40]. Second, a working document of the Commission states that the aim of the revised directive is to include public administrations "in its function of provider of services to citizens

---

[7] Recital 34 NIS directive.

[8] See the title of the NIS directive.

[9] Art. 2 (1), (2) and Art. 4 (23) Regulation (EU) 2019/881. This can also be read from the detailed explanation of the proposal p. 9: Annex I (energy; transport; banking; financial market infrastructures; health, drinking water; waste water; digital infrastructure; public administration and space).

[10] Art. 4 (23) Regulation (EU) 2019/881. "Public administration entities that carry out activities in the areas of public security, law enforcement, defence or national security are excluded".

and businesses that are essential for the functioning of the internal market" [41]. Tax administrations are generally not considered to be service providers. Their main aim is to collect taxes for the State. This may contribute for the well-functioning of the internal market, for example by guaranteeing financial stability in the EU, but is not essential in the sense of an economic driver. Lastly, even if tax administrations would be considered as public administrations that provide services, they would fall under the exception of law enforcement foreseen in Art. 4 (23). Therefore, there is no cybersecurity right based on the NIS directive that would apply in a tax law field and eventually grant taxpayers a right to cybersecurity. This can be explained by the fact, that the EU is still mainly driven by economic considerations. It is a priority of the EU to regulate the life of economically relevant subjects, such as companies or entrepreneurs. One could argue that a general cybersecurity legislation applicable to all actors, including tax administrations would be beneficial for cross-border workers and companies. It would provide legal certainty and trust in all Member States and contribute to the freedom of movement of workers and the freedom of establishment. But the harmonization has not still achieved this level. The public opinion is still divided on the question of whether the NIS Directive should or should not include further public sectors into its scope of application [41]. While cyber professionals approve such a wide-reaching cybersecurity directive, OESs, DSPs and trade associations are against it ("Cyber professionals were more likely to agree to extend the scope of the NIS Directive to include further sectors and types of digital service at risk of cyber threats. On the other hand, OESs, DSPs and trade associations were far less likely to agree with 22.8% and 25% of them respectively disagreeing with the prospect of including further digital services within the scope of the NIS Directive") [41]. It is therefore very unlikely that a taxpayers' right to cybersecurity will see the light under cybersecurity legislation.

This does not mean that taxpayers are denied cybersecurity. All States across the world are aware of the risks and costs of an insufficient cybersecurity protection. Regrettably, it is difficult to say with certainty how much the Member States spend on cybersecurity and the investment in strong cybersecurity can only be guessed relying on different factors [42]. To reassure the taxpayers, the cybersecurity guidelines of the NIS directive through the application to businesses are believed to create a certain level of herd immunity in a cyberspace where everything is interlinked [43]. Finally, a taxpayers' right to cybersecurity could be deduced from the GDPR, or lastly from a national or an international law.

4.2 Can a Taxpayers' Right to Cybersecurity Be Deducted from Data Protection Law?

On the one hand, the link between cybersecurity and data protection is undeniable. For instance, the proposal for the NIS directive mentions the improved personal data protection for citizens as its indirect benefit [38]. A Commission's communication reads: "Cybersecurity is essential … for safeguarding fundamental rights and freedoms, including the rights to privacy and to the protection of personal data" [44]. In a digital world, there is no data protection without a strong cybersecurity regulation. On the other hand, the data protection law and the cybersecurity law have different legal bases. Despite their intersections, they do not cover the same situations and pursue different aims. One striking difference is that the fundamental right to data protection in Art. 8 of the Charter does not mention cybersecurity at all. The cybersecurity aspects of the right to data protection are only addressed in the GDPR. There is therefore no taxpayers' fundamental right to cybersecurity in EU law but a legal claim to cybersecurity in certain situations granted to natural taxpayers based on the GDPR.

The GDPR provides for cybersecurity guidelines in Articles 25 and 32 of the GDPR. Art. 25 GDPR is the legal basis for the by design and by default principle. By design means that the data protection considerations need to be incorporated at the stage of designing the products [23]. According to Art. 25 GDPR controllers have to implement adequate technical solutions to guarantee the rights of the data subjects [45]. The protection by design and by default principle is considered to encourage "to take into account the right to data protection when developing and designing such products"[11] and therefore to have a preventive and proactive effect on the data protection of data subjects. The GDPR gives examples of data protection by design, such as "minimising the processing of personal data, pseudonymising personal data as soon as possible, transparency with regard to the functions and processing of personal data, enabling the data subject to monitor the data processing, enabling the controller to create and improve security features".[12] More specifically, Art. 32 relates to the security of processing and forces the controllers and the processors to foresee technical measures such as "(a) the pseudonymisation and encryption of personal data (b) the ability to ensure the ongoing confidentiality, integrity, availability and resilience of processing systems and services; (c) the ability to restore the availability and access to personal data in a timely manner in the event of a physical or technical incident; (d) a process for regularly testing, assessing and evaluating the effectiveness of technical and organisational measures for ensuring the security of the processing." These are technical provisions relating to cybersecurity. In both provisions, the obligation goes only as far as the state of the art permits it and "the costs of implementation and the nature, scope, context and purposes of processing as well as the risk of varying likelihood and severity for the rights and freedoms of natural persons" are balanced.

The state-of-the-art concept is intended to be broad and dynamic evolving through space and time, to keep pace with the technological developments in the IT security field. The understanding of this concept is based on practice. The Guideline "State of the art" published by the German IT Security Association TeleTrusT in cooperation with the European Network and Information Security Agency (Enisa) provides for an orientation for practitioners and other interested parties on the current understanding of the state of the art.[13] Taxpayers can also rely on the state-of-the-art concept to claim the protection of their data based on the GDPR. Art. 25 and Art. 32 of the GDPR oblige the controllers and/or processors to take "into account the state of the art" when elaborating the data protection by design and by default, and the security of processing.

The tax administrations need to guarantee this level of cybersecurity protection at least to the taxpayers that are natural persons. Another interesting fact is that the restrictions to some rights and obligations of the Regulation foreseen in Art. 23 GDPR do not

---

[11] Recital (78) GDPR.

[12] Recital (78) GDPR, these examples are also in Art. 25 (1) GDPR.

[13] The Guideline dates from 2021, an update is foreseen every two years.

apply to cybersecurity guidelines. This can be explained by their specific nature that need to be technically implemented without exception.

Comparing the technical implementation of cybersecurity requirements between the NIS directive and the GDPR, one can conclude that even here the GDPR goes further than the NIS does. While Art. 14 and Art. 16 of the NIS Directive mention that cybersecurity must go as far as the state of the art permits it, they do not go further into details. They also impose obligations on the Member States. They have to ensure that "operators of essential services take appropriate and proportionate technical and organisational measures to manage the risks posed to the security of network and information systems which they use in their operations" (Article 14(1) NIS) or "that digital service providers identify and take appropriate and proportionate technical and organisational measures to manage the risks posed to the security of network and information systems" (Article 16(1) NIS). Compared to the GDPR, the NIS directive creates rather vague obligations and makes it clear that is up to the Member States to assure the security of the network and information systems. This is not surprising and can be explained by the fact that the NIS directive is a directive, which in its nature leaves the implementation of harmonized principles up to the Member States. The GDPR is a regulation, therefore directly applicable and transposable as such in the Member States. Considering the aforesaid, the fact that the NIS directive does not apply to tax administrations and grants no claim to taxpayers to cybersecurity, has no impact on taxpayers. Compared to the NIS directive, the GDPR seems to be more appropriate in its aim and scope of protection to defend taxpayers' rights regarding data protection and cybersecurity.

The GDPR is an instrument like no other and is sometimes referred to be the law of everything [46]. With its broad scope of application and its content in relation to data protection and cybersecurity, it guarantees taxpayers cybersecurity protection even if only within the limits of the GDPR. This does not create a new taxpayers' right to cybersecurity, but rather addresses cybersecurity as a technical aspect of the taxpayers' right to data protection. For example, a taxpayer can claim from the tax administrations to guarantee the pseudonymisation or encryption of personal data. But these cybersecurity measures operate only in the scope of the GDPR. This means that from a strict legal point of view there is no general legal obligation to adapt this cybersecurity measure, but only a specific one in the limits of the processing of personal data and only as far as the GDPR applies. Although it is desirable to have a general obligation to cybersecurity in all fields of data processing, this is still not the case. As the Working Party 29 declares in one of its statements, "the availability of strong and efficient encryption is a necessity in order to guarantee the protection of individuals with regard to the confidentiality and integrity of their data" [47]. Encryption being one of the cybersecurity obligations in the GDPR, it is presented as a means to a greater end.

5   Conclusion

The limited competence of the EU in the EU tax field makes the application of taxpayers' rights a complex matter. The application of EU law and the scope of application of the relevant legislation has always to be carefully tested before a taxpayer can have the certainty to claim rights. The right to data protection is guaranteed in the Charter, the

TFEU and secondary legislation and generally applies to taxpayers. This is not the case for cybersecurity. The NIS directive, which harmonizes cybersecurity guidelines in the EU, does not pursue the aim to secure personal data and does not apply to tax administrations. Even if there is a link between data protection and cybersecurity, there are also striking differences in their legal meaning and application. While there is a fundamental right to data protection, there is no fundamental right to cybersecurity. The fundamental right to data protection of the Charter does not foresee any requirements relating to cybersecurity. As to the secondary law, taxpayers can claim the application of certain cybersecurity measures when the GDPR applies. The GDPR only ensures that tax administrations implement cybersecurity guidelines when acting as controllers or processors and when processing personal data. This is not a general right and is only applicable to situations falling under the scope of the GDPR. The author therefore reaches the conclusion that there is no stand-alone taxpayers' right to cybersecurity.

Looking back to the last century, there was no fundamental right to data protection. However, with the changing digital environment it cut itself off from the more general right to privacy. Cybersecurity becoming more and more important in our society, the question comes up whether it could become a stand-alone right over time? Some want cybersecurity to be recognized as a human right, [43, 48] some do not want that the scope of its application expands further [41]. And should cybersecurity become a general fundamental right applicable to all, what should it look like? As for now, cybersecurity is far from being a general right and even further from becoming a fundamental right of EU law.

References

1. Lexikon der Wirtschaft. https://www.bpb.de/nachschlagen/lexika/lexikon-der-wirtschaft/20760/steuerzahler. Accessed 01 Sep 2021
2. Brzezinski, B.: Taxpayers' rights: some theoretical issues. In: Nykiel, W., Sek, M. (eds.) Protection of taxpayer's rights, European, International and Domestic Tax Law Perspective, pp. 17–32. Oficyna Wolters Kluwer Business, Warsaw (2009)
3. Confédération Fiscale Européenne: Model Taxpayer Charter. http://www.taxpayercharter.com/charter.asp?id=15. Accessed 10 May 2021
4. Platform for Tax Good Governance: Corporate Tax Policy Key Priorities Q&As September 2020. https://ec.europa.eu/taxation_customs/sites/default/files/confederation_fiscale_europeenne_tax_advisers_europe.pdf. Accessed 10 May 2021
5. Savvas, K.: European Union - EU whistle-blower directive: taking taxpayers' rights seriously. World Tax J. 13(2), 30 (2021)
6. Pistone, P., Baker, P.: The Practical Protection of Taxpayers' Rights. IFA cahiers de droit fiscal international 100b, (2015)
7. Bowal, P., Wanke, I.: Taxpayers' rights. Law. Now. 23(4), 1–4 (1999)
8. Judgment of the Court (Grand Chamber): Berlioz Investment Fund SA v Directeur de l'administration des contributions directes. Case C-682/15. ECLI:EU:C:2017:373, 16 May 2017
9. Judgment of the Court (Grand Chamber): Jiří Sabou v Finanční ředitelství pro hlavní město Prahu. Case C-276/12, ECLI:EU:C:2013:678, 22 October 2013
10. European Commission Press Release, July 2020. https://ec.europa.eu/commission/presscorner/detail/en/ip_20_1334. Accessed 01 Sep 2021

11. Brussels, 15.7.2020 COM: 312 Final Communication from the Commission to the European Parliament and the Council, an action plan for fair and simple taxation supporting the recovery strategy (2020)
12. Confédération Fiscale Européenne: Towards greater fairness in taxation, A Model Taxpayer Charter, Presentation to the members of the Platform for Tax Good Governance (2014). https://ec.europa.eu/taxation_customs/sites/default/files/resources/documents/taxation/gen_info/good_governance_matters/platform/meeting_20140610/cfe.pdf. Accessed 10 Feb 2021
13. EU Commission: Guidelines for a Model for a European Taxpayers' Code, Ref. Ares (2016) 6598744 - 24/11/2016. https://ec.europa.eu/taxation_customs/sites/default/files/guidelines_for_a_model_for_a_european_taxpayers_code_en.pdf. Accessed 01 Sep 2021
14. Brussels, 15.7.2020 COM: 312 final Annex, annex to the Communication from the Commission to the European Parliament and the Council, an action plan for fair and simple taxation supporting the recovery strategy (2020)
15. Brussels, taxud/d1: summary record of the meeting of the platform for tax good governance, 10 March 2021
16. Initiative for Taxpayers' Rights - Proposal for a Recommendation to improve the Situation of EU Citizens as Taxpayers for Direct and Indirect Tax. https://ec.europa.eu/taxation_customs/sites/default/files/210310_platform_meeting_-_taxpayers_rights_paper.pdf. Accessed 01 Sep 2021
17. Questions and Answers on the Tax Package, July 2020. https://ec.europa.eu/commission/presscorner/detail/en/qanda_20_1337. Accessed 01 Sep 2021
18. Chaouche F., Haslehner, W.: Cross-border exchange of tax information and fundamental rights. In: Haslehner, W., Kofler, G., Rust, A. (eds.) EU Tax Law and Policy in the 21st Century, EUCOTAX Series on European Taxation, vol. 55, pp. 179–212. Wolters Kluwer, Alphen aan den Rijn (2017)
19. GonzálezFuster, G.: The materialisation of data protection in international instruments. In: GonzaFuster, G. (ed.) The Emergence of Personal Data Protection as a Fundamental Right of the EU. LGTS, vol. 16, pp. 75–107. Springer, Cham (2014). https://doi.org/10.1007/978-3-319-05023-2_4
20. Directive 97/66/EC of the European Parliament and of the Council of 15 December 1997 concerning the processing of personal data and the protection of privacy in the telecommunications sector
21. Directive 2002/58/EC of the European Parliament and of the Council of 12 July 2002 concerning the processing of personal data and the protection of privacy in the electronic communications sector (Directive on privacy and electronic communications) Official Journal L 201, pp. 37–47, 31 July 2002
22. Schaumburg, H.: Einführende Grundlagen. In: Schaumburg, H., Englisch, J., Fehling, D., Kofler, G., Oellerich, I., Reimer, E. (eds.) Europäisches Steuerrecht, Otto Schmidt KG Verlag, Köln (2015)
23. Savin, A.: EU Internet Law. 2nd edn. Elgar European Law, Massachusetts (2017)
24. Charter of Fundamental Rights of the European Union OJ C 326, pp. 391–407, 26 October 2012
25. Docksey, C.: Articles 7 and 8 of the EU Charter: two distinct fundamental rights. In: Grosjean, A. (ed.) Enjeux européens et mondiaux de la protection des données personnelles, pp. 71–97. Larcier, Brussels (2015)
26. Regulation (EU) 2016/679 of the European Parliament and of the Council of 27 April 2016 on the protection of natural persons with regard to the processing of personal data and on the free movement of such data and repealing Directive 95/46/EC (General Data Protection Regulation)
27. Ausloos, J.: Foundations of Data Protection Law. Oxford University Press, New York (2020)

28. Judgment of the Court of 18 June 1991, Elliniki Radiophonia Tiléorassi AE and Panellinia Omospondia Syllogon Prossopikou v Dimotiki Etairia Pliroforissis and Sotirios Kouvelas and Nicolaos Avdellas and others (ERT). Case C-260/89. ECLI:EU:C:1991:254
29. Judgment of the Court (Third Chamber) of 13 July 1989, Hubert Wachauf v Bundesamt für Ernährung und Forstwirtschaft. Case 5/88. ECLI:EU:C:1989:321
30. Judgment of the Court (First Chamber) of 18 December 1997, Daniele Annibal-di v Sindaco del Comune di Guidonia and Presidente Regione Lazio. Case C-309/96. ECLI:EU:C:1997:631
31. Judgment of the Court (Grand Chamber) of 26 February 2013, Åklagaren v Hans Åkerberg Fransson. Case C 617/10. ECLI:EU:C:2013:105
32. Judgment of the Court (First Chamber) of 10 December 2020, Land Nordrhein-Westfalen v D.-H. T. as liquidator of J & S Service UG. Case C-620/19, ECLI:EU:C:2020:1011
33. Kokott, J.: European union - taxpayers' rights. Eur. Tax. **60**(1), 1–7 (2020)
34. Placco, A.: La protection des données à caractère personnel dans le cadre de la jurisprudence de la cour de justice de l'Union Européenne relative aux droits fondamentaux. In: Grosjean, A. (ed.) Enjeux européens et mondiaux de la protection des données personnelles, pp. 31–50. Larcier, Bruxelles (2015)
35. Directive (EU) 2016/1148 of the European Parliament and of the Council of 6 July 2016 concerning measures for a high common level of security of network and information systems across the Union OJ L 194, 19.7.2016, pp. 1–30
36. NIS Directive, 17 June 2021. https://digital-strategy.ec.europa.eu/en/policies/nis-directive
37. Cole, M., Schmitz, S.: The Interplay between the NIS Directive and the GDPR in a Cyber-security Threat Landscape. University of Luxembourg Law Working Paper No. 2019–017, (2019)
38. Proposal for a Directive of the European Parliament and of the Council on measures for a high common level of cybersecurity across the Union, repealing Directive (EU) 2016/1148 COM/2020/823 final
39. Regulation (EU) 2019/881 of the European Parliament and of the Council of 17 April 2019 on ENISA (the European Union Agency for Cybersecurity and on information and commu-nications technology cybersecurity certification and repealing Regulation (EU) No 526/2013 (Cybersecurity Act) (OJ L 151, 7.6.2019, p.15)
40. Regulation (EC) No 1059/2003 of the European Parliament and of the Council of 26 May 2003 on the establishment of a common classification of territorial units for statistics (NUTS) (OJ L 154, 21.6.2003, p. 1)
41. Brussels, 16.12.2020 SWD: 345 final Part 2/3 Commission Staff Working Document Impact Assessment Report (2020)
42. Antczak, J., Kamiński, K.: Cybersecurity Expenditure in the EU Member States for the non-profit organisation. New Direction, Brussels (2018)
43. Shackelford, S.: Should cybersecurity be a human right: exploring the shared responsibility of cyber peace. Stan. J. Int. L. **55**, 155 (2019)
44. Joint Communication to the European Parliament and the Council, The EU's Cybersecurity Strategy for the Digital Decade JOIN/2020/18 final
45. Tamò-Larrieux, A.: Privacy and data protection regulation in europe. In: Tamo-Larrieux, A. (ed.) Designing for Privacy and its Legal Framework. LGTS, vol. 40, pp. 73–100. Springer, Cham (2018). https://doi.org/10.1007/978-3-319-98624-1_5
46. Purtova, N.: The law of everything. broad concept of personal data and overstretched scope of EU data protection law. Law. Innov. Technol. **10**(1), 40–81 (2018)
47. Statement of the WP29 on encryption and their impact on the protection of individuals with regard to the processing of their personal data in the EU, Brussels, 11 April 2018
48. Human Rights Watch, 26 May 2020. https://www.hrw.org/news/2020/05/26/its-time-treat-cybersecurity-human-rights-issue. Accessed 01 Sep 2021

Usable Privacy and Security from the Perspective of Cognitive Abilities

Joakim Kävrestad[1]([✉])(iD), Allex Hagberg[2], Robert Roos[2], Jana Rambusch[1], and Marcus Nohlberg[1](iD)

[1] University of Skövde, Skövde, Sweden
{joakim.kavrestad,jana.rambusch,marcus.nohlberg}@his.se
[2] Xenolith AB, Skövde, Sweden
{allex,robert}@iodesk.net

Abstract. Privacy, Information, and Cybersecurity (PICS) are related properties that have become a concern for more or less everyone. A large portion of the responsibility for PICS is put on the end-user, who is expected to adopt PICS tools, guidelines, and features to stay secure and maintain organizational security. However, the literature describes that many users do not adopt PICS tools and a key reason seems to be usability. This study acknowledges that the usability of PICS tools is a crucial concern and seeks to problematize further by adding cognitive ability as a key usability aspect. We argue that a user's cognitive abilities determine how the user perceives the usability of PICS tools and that usability guidelines should account for varying cognitive abilities held by different user groups. This paper presents a case study with focus on how cognitive disabilities can affect the usability of PICS tools. Interviews with users with cognitive disabilities as well as usability experts, and experts on cognitive disabilities were conducted. The results suggest that many of the usability factors are shared by all users, cognitive challenges or not. However, cognitive challenges often cause usability issues to be more severe. Based on the results, several design guidelines for the usability of PICS tools are suggested.

Keywords: Privacy · Security · Usability · User · Cognitive · Ability · Disability

1 Introduction

Privacy, Information, and Cybersecurity (PICS) are related properties that have become a concern of more or less everyone [26]. Privacy is typically discussed as the individuals right to their personal information [35]. Information security

---

Supported by the Swedish Post and Telecom Authority, and Begripsam.

and cybersecurity are terms that are often used interchangeably even if information security relates to the security of information regardless of how it is stored while cybersecurity concern the security of information and devices connected to cyberspace [16]. The three concepts are discussed together under the term PICS in this paper. The reason is that many safeguards and concept are the same for the domains of privacy, information, and cybersecurity.

In our personal lives, we rely upon digital services for banking, social contacts, dating, shopping, and more. Consequently, personal data is stored in a multitude of locations worldwide, and the confidentiality, integrity, and availability of it can be compromised in several ways unless PICS is ensured. Moreover, PICS is high on the agenda of modern organizations. Different types of adversaries, ranging from nation-states and organized crime units to less sophisticated script kiddies attempt to compromise organizations in various ways [5]. Common motives for those attacks include financial gain, destabilization of nation-critical systems, and political motivation. A successful attack against an organization can result in severe damages such as system malfunction, loss of money or intellectual property, or disclosure of personal information stored by the organization [1,14, 24]. While service providers or organizational IT departments typically handle some aspects of PICS, a large part of the responsibility is put on the users who are expected to behave securely by use of tools, features, and procedures that intend to ensure privacy or cybersecurity (from hereon, denoted PICS tools).

PICS tools are tools, features and procedures designed to ensure or increase privacy or cybersecurity. This includes special purpose software such as password managers or encryption software [8], built in features such as password complexity requirements, captcha or privacy settings [12,43], and policies and procedures such as password use recommendation or guidelines on phishing detection [44].

It is well known that it is hard to get users to use PICS tools. Unsurprisingly, the usability of such tools has been the attention of much research, and it is obvious that usability of PICS tools is a factor that determines what tools and features users choose to adopt or not [3,19,31,41]. A related discussion is that of the digital divide, a phenomenon that can be described as some people being excluded from the digital world for various reasons [32]. One such reason, discussed in previous literature, is disabilities that impact the ability to use technology [17]. Along that line, cognitive workload and fatigue have been discussed in previous research as important factors that influence security behaviour [11,33]. In essence, the use of PICS tools requires cognitive resources from the user. If those resources are depleted, so is the users' ability to use PICS tools [15]. For instance, previous research has found that cognitive depletion leads to creation of worse passwords [10], that cognitive ability affects the ability to solve captcha functions [2] and detect phishing [39], and that use of privacy settings can be increased by minimizing cognitive effort needed to use such settings [36]. Consequently, cognitive ability should be a factor of importance when researching the usability of PICS tools. The reasons are several:

- A user's cognitive abilities determine the amount of effort a user can spend using PICS tools. Thus, PICS tools requiring less cognitive effort can be used by more users and with better results.
- Users with cognitive disabilities run the risk of being excluded from using PICS tools, which is an inclusion problem. An example can be that the ability to solve a captcha can be limited due to a cognitive disability. In such a case, the captcha can exclude a user from using the service protected by the captcha.
- Since people with cognitive disabilities are working in organizations, just like anyone else, excluding them from the design of PICS tools becomes an organizational cybersecurity problem. The rationale is that excluding this group from design of PICS tools makes the effect of those tools unknown for this group of users, with possible PICS issues as a consequence.
- With or without a disability, a user's cognitive abilities vary over time. Since the need for security does not, a PICS tool must be usable even when a user's cognitive ability is lowered. It can, for instance, be assumed that a user's ability to detect phishing is lower when the user is tired as the end of a working day.

Our research specifically highlights users with cognitive disabilities, and the goal of this study is to provide insight into how users with cognitive disabilities perceive PICS tools by identifying usability requirements considered important by this group. This study was carried out as a case study where data was gathered from domain experts and people with cognitive disabilities. The results are expressed as design guidelines that PICS tools should meet in order to be considered inclusive with regard to users with cognitive disabilities. Those guidelines are discussed in relation to a commonly used framework for web accessibility, Web Content Accessibility Guidelines 2.1 (WCAG 2.1) [40]. This research contributes with increased understanding of the importance of usability in PICS. Specifically, the implications that a lack of usability has for users with cognitive challenges are highlighted and guidelines for increased usability are proposed.

The research was supported by Begripsam, a non-profit organization specializing in inclusive design with regard to users with cognitive disabilities. Begripsam specializes in usability testing for cognitive inclusion and helped the research by recruiting participants from their network.

The rest of the paper is structured as follows: A background to concepts used in the paper is provided in Sect. 2. Section 3 describes the used methodology before the results are presented in Sect. 4. The results are discussed in Sect. 5. Section 6 outlines the contributions of this paper and directions for future work.

2 Background

Cognitive ability includes a person's ability to reason, plan, solve problems, and more [18]. It also affects a person's memory and ability to concentrate [25]. Cognitive abilities can be affected by several conditions such as autism and attention deficit hyperactivity disorder (ADHD) [13,45]. It is also affected by other factors such as stress and fatigue, [28] which clearly shows that it is not constant but rather a dynamic spectrum. In fact, cognitive ability can shift during the day based on numerous factors including not only fatigue and stress but also mood, anxiety and more [38].

While someones cognitive abilities varies over time, there are several conditions, in this paper discussed as cognitive disabilities, that affects cognitive abilities more permanently [42]. A cognitive disability is, in this paper, defined as a condition that impacts on a person's cognitive abilities [27]. Someone without such a condition is denoted neurotypical. While cognitive disabilities are highly individual, they impact a persons cognitive abilities in one or more ways [7]. Lundin and Mellgren describe that a person with a cognitive disability may experience difficulties with one or more of memory, problem-solving, attention, linguistic comprehension, math comprehension, or visual comprehension [23]. As exemplified by Rabiee et al., the level of cognitive impairment, in addition to what cognitive abilities that are impacted, is also individual [30]. Consequently, the impact of a cognitive disability will vary greatly depending on the specific disability, and how that disability is manifested.

The focus of this research is on users with cognitive disabilities who are able to autonomously use computers. The rationale is that this user group is required to handle PICS on their own. Further, a focus on users with cognitive disabilities is imperative in order to understand the cognitive challenges that may come with the use of PICS tools. We argue that this user group is underrepresented in past PICS research discussing usability of PICS tools which is typically focused on the users in general and treats users as one homogeneous group. Given the individuality of cognitive disabilities the research focus is the cognitive implications of cognitive disabilities rather than cognitive disabilities themselves. While participants included in the research cover different cognitive conditions, including dyslexia, ADHD, autism, language impairment, and brain fatigue, the results are discussed in relation to impact on memory, cognitive processing etc., rather than individual conditions.

3   Methodology

An interpretative research approach using qualitative data was used. The rationale was that previous research in this domain is scarce, making it important to understand the individual experiences of members of the target population.

As shown in Fig. 1, the research began with semi-structured interviews with domain experts. Those guided target group workshops that were held next. The data from all sessions were used to identify requirements on PICS tools that were in turn used to propose guidelines. The methodology is described in more detail in the rest of this section.

We employed a purposeful sampling approach where we selected to include study participants who were expected to provide valuable input to the research. We included experts in the domain to acquire data from professionals working

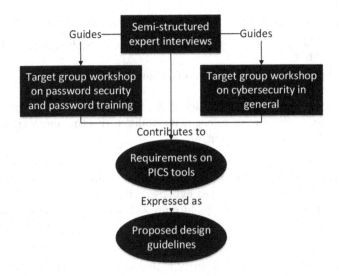

Fig. 1. Overview of methodology

with the topic discussed in this research as suggested by Etikan et al. [6]. We further included participants from the target group, namely users with cognitive disabilities. The rationale was that it allowed for recruitment of participants that were able to contribute to the study with first-hand experiences. While the study design does not allow for generalization, the study aim was to provide a basis for further research and generate a better understanding of problems faced by the target group, rather than quantifying the occurrence of the problems. Further, including both members of the target group and domain experts served as a means of triangulation as suggested by Lincoln and Guba [22]. This allows for comparison of the results and intends to make the combined results more reliable.

The expert interviews included four participants and were held as semi-structured interviews. The participants were identified for inclusion by considering domain experts already known to the research group. Semi-structured interviews were used since it allowed for pre-defined interview themes that guided the interviews in a uniform direction while allowing for follow-up questions based on the answers from the participants. Three interviews were held with one participant working as a coordinator for university students with disabilities, one user experience design expert with personal experience supporting close relatives with cognitive disabilities, and two participants who organize and lead usability evaluations with participants with cognitive disabilities as their profession. The interview with organizers of usability evaluations included two participants upon request from the participants.

The topics discussed during the semi-structured interviews were:

- Differences between neurotypical users and users with cognitive disabilities regarding PICS.
- How different cognitive disabilities can impact a user to be more or less susceptible to risks.
- If users with cognitive disabilities differ from neurotypical users regarding training, use of PICS tools or cognitive abilities affecting memory, willingness to take risks, and impulse control.

The workshops with members of the target group included ten participants. They were organized as two workshops where one discussed password security specifically and the other described cybersecurity in general. The rationale was that a more specific topic would yield more detailed data while a broader topic would also result in broader discussions. The workshops were carried out as follows:

- The workshop on password security included four participants and took the form of a usability analysis of a security education, training, and awareness (SETA) method called Context Based Micro training (CBMT) used to train users on password security [20]. The implementation is described in detail in Kävrestad and Nohlberg [20]. Framing the workshop as a usability analysis intended to spark a discussion on the usability of password guidelines and methods for presenting security related information to users.
- The general workshop included six participants and was arranged as a discussion on cybersecurity topics and problems encountered by the participants relating to security features. Questions were asked about the participants experiences with various PICS tools and situations. The topics included passwords, phishing, fake news, fraud, multi-factor authentication, privacy, and more. Having a more general theme intended to make the participants describe the topics they considered as most important.

Workshops were used with the intention of revealing the participants spontaneous reactions to the workshop topics [9]. Begripsam supported the design and execution of the workshops. All workshop participants were included in Begripsams network of users and Begripsams participation in the workshops intended to make the participants more comfortable while sharing their experiences. It should also be mentioned that the participants were used to discussing design issues as part of their involvement with Begripsam. They should therefore be considered as more knowledgeable than the average user.

All interview and workshop participants consented to participate in the study via e-mail before the sessions. The study purpose and data collection procedures were described to the participants again at the beginning of each session and the participants confirmed their consent to participate before the sessions started. Note that all participants were capable of giving consent to participate on their own.

All interviews and workshops were held by the same researcher (A) to maintain consistency and then transcribed by another member of the research group

(B). The analysis was then conducted by researcher A and reviewed by researcher B, and finally reviewed by the rest of the research group. The video conferencing software Zoom was used to hold and record all sessions since the ongoing Covid-19 pandemic did not allow for physical sessions.

The analysis used an inductive thematic approach [4] employed to identify requirements that users with cognitive disabilities consider important. The identified requirements were then transformed to design guidelines presented as the conclusion of this study. The analysis was carried out in three steps with different purposes as follows:

1. The transcripts were first read and all sections where respondents described something that was positive or negative with regards to usability were extracted.
2. The marked sections were reread and assigned a descriptive label. The descriptive labels formed themes expressed as requirements that PICS tools should follow to be usable.
3. The sections in each theme were analyzed again, and the data in each theme was summarized and related to WCAG 2.1.

The expert interviews were analyzed before the target group workshops were held, and the output guided the workshops. The expert interviews emphasized that cognitive disabilities are very individual and that many users have more that one cognitive disability. As a result, it was not considered meaningful to discuss the impact of individual conditions and the workshops rather considered the impact of cognitive disabilities at a general level. During the workshops, the participants described how their cognitive abilities, rather than conditions, impacted their way of using PICS tools. The target group workshops were then analyzed separately before the results from the two steps were compared and used to propose guidelines for the inclusion of users with cognitive challenges.

4   Results

This section outlines the results from the individual research steps and their combined results.

4.1   Expert Interviews

Three expert interviews were held and covered four participants as described in the section Methodology. The transcription of the interviews totaled 10741 words, and the total time of the interviews was 79 minutes. The combined result of the three interviews revealed four different themes of requirements that PICS tools should follow to be perceived as usable for users with cognitive disabilities.

The themes were established by categorizing and aggregating quotes from the participants. Table 1 shows the themes and a subset of the quotes leading up to the themes. Note that the interviews were held in Swedish, and quotes are translated by researcher A.

Table 1. Part of data set from the expert interviews. *Bank-ID is a national authentication feature in Sweden. It is issued by banks and therefore requires a bank account. It is not available for users who cannot get a bank account, or who are not allowed to control their own bank account.

Quote	Theme	Summary
It must be clear and well-structured	Clarity and simplicity	Informative elements must be short and easy to read, and that tools should behave predictably. It should also be well-structured. Confusing elements and lack of control are perceived as bad and may result in paralysis
..it is too much information....many with ADHD does not read it	Clarity and simplicity	
I think it is good if it is clear	Clarity and simplicity	
Reasonable amount of information in small chunks	Clarity and simplicity	
Then you don't need to rethink or learn	Low memory load	It should not require users to learn or re-learn
Limited memory capacity	Low memory load	
Storing in memory is a hard process	Low memory load	
Tasks that are slightly different appear completely new and require re-learning	Low memory load	
Access to reading of text	Availability functions	It should have text-to-speech functionality that supports users with a wide range of disabilities
Functions that everyone can use	Availability functions	
Users with autism may experience anxiety when unexpected events happen	Discriminating design	Design that is impossible for some user groups to use should be avoided. In Sweden, this includes Bank-ID, which is an authentication feature that is not available for all users, for instance, users who are declared incapacitated
Don't like when things happen without your control	Discriminating design	
Not everyone is allowed to use Bank-ID* even if it is used for increased security	Discriminating design	

4.2   Target Group Workshops

Following the expert interviews, two group workshops with participants with different cognitive disabilities were held. The first workshop included four participants and the second included six participants. The transcription of the workshops totaled 17913 words, and the total time of the workshops was 181 minutes.

The analysis was based on the four themes developed during the analysis of the expert interviews. Quotes from the workshops were labeled using the four themes. Two themes, *Availability functions* and *Low memory load*, were discussed in a broader sense during the workshops compared to the interviews. The themes were renamed to better capture the full meaning of the interviews and workshops combined. *Availability functions* was renamed because the expert interviews only described availability functions while the workshop participants also described the usefulness of different kinds of media. The new name *Media diversity* intends to reflect the richer meaning of the combined data. Likewise, *Low memory load* was renamed to *Limit cognitive load* because the workshops suggested that the key aspect of the category was to minimize need for cognitive processing in a broader sense then to just avoid the need for learning and re-learning. The new label better captures that nuance. The analysis of the workshops is summarized in Table 2 which shows summaries of the four themes and examples of quotes, for each theme, from the participants.

4.3   Combined Results and Proposed Guidelines

This research aimed to identify inhibitors and enablers for the usability of PICS tools with regards to users with cognitive challenges and use that data to draft design guidelines intending to support the design of inclusive and usable PICS tools. This section will describe the identified themes presented above further and propose guidelines that seek to address the identified inhibitors and enablers. The guidelines will be discussed in relation to WCAG 2.1.

The first theme is *Media diversity* where the expert interviews suggested that text-to-speech functions are crucial for several users, and that was emphasized further during the target group workshops. Text-to-speech functions enable users with various challenges such as dyslexia to understand masses of text with lower effort. While not a cognitive condition, several participants highlighted that text-to-speech is also beneficial for users with visual impairment. The first suggested design guideline is, therefore, to *include text-to-speech functionality in tools, functions, and guidelines that requires the users to read text.*

The workgroups further made it obvious that different users want to process information in different ways. While some users may benefit from having a video present information, others may get stressed by not being able to control the pace that information is presented with. It was made clear during the interviews that informative elements must be concise, well-structured, and relevant. However, different media formats benefit different user groups, and a resulting guideline is to *present information in different formats and allow for the user to choose the preferred format..* An example could be to have information displayed as text as a

Table 2. Part of data set from the workshops

Quote	Theme	Summary
I don't understand the purpose of that picture ... it confuses and takes energy	Clarity and simplicity	The respondents describe that informative elements must be short and easy to read and that tools should behave predictably. Further, unnecessary design elements such as animations or images that do not provide additional content should be avoided since they require unnecessary cognitive processing. The respondents also emphasize that it is beneficial to use simplistic language
It is distracting that it starts moving automatically .... takes focus completely	Clarity and simplicity	
It should be coherent so I know what to expect	Clarity and simplicity	
In general ... good with limited text and short sentences	Clarity and simplicity	
I want information but ... prefer it short and to the point	Limit cognitive load	Minimize cognitive load by using consistent design choices, avoiding flashy design elements, and minimize the choices the user has to make. It was also mentioned that spelling errors could take a lot of energy
Security is important, but it should be fewer options....it should not be so hard	Limit cognitive load	
It is always good with a text to speech function	Media diversity	Using different media to provide information is beneficial since different user groups may benefit from consuming information differently. For instance, text to speech is crucial for users with language difficulties, while some users may prefer video or text. This is exemplified by the respondents who express different preferences and needs
..no not a lot of text...I would rather have a video	Media diversity	
It is good with large font size and short texts	Media diversity	
...good with a video...I should be the one starting the video, and it should read the text next-by	Media diversity	
You can be denied access if you are not allowed to have Bank-ID	Discriminating design	Design that is impossible for some user groups to use should be avoided. In addition to Bank-ID, hidden text fields and captcha are described as close to impossible for some participants to use. The participants suggest that tools should support different forms of authentication to be more inclusive
I misspell every tenth word....my email ended up in the trash folder	Discriminating design	
I went to a webpage that said "I am not a robot" and "which of these pictures are bridges" ... do you see a bridge or not?	Discriminating design	

default setting, but allow a user to configure that information is instead presented as audio. The guidelines in the *Media diversity* share commonalities with the WCAG 2.1 chapter named *perceivable* that outlines ways to make information easy to perceive. The results, in this theme, therefore serves to emphasize the need of following accessibility frameworks when designing PICS tools.

The second theme was *Clarity and simplicity*, and all respondents describe that information must be relevant, easy to understand, and well-structured. They emphasize that processing information is very energy consuming, and one respondent described that processing badly worded information can be so exhaustive that they need to rest afterwards. The expert interviews further describe that a common reaction to tools that are seen as too hard to understand is not to use them at all. A resulting guideline is to *only provide the most important information, and in an easy-to-digest manner.*

The workshop part made it evident that the participants experienced processing of information as very energy-consuming. They described that moving design elements such as animations or videos required a lot of cognitive work. They further described that images that do not provide information or did not make sense were disruptive and caused them to consider their purpose. In summary, a PICS tool should *avoid unnecessary design elements* and *allow the user to control moving media.* The rationale behind those guidelines is to emphasize that design elements that are created just to make a tool look fancy, but with no added functionality still require cognitive processing and can have a negative impact on the usability of the tool. Providing information that is easy to understand, allow users to control media, and avoiding unnecessary design elements make part of WGAC 2.1 emphasizing their importance for PICS tools. Keeping to the most important information and thereby minimizing the need for cognitive processing is, is not a focus of WCAG 2.1 and in that regard, this results makes an addition.

The third theme, *limit cognitive load* further emphasizes the importance of the guidelines just presented. Under this theme, the expert interviews describe learning and re-learning as energy-consuming processes. Further, they have shown that it is beneficial for users to limit the need to memorize new things. Similarly, the target group workshops suggest that tools with as little interaction as possible is favorable. The respondents describe that security is important, but seldom their primary target and a tool that adds security without involving the user is wanted, as long as that tool is indeed able to do its intended job. A further insight that became evident during the first workshop was that consistent design within a tool is also important. If a user quickly understands how the tool works, and the tool continues to work in the same way, it becomes intuitive to use and the need for cognitive processing is limited. Added guidelines under this theme are to *use consistent design choices* and *minimize the need for user interaction.* In regards to the second guideline, this research differs from WCAG 2.1 in that it suggests minimizing user interaction whereas WCAG 2.1 emphasize making interaction possible for different user groups [40]. While enabling different user groups to use a system is important, this research highlight the value of minimizing interactions to minimize cognitive load.

Discriminating design was the final theme and included two main discussions. First, some tools and designs are simply impossible to use for some user groups. The reasons can be that some user groups are simply excluded because of legal reasons or similar, as is the case with the Swedish national identification system "Bank-ID." Another reason for exclusion is that some design elements are impossible or close to impossible for users to use because of a cognitive challenge. The most persistently described examples where:

- Hidden text fields which are extremely difficult to use for users with dyslexia where writing in the blind becomes an additional challenge. If it is hard to spell passwords normally, it is almost impossible when the input is hidden.
- Captchas, which requires cognitive processing and good vision.
- Text elements with small font size are hard to notice and hard to read by a user with limited vision.

The workgroup participants further described that allowing different forms of authentication helped different user groups since it allows each user to select a method that works for them. On this topic, some participants did prefer password-based authentication while others preferred biometric options or Bank-ID. In summary, two additional guidelines were developed under this theme. *Avoid design elements or functions that are unreasonably hard, or impossible for some user groups to use* is the first guideline. It requires that user groups are identified with inclusion in mind, and that accessibility is considered from the viewpoint of each user group. Elements that are hard or even impossible for one or more groups to use should be removed or complemented with an additional element that meets the requirements of the identified group. The last guideline is to *allow for various forms of authentication*. It is proposed since authentication forms were central to the workshop discussions and make a central function in the use of information systems. Ensuring that various user groups can be authenticated securely and conveniently should therefore be seen as a key usability factor. An example can be to allow for biometric authentication instead of password based since using a biometric reader can be easier than to remember a password for some users.

5   Discussion

This research employed an interpretative approach using interviews. As a consequence, the degree to which the data is representative beyond the participants is unknown. However, the study's intent was not to gather a representative dataset but to gain a deeper understanding of the target group's experiences. No effort has been made to generalize the results in this study outside of the targeted population. The study presents results in the form of guidelines, and while the guidelines are designed to meet the needs of the target group, they are not validated in this work. We further acknowledge that the guidelines may not cover all usability requirements faced by users with cognitive challenges. Future endeavors in this domain could use the results of this study as a starting point and extend and validate the results presented here. A natural extension could be to conduct additional data gathering to further understand the impact of usability issues. An especially interesting direction would be to research how implementation of usability guidelines in the PICS domain impacts security. A second effect of the research design is that it is not possible to track the results to individual disabilities or challenges. It was decided to not collect or describe the participants individual disabilities to safeguard the individuals privacy. However, that means that any inference as to if and how the recommendations should be modified for different groups is impossible. The intent of the research is to provide results that describe users with cognitive difficulties on a general level and a second natural extension of this work would be continued research with more specific populations.

Previous research describes that security is only as strong as the weakest link [29] and that user behavior is a key aspect of security [34]. User behavior includes that users adopt procedures and guidelines, and use tools designed to increase cybersecurity. Usability is a key factor for such adoption [31]. Since PICS tools are expected, or even required, to be used by all users, it is important to discuss the implication of our results on the general population. The proposed guidelines are intended to increase usability for users with cognitive challenges, but they must do so without negatively impacting usability for other user groups. The results in this study align well with previous research conducted on the same topic, but with a focus on the general user rather than on users with cognitive challenges [21]. Further, the interviews in this study suggest that all users face similar usability challenges when it comes to PICS tools. The main difference identified is that the impact of those challenges is more severe for users with cognitive challenges. Thus, we suggest that the guidelines presented in this study will positively affect the usability of PICS tools for all user groups. It should, however, be noted that this makes a natural area for future research were the security implications of the guidelines should be given attention. It can also be noted that some functions may render users with cognitive challenges unable to use some services, highlighting the importance of accessibility. Ensuring that a cognitive challenge does not exclude someone from using a particular service should be given high priority. The guideline proposed for this purpose posits that a PICS tool developer should consider all potential user groups and their challenges. While that can be a difficult task, different frameworks exist and can provide support. One such example is WCAG 2.1 [40]. While WCAG 2.1 is not specifically designed for PICS tools, this research showcase that many usability problems are the same in the PICS domain as in other domains. However, this research suggests that limiting cognitive load is a key usability issue for PICS tools and that is not a top priority of WCAG 2.1. As such, a call for a focus on minimizing cognitive load makes a contribution of this research.

The consistent theme through the interviews were that simplicity and minimal requirement for interaction from the user were sought-after properties that

PICS tools should strive to achieve. However, the respondents also describe a desire for pluralism. Here, the respondents describe that it is good if the information is presented in different media and if different ways for performing the same task (e.g., authentication) is provided. Combining pluralism and simplicity could be challenging, and it seems natural that a feature added to accommodate one user group can be seen as redundant for another group. It also adds complexity in terms of development, where developers may need to implement more features than they would if they choose not to adopt the guidelines proposed in this paper. Future work considering the implementability of the proposed guidelines would make a natural extension of this study. Further, one could imagine a dilemma where a developer may opt not to adopt the guidelines even if that means that the product developed can be used by less users. The added userbase may be to small to financially motivate adoption of the guidelines if that requires additional work. While research into this dilemma is a natural direction for future work, we argue that inclusion should be a natural part of many development projects. Not least considering the United Nation goals for sustainable development where inclusive societies are promoted [37].

6   Conclusions

This study aimed to propose design guidelines that PICS tools should meet to be considered usable for users with cognitive challenges. Data was gathered from domain experts and the target group, and the data from the two participant groups revealed similar findings. The results showcase that the target group is heterogeneous in regards to the challenges they face. Nevertheless, while there are individual differences this study supports the notion that most solutions are beneficial for most users. A conclusion that can be drawn from the requirements described by the participants is that simplicity and clarity are crucial properties. Further, some commonly used design elements such as captchas or hidden text elements may render a function hard, or even impossible, for some users to use and should be avoided or combined with alternative functions for the same purpose. A further conclusion of this study is that users with cognitive disabilities to a large extent experience similar difficulties as neurotypical users, regarding the usability of PICS tools. However, the consequences of these usability issues are often more severe for users with cognitive disabilities. A usability issue that is annoying for a neurotypical user may render a user with a cognitive disability unable to use a service. This conclusion warrants further studies into how current design of PICS tools presents an inclusion problem, and how that problem can be addressed with maintained level of security.

There are few, if any, previous studies that specifically address the usability of PICS tools and features from the perspective of users with cognitive challenges. This study contributes to the scientific community with insights into how the usability of such functions is perceived from this perspective. As a contribution to the community of practitioners, this study proposes guidelines that can be used when developing future PICS tools, functions, and features. Needless to say, people with cognitive disabilities are using digital services and working in organizations world-wide. On the back of that, this study highlights that including this user-group in the design of PICS tools is an important matter for inclusion as well as PICS.

References

1. Andreasson, A., Blix, F.: "Special commando move"-when informal, formal and technical cybersecurity components fail. In: Proceedings of the 5th International Workshop on Socio-Technical Perspective in IS Development, pp. 26–33 (2019)
2. Belk, M., Fidas, C., Germanakos, P., Samaras, G.: Do human cognitive differences in information processing affect preference and performance of captcha? Int. J. Hum. Comput. Stud. **84**, 1–18 (2015)
3. Bhagavatula, R., Ur, B., Iacovino, K., Kywe, S.M., Cranor, L.F., Savvides, M.: Biometric authentication on iphone and android: usability, perceptions, and influences on adoption. In: USEC'15: Workshop on Usable Security, pp. 1–10 (2015)
4. Braun, V., Clarke, V.: Using thematic analysis in psychology. Qual. Res. Psychol. **3**(2), 77–101 (2006)
5. Canadian Centre for Cyber security: Cyber threat and cyber threat actors (2020). https://cyber.gc.ca/en/guidance/cyber-threat-and-cyber-threat-actors
6. Etikan, I., Musa, S.A., Alkassim, R.S.: Comparison of convenience sampling and purposive sampling. Am. J. Theor. Appl. Stat. **5**(1), 1–4 (2016)
7. Gazzaniga, M.S., Ivry, R.B., Mangun, G.: Cognitive Neuroscience. The Biology of the Mind. Norton, New York (2006)
8. Gerber, N., Zimmermann, V., Henhapl, B., Emeröz, S., Volkamer, M.: Finally Johnny can encrypt: but does this make him feel more secure? In: Proceedings of the 13th International Conference on Availability, Reliability and Security, pp. 1–10 (2018)
9. Gibbs, A.: Focus groups. Soc. Res. Update **19**(8), 1–8 (1997)
10. Groß, T., Coopamootoo, K., Al-Jabri, A.: Effect of cognitive depletion on password choice. In: The {LASER} Workshop: Learning from Authoritative Security Experiment Results ({LASER} 2016), pp. 55–66 (2016)
11. Gutzwiller, R., Dykstra, J., Payne, B.: Gaps and opportunities in situational awareness for cybersecurity. Digit. Threats: Res. Pract. **1**(3), 1–6 (2020)
12. Habib, H., et al.: "It's a scavenger hunt": usability of websites' opt-out and data deletion choices. In: Proceedings of the 2020 CHI Conference on Human Factors in Computing Systems, pp. 1–12 (2020)
13. Happé, F.G., Mansour, H., Barrett, P., Brown, T., Abbott, P., Charlton, R.A.: Demographic and cognitive profile of individuals seeking a diagnosis of autism spectrum disorder in adulthood. J. Autism Dev. Disord. **46**(11), 3469–3480 (2016). https://doi.org/10.1007/s10803-016-2886-2
14. Henriquez, M.: The top 12 data breaches of 2019 (2019). https://www.securitymagazine.com/articles/91366-the-top-12-data-breaches-of-2019
15. Horcher, A.M., Tejay, G.P.: Building a better password: the role of cognitive load in information security training. In: 2009 IEEE International Conference on Intelligence and Security Informatics, pp. 113–118. IEEE (2009)
16. ISO 27000:2018(EN). Standard, International Organization for Standardization, Geneva, CH (2018)

17. Johansson, S., Gulliksen, J., Gustavsson, C.: Disability digital divide: the use of the internet, smartphones, computers and tablets among people with disabilities in Sweden. Univ. Access Inf. Soc. **20**(1), 105–120 (2021). https://doi.org/10.1007/s10209-020-00714-x

18. Karwowski, M., Kaufman, J.C.: The Creative Self: Effect of Beliefs, Self-Efficacy, Mindset, and Identity. Academic Press, Cambridge (2017)

19. Kävrestad, J., Eriksson, F., Nohlberg, M.: Understanding passwords-a taxonomy of password creation strategies. Inf. Comput. Secur. (2019)

20. Kävrestad, J., Nohlberg, M.: ContextBased microtraining: a framework for information security training. In: Clarke, N., Furnell, S. (eds.) HAISA 2020. IAICT, vol. 593, pp. 71–81. Springer, Cham (2020). https://doi.org/10.1007/978-3-030-57404-8_6

21. Lennartsson, M., Kävrestad, J., Nohlberg, M.: Exploring the meaning of "usable security". In: Clarke, N., Furnell, S. (eds.) HAISA 2020. IAICT, vol. 593, pp. 247–258. Springer, Cham (2020). https://doi.org/10.1007/978-3-030-57404-8_19

22. Lincoln, Y.S., Guba, E.G.: Naturalistic Inquiry. Sage, Thousand Oaks (1985)

23. Lundin, L., Mellgren, Z.: Psykiska funktionshinder: stöd och hjälp vid kognitiva funktionsnedsättningar. Studentlitteratur (2012)

24. McLean, R.: A hacker gained access to 100 million capital one credit card applications and accounts (2019). https://edition.cnn.com/2019/07/29/business/capital-one-data-breach/index.html

25. Oberauer, K., Süß, H.M., Schulze, R., Wilhelm, O., Wittmann, W.W.: Working memory capacity–facets of a cognitive ability construct. Pers. Individ. Differ. **29**(6), 1017–1045 (2000)

26. OECD: Hows Life in the Digital Age? (2019). https://www.oecd-ilibrary.org/content/publication/9789264311800-en

27. Olney, M.F., Kim, A.: Beyond adjustment: integration of cognitive disability into identity. Disab. Soc. **16**(4), 563–583 (2001)

28. Palmer, L.: The relationship between stress, fatigue, and cognitive functioning. Coll. Stud. J. **47**(2), 312–325 (2013)

29. Pfleeger, C.P., Pfleeger, S.L., Margulies, J.: Security in Computing, 5th edn. Prentice Hall, Upper Saddle River (2015)

30. Rabiee, A., et al.: The cognitive profile of people with high-functioning autism spectrum disorders. Behav. Sci. **9**(2), 20 (2019)

31. Ramokapane, K.M., Mazeli, A.C., Rashid, A.: Skip, skip, skip, accept!!!: a study on the usability of smartphone manufacturer provided default features and user privacy. Proc. Priv. Enhancing Technol. **2019**(2), 209–227 (2019)

32. Ramsetty, A., Adams, C.: Impact of the digital divide in the age of COVID-19. J. Am. Med. Inform. Assoc. **27**(7), 1147–1148 (2020)

33. Reeves, A., Delfabbro, P., Calic, D.: Encouraging employee engagement with cybersecurity: how to tackle cyber fatigue. SAGE Open **11**(1) (2021)

34. Safa, N.S., Von Solms, R.: An information security knowledge sharing model in organizations. Comput. Hum. Behav. **57**, 442–451 (2016)

35. Solove, D.J.: A taxonomy of privacy. U. Pa. L. Rev. **154**, 477 (2005)

36. Stern, T., Kumar, N.: Improving privacy settings control in online social networks with a wheel interface. J. Am. Soc. Inf. Sci. **65**(3), 524–538 (2014)

37. United Nations: Sustainable development (2021). https://sdgs.un.org/

38. Verhagen, S.J., et al.: Measuring within-day cognitive performance using the experience sampling method: a pilot study in a healthy population. PloS One **14**(12) (2019)

39. Vishwanath, A., Harrison, B., Ng, Y.J.: Suspicion, cognition, and automaticity model of phishing susceptibility. Commun. Res. **45**(8), 1146–1166 (2018)
40. W3C: Web content accessibility guidelines (wcag) 2.1 (2018). https://www.w3.org/TR/WCAG21
41. Whitten, A., Tygar, J.D.: Why Johnny can't encrypt: a usability evaluation of PGP 5.0. In: USENIX Security Symposium, vol. 348, pp. 169–184 (1999)
42. World Health Organization: International statistical classification of diseases and related health problems 10th revision (icd-10) (2019)
43. Yan, J., El Ahmad, A.S.: Usability of CAPTCHAs or usability issues in CAPTCHA design. In: Proceedings of the 4th Symposium on Usable Privacy and Security, pp. 44–52 (2008)
44. Yıldırım, M., Mackie, I.: Encouraging users to improve password security and memorability. Int. J. Inf. Secur. **18**(6), 741–759 (2019). https://doi.org/10.1007/s10207-019-00429-y
45. Young, S.: Coping strategies used by adults with ADHD. Pers. Individ. Differ. **38**(4), 809–816 (2005)

Cloud Native Privacy Engineering through DevPrivOps

Elias Grünewald[✉][iD]

Information Systems Engineering, Technische Universität Berlin, Berlin, Germany
gruenewald@tu-berlin.de

Abstract. Cloud native information systems engineering enables scalable and resilient software architectures powering major online offerings. Today, these are built following agile development practices. At the same time, a growing demand for privacy-friendly services is articulated by societal norms and policy through effective legislative frameworks. In this paper, we (i) identify conceptual dimensions of cloud native privacy engineering – that is, bringing together cloud computing fundamentals and privacy regulation – and propose an integrative approach to be addressed to overcome the shortcomings of existing privacy enhancing technologies in practice and evaluating existing system designs. Furthermore, we (ii) propose a reference software development lifecycle called DevPrivOps to enhance established agile development methods with respect to privacy. Altogether, we show that cloud native privacy engineering opens up key advances to the state of the art of privacy by design and by default using latest technologies.

Keywords: Cloud native · DevOps · Privacy · Privacy engineering · Data protection · Software engineering · Privacy enhancing technologies · DevPrivOps

1 Introduction

The enormous and unstoppable rise of digital services for people's lives already resulted in globally interconnected digital societies. During this long-lasting process the inter- and trans-disciplinary questions on how to achieve an adequate level of privacy are still to be solved – while privacy itself is an essentially contested concept [46]. Although some seem to have accepted sheer insurmountable hurdles or are actively supporting a post-privacy age (as shown by [55]), many others, fortunately, fight for autonomy and against a "surveillance capitalism" [74]; may it be through political advocacy, privacy law, or key technological advances. In this paper, we mainly focus on the latter with respect to current trends in the field of privacy engineering.

All major digital service offerings are enabled through the extensive use of highly distributed cloud computing systems. These provision compute, storage,

© IFIP International Federation for Information Processing 2022
Published by Springer Nature Switzerland AG 2022
M. Friedewald et al. (Eds.): Privacy and Identity 2021, IFIP AICT 644, pp. 122–141, 2022.
https://doi.org/10.1007/978-3-030-99100-5_10

and network resources, that are used to build and run scalable and dynamic infrastructure and applications [10]. Within the last decade, the service portfolio of public cloud vendors has bloomed from distributed databases over service meshes to highly-specific AI-based programming and execution platforms. However, not only the technical infrastructure has drastically changed, but also development models to create and operate distributed services. Software is crafted by diverse teams in agile programming, testing and design prototyping phases, and through iterative requirements engineering and using project management tools. Namely, agile development processes like scrum allow to develop and deploy new functionalities and complete services to production continuously (DevOps), i.e. potentially multiple times per hour [5].

Inherently, distributed services are highly complex, which is why software engineering increasingly focuses on manageability, resilience and robustness, or observability to cope with the engineering challenges and – as a secondary concern – legal obligations of privacy and cloud computing. At the same time, the still emerging field of privacy engineering [29] has to provide the most accessible conceptual methods and technical tools to achieve privacy by design and by default, as legally required by the European General Data Protection Regulation (GDPR) [20] and commonly agreed upon in privacy research. Although, fundamental privacy principles [8] such as transparency, purpose limitation, and accountability, have been long established and are more often enforced [67], so far, many developers lack a solid understanding and the concrete technologies to construct privacy-friendly cloud native systems. In short, we observe three major challenges:

- **Cloud native application architectures introduce new privacy challenges** w.r.t. distributed (personal) data management across countries, availability under immense loads, compliant information flow control, restrictive access policies et cetera.
- **Software engineers are ill-equipped with privacy-preserving methods and tools addressing *all* privacy principles**, including, among others, lawfulness, transparency, or accountability; while privacy is often misinterpreted as only subject to security-related research.
- **Agile development practices still (mostly) neglect or even contradict privacy principles** (beyond data minimization and security) as crosscutting themes of software engineering.

Addressing these issues well aligns with related work on privacy and (early) cloud computing [72], engineering privacy by design [6,7], and, how privacy is affected by agile development practices [31]. In a similar vein, this paper aims to provide a more clear viewpoint on the term of cloud native privacy engineering through a two-fold contribution:

- A conceptual model on the **dimensions of cloud native privacy engineering** accompanied by different use case scenarios from an information systems engineering perspective, and

- Proposing a **privacy-aware *DevPrivOps* reference lifecycle** addressing the shortcomings of established agile practices explicitly tailored to cloud native environments.

The journey through this paper takes place as follows: First, we briefly introduce the established concepts of cloud native application architectures and agile software development and, further, compare to related work in Sect. 2. On this basis, we observe the dimensions of cloud native privacy engineering in Sect. 3 illustrated by several use case scenarios. Afterwards, we introduce the software development cycle called *DevPrivOps* proposed for privacy-aware information systems engineering in Sect. 4. Finally, we discuss our findings and conclude in Sect. 5.

2   Background and Related Work

This section introduces a brief background on the field of cloud native engineering and agile software development. Moreover, we summarize the latest findings in the field of privacy engineering.

2.1   Cloud Native and Agile Software Development

Within the last decade, the technical evolution of distributed service-oriented architectures has been rapid and disruptive [47]. The emergence of cloud computing, mainly characterized by on-demand access to shared compute, storage, and network resources [44,45], has led to a diverse and powerful infrastructure, platform, and software service portfolio [41,62]. Without doubt, the transformative power of cloud-based systems serves as an important utility across many dimensions of today's societies [25]. Most prominently, major public cloud vendors such as Amazon Web Services, the Google Cloud Platform, Microsoft Azure, and IBM Cloud, showcase their offerings, which are adopted by a multitude of private and governmental customers. Furthermore, private and hybrid cloud approaches also enable online services. The latter are often powered by open source projects such as OpenStack[1].

To build and operate applications, which are scalable for millions of users, developers rely on so-called cloud native technologies. The Cloud Native Computing Foundation (CNCF) highlights the usage of "containers, service meshes, microservices, immutable infrastructure, and declarative APIs" [10]. In practice, modern applications may consist of hundreds of loosely-coupled microservices that communicate through well-defined programming interfaces following paradigms such as REST [16] or (g)RPC[2].

At the same time, we observe a transformation from a (often waterfall-like) legacy software development culture towards a more flexible, iterative and agile

---

[1] See https://www.openstack.org/.

[2] See, e.g., https://developers.googleblog.com/2015/02/introducing-grpc-new-open-source-http2.html.

organizational setup [5,54]. DevOps is widely acknowledged as the best way to deal with the complexity of large microservice architectures [19]. In doing so, the development team should be responsible for the entire lifecycle (incl. plan, code, build, test, release, deploy, operate, and monitor phases) of a software component and their expertise may be used to make individual technology decisions [38]. Together with an adhered framework for managing tasks and responsibilities (such as scrum [56]), which integrates reasonable tool support for assisting all phases, fast-paced development with which high quality software can be achieved.

Finally, cloud native architecture, engineering, and management techniques heavily focus on the possible trade-offs between different software qualities and, moreover, ultimate technology decisions [4,24]. Such trade-offs occur in different shapes and sizes. They vary from evidence-based benchmarking experiments for choosing a best-fit technology to multilateral discussions on, e.g., what an adequate level of fair computing practice actually is in the context of cloud-based systems [65].

2.2 Privacy

Privacy is a fundamental human right according to Art. 12 of the Universal Declaration of Human Rights [66]. Moreover, it has an even longer tradition as a societal norm and guideline for legislation and jurisdiction [69]. Consequently, it is subject to inter- and trans-disciplinary research with legal, social, economic, political, psychological, and technical discourse. Predominantly, the notion of privacy is shaped by two different western cultures [70]. Being well aware of the different interpretations of privacy and data protection (including informational self-determination), hereafter we use these terms interchangeably.

Today, privacy law (and the public discussion it is complemented by[3]) significantly influences business practices. Regulations, such as the GDPR or the California Consumer Privacy Act (CCPA) [11] provide strong regulatory frameworks which are accompanied by landmark case law decisions (such as "Schrems II"[4]). Eventually, the legal perspective of privacy boils down to several foundational principles (e.g., transparency, data minimization, or accountability) which have been accepted as common ground (inter alia, [8,48]). Therefore, in Sect. 3 we extract the central privacy principles which are encoded in the GDPR to be reflected with the cloud native and agile software development trends laid out above. Before that, we briefly introduce the discipline of privacy engineering.

2.3 Privacy Engineering

Privacy engineering is the discipline of technically addressing the aforementioned privacy principles to protect data subjects and to avoid threats and vulnerabili-

---

[3] As prominent examples may serve the Snowden, Cambridge Analytica, or lately, Pegasus revelations.

[4] See https://curia.europa.eu/juris/document/document.jsf?text=&docid=228677& doclang=en.

ties (inducing risks) while meeting all functional and non-functional requirements of data controllers and processors. Clearly, this does not only include the operationalization of producing source code, but also encompasses the holistic view on software architecture, business organization and culture including all stakeholders. This perspective led to the umbrella term *Privacy by Design and By Default* [8,30,32,59]. From a legal perspective, privacy engineering is motivated through said motto in Art. 25 GDPR. Controllers, therefore, have to take into account the "state of the art, the cost of implementation and the nature, scope, context and purposes of processing as well as the risks of varying likelihood and severity" of processing personal data. Further, "appropriate technical and organisational measures" need to be implemented. As a consequence, there is a steady and momentous incentive for building applicable technical components. Since they may advance the state of the art, they then have to be used by data controllers in practice to protect data subjects. Naturally, when exactly the state of the art might be significantly advanced is questionable from case to case. However, the GDPR, for instance, enables certification procedures in Art. 42, which also take into consideration the differences between dominant economic players and small and medium-sized enterprises. Additionally, among others, the European Data Protection Board, constantly publishes guidelines and recommendations which are clear indicators on compliant technical and organizations measures. Likewise, other civic or research institutions provide their expertise to the public.

Focusing on the implementation, Privacy Enhancing Technologies (PETs) are subject to the core of privacy engineering research. With each generation of new technologies, the conceptual frameworks further matured: From early visions [26], over elaborated strategies for software architecture in practice [32,34,35] and related privacy patterns[5], to topical challenges of software engineering and service architectures [37].

Reputed early projects such as Cranor's P3P [13] or the European PRIME [33] and PrimeLife [52] catalysed the discourse around PETs further. More recent projects then focused on privacy and especially transparency, also in distributed contexts (e.g., Privacy & Us[6], PRISMACloud[7], SPECIAL[8], or DaSKITA[9]). While many approaches focus on (not less important) data subject facing technologies (such as privacy dashboards), key advances that keep pace with the rising complexity of distributed cloud native systems are hard to identify.

Still, product managers and software engineers are ill-equipped with the right tools to put privacy by design in practice. Studies show, that there is a fundamental responsibility issue among engineers [61].

Although the majority of them is aware of the threats of non-compliant software systems and the potential harm they could produce to data subjects, they lack the means to proactively implement countermeasures against attack

---

[5] See https://privacypatterns.org/.
[6] See https://privacyus.eu/.
[7] See https://prismacloud.eu/.
[8] See https://specialprivacy.ercim.eu/.
[9] See https://daskita.github.io/.

vectors or the ethical design of IT infrastructures [61]. Further, extensive literature review reveals that there are *(i)* a lack of viable tools and practices for the complete software development cycle, and *(ii)* misconceptions when such implementations achieve their goals [2].

As introduced above, the way software is developed has fundamentally changed ("The Agile Turn"). Traditional shrink-wrap products are to be replaced by interconnected online service offerings powered by cloud native architectures [31]. This, in turn, makes it inevitable to rethink both, the complexity of interrelations of data processors and the functional and non-functional requirements the future generation of PETs needs to address. The same is true for the resulting automation potentials, e.g., within data protection impact assessments [73]. Furthermore, cloud native engineering is constantly in flux and will be extended through IoT and fog computing scenarios [50]. Therefore, we continue examining which dimensions cloud native privacy engineering is subject to in the following section.

3   Dimensions of Cloud Native Privacy Engineering

In the following section, we propose a cloud native privacy engineering matrix, that illustrates conceptual dimensions, which will be exemplified by subsequent use case scenarios.

First, we reiterate the importance of regulatory frameworks such as the GDPR [20] or the CCPA [11] in the context of privacy-aware cloud systems – we refer to legislation . Through further legislative proposals such as the European ePrivacy Regulation[10], Data Governance Act[11], and the Digital Services Act[12] the future guidelines will be complemented. Together with evolving social norms and expectations or professional privacy threat analysis frameworks, such as LINDDUN [14], these will and already are highly influencing the compliance strategies of enterprises. Therefore, the discipline of privacy engineering has to keep track of all these legal requirements to be implemented in their software products.

Second, enterprises are changing their organization through more innovative workforce structures. On the one hand, many firms are no longer just supported by software, but software development is at the core of their business activity. With these changes come shifts in personnel and governance structures, roles and responsibilities, and more flexible methods of operation. This is why, from a business perspective, established models to integrate privacy need to be reviewed. These concerns are of utmost importance for decision-makers and strategists within companies to align with the aforementioned regulatory requirements (i.e. in order to avoid penalties), but also to keep being competitive. In

---

[10] See https://eur-lex.europa.eu/legal-content/EN/TXT/?uri=CELEX%3A52017PC
0010.

[11] See https://eur-lex.europa.eu/legal-content/EN/TXT/?uri=CELEX%3A52020PC
0767.

[12] See https://eur-lex.europa.eu/legal-content/en/TXT/?uri=COM:2020:825:FIN.

the cloud native context, this includes, for instance, make-or-buy or vendor lock-in decisions with regard to (multi-/hybrid-) cloud computing infrastructure or (external) privacy consulting.

Third, we emphasize a `process`-related dimension. Closely related to the organizational questions are the handling of effective communication and clear privacy by policy [60] responsibilities. From a computer science and engineering perspective, technical components are aspired to automate as many things as possible. As we will see later on, the smart implementation of privacy-related tools into the continuous integration and deployment (CI/CD) workflows can greatly heighten the level of data protection. However, "purely technical approaches might prove insufficient for aligning nuanced legal policies with engineering artifacts" [29]. As a consequence, engineers need to be engaged and cherished for their individual contributions to all cloud native privacy engineering efforts. This can be done through a supportive and efficient culture, incentive schemes and, most importantly, developer-centric privacy engineering solutions. These are primarily characterized through developer-friendliness (including intuitive usage, appropriate documentation etc.) and low implementation overhead [27,51]. At the same time, already established cloud native tooling provides tremendous potential to be unlocked for *(i)* aligning with privacy law, *(ii)* supporting organizational efficacy, and *(iii)* automating many steps of the process of dealing with hundreds of services. All of these reflect the highly-specific perspectives driven by the business model and implementation of fulfillment processes of a data controller.

Furthermore, cloud native engineering is heavily focused on the specifics of (at least) three different layers. Usually, these layers are denoted as Infrastructure, Platform, and Software as a Service (XaaS). These terms emphasize the share between self-managed and fully provided solutions by the cloud provider. Since we are discussing software development in general, we rename "Software" to "Application" layer to avoid confusion. Thus, all major cloud vendors offer[13] three layers:

- `Infrastructure` that consists of compute, storage, and network resources (virtual and/or pooled)
  - *Examples: Virtual machines, Storage buckets, Software Defined Networks*
- `Platform` for building, testing, deploying, running, and scaling services on managed infrastructure
  - *Examples: Container orchestrators, Serverless/Functions as a Service, Pre-trained machine learning environments, Managed databases, Elastic load balancers*
- `Application` that is handling the business logic and may contain several user or application programming interfaces.

---

[13] Note that some of these example attributions may differ in details depending on their concrete system design. Some of the abstraction levels also increasingly blur together.

- *Examples: Depending on the business scenario, any application written in any programming language incl. interface and communication specifications.*

All of the latter are building blocks for large-scale data processing. From this follows, privacy engineering needs a bouquet of solutions to cope with the different deployment models and configurations of cloud native architecture, since personal data is processed in many different ways. We have now identified the first six dimensions of cloud native privacy engineering. Three of them (Legislation, Organization, and Process) are addressing mainly the external factors privacy engineers are influenced by.

Oriented orthogonally to the dimensions already mentioned, we will therefore now add 10 more to complete the proposed view of cloud native privacy engineering. All of the following ones are distilled from both literature and the GDPR, who we denote as essential privacy principles. Note that none of the following principles is new per se, however, it is of utmost importance to see them in conjunction with the aforementioned cloud engineering layers of abstraction. For an in-depth study, we refer to extensive related work [8,39,68]. We only list them very briefly for the sake of simplicity:

- Lawfulness (Art. 5(1a), 6–11 GDPR) comprises the prohibition of all personal data processing activities *unless* there is one of the well-defined permission options present (e.g. consent).
- Fairness (Art. 5(1a) GDPR) refers to proportionality between interests and necessities of both data controllers and data subjects. Moreover, it can be interpreted as procedural fairness which includes timeliness or burden of care [9]. Fairness is also an umbrella term for multiple concepts as defined by the OCED guidelines [48] and the Fair Information Practices [21].[14]
- Transparency (Art. 5(1a), 12, 13, 14, 30 GDPR) includes transparent information, communication and modalities for the exercise of data subjects and the respective obligations for data controllers or processors which allows independent verification and enables trust [8].
- Accountability (Art. 5(2), 24 GDPR) entails the responsibility and ability for demonstration of compliance with all the other principles. Therefore, it is closely related to enforcement and audit strategies of supervisory authorities.
- Purpose limitation (Art. 5(1b) GDPR) requires specific, explicit, and legitimate purpose specifications. This prohibits overly broad statements and data processing upon retrospective amendments or further incompatible processing with the initially stated purpose.
- Data minimization (Art. 5(1c) GDPR) limits the collection of personal data for further processing. Frequent tactics are excluding, selecting, stripping, perturbating, and deleting personal data as much as possible [35]. Possible safeguards include anonymization and (to a limited degree) pseudonymization.

---

[14] Note, although fairness "remains under-defined from a legal perspective", it still has to be considered in explicit design trade-offs; see also [23].

- **Accuracy** (Art. 5(1d) GDPR) determines that all personal data are to be kept up-to-date and correct. Therefore, data subjects have the right to rectification (Art. 16), which is important to reduce possible algorithmic discrimination because of false assumptions.
- **Storage limitation** (Art. 5(1e) GDPR) specifies period for which personal data can be processed. This period is strongly coupled to the lawfulness and the specific purpose for which the processing is permitted.
- **Security** (Art. 5(1f), 32 GDPR) safeguards against unauthorized and unlawful data processing. The technical and organizational measures need to ensure confidentiality, integrity, and availability (CIA triad) [1].
- **Access & Data portability** (Art. 15, 20 GDPR) refer to all data subjects' right to get a copy of all personal data relating to them. Closely related, the GDPR guarantees the freedom - where technically feasible - to transmit their personal data from one controller to another. The latter also enables a (in theory) effective mean against dominant market positions [15].

Privacy by design needs to target a positive-sum, not zero-sum to unfold its real societal impact [8]. Although within systems engineering trade-offs need to be discussed during the development process, the ultimate goal has to be to align with *all* the privacy principles best. In this context, we also acknowledge the classifications of privacy engineering *by architecture* [60], *policy* [60], and *interaction* [29] which clear the mist for evaluating proposed systems. In addition, we can contextualize (again) the privacy design strategies [35] that can be directly mapped to many of the resulting matrix elements which are depicted in Fig. 1.

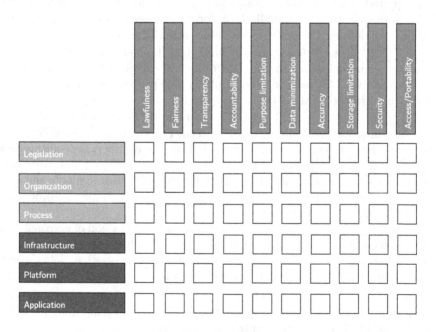

Fig. 1. Dimensions of cloud native privacy engineering

We now examine two different use cases, illustrating the range of different privacy engineering mechanisms:

Use Case 1. Transparency in large service-based cloud architectures is key to strengthen data subjects' level of informedness. Traditionally, written privacy policies try to convey transparency information in legalese language. However, they are not only hard to understand for users, but also incompatible with agile development practices, as they 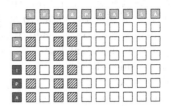 – by design – cannot be changed multiple times per day. Cloud native architectures, in turn, need a machine-readable representation and additional tooling for processing said transparency information in order to describe the multitude of services in real-time. TILT [27] and TIRA [28], as technical mechanisms, address this issue being explicitly tailored to large-scale cloud native systems, agile development practices, and the legal requirements. Consequently, the proposed policy language and programming toolkit of TILT, and the OpenAPI extension and dashboard of TIRA address transparency, accountability, and lawfulness on many different levels.

Use Case 2. The Right to Data Portability (RtDP) is still uncharted territory in real-world systems. At least, many data controllers provide so-called takeouts[15] for semi-automatically fulfilling the right to access according to Art. 15 GDPR. Also the CCPA clearly specifies in Sec. III that data controllers "shall promptly take steps to disclose and deliver, free of charge to the consumer, 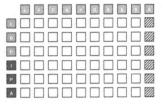 the personal information required". Closely related, Art. 20 GDPR states the right to data portability. As a consequence, the data also has to be provided in a machine-readable format. However, the automatic transfer of all personal data from controller A to B is still somewhat disregarded. At least, one major PET has been proposed by a consortium of big technology companies, namely the Data Transfer Project (DTP)[16]. The DTP addresses the RtDP through three main components. First, there are several data models that can be extended by the community, and are to be used for describing the personal data to be transferred. Next, they propose company-specific adapters for authentication and how to communicate with the provider's core infrastructure (preferably through well-defined APIs). Third, they connect these components through various middleware components enabling in-transit encryption or failure handling. The project is in an experimental state, however, it is a serious attempt to enable the RtDP. Notably, the tool is built using common cloud native techniques such

---

[15] E.g. Google's takeout under https://takeout.google.com/settings/takeout.
[16] See https://datatransferproject.dev/.

as containerization and well-defined web APIs for developer-friendly integration at application level.

As we can infer from these two examples, cloud native privacy engineering is still a difficult endeavour. On the one hand, there is no such option as free lunch, since not a single or two tools can possibly cover the complete range of the dimensions at hand. Secondly, a remaining question is as to whether a PET is considered as "appropriate" measure. Calculating the security-related risk of a password brute-force attack is fairly easy, while, in comparison, measuring an adequate level of *fair* or *transparent* data processing is an unsolved problem. Especially in these cases, as in other compliance contexts, we need to put the organizational and process-related dimensions into the center of attention. Notwithstanding, by the help of the proposed model, we can now compare different architectures by checking how sparse or dense the matrix is filled. As a rule of thumb, the more privacy principles at different levels are met (indicated by a colored matrix element), the better is the overall rating. Salient privacy engineering solutions then cover complete columns or even span rows. In contrast, a system described by a sparse matrix faces a substantial need for remedial action. In a second step, case-specific data protection impact assessments (DPIAs) following a risk-based approach should be carried out. By its very nature, the level of ensured privacy cannot be put into a single evaluation model. However, evidence-based experiments and research shall complement the discussion: On the one hand, we need to consider the cost of implementation efforts according to Art. 25(1) in relation to the (risks associated with the) processing. On the other hand, we argue that all phases of development and operations need to be taken into account. Consequently, we need empirical studies for various kinds of PETs relating to all dimensions of cloud native privacy engineering. Having these, we can better compare and evaluate complete systems w.r.t. to architecture, engineering, and management.

After having discussed the dimensions of cloud native privacy engineering, we head over towards the software development cycle to demonstrate the implementation in practice.

4   DevPrivOps: Privacy Engineering in Practice

In this section, we suggest an enhanced *DevPrivOps* lifecycle complementing the model of [57], that illustrates how privacy can be ensured in cloud native architectures and through which tools the privacy-friendly and agile development of large-scale service infrastructures can be exemplified.

DevOps emphasizes cross-functional collaboration to operate systems and accelerate delivery of any occurring changes [17]. For this purpose, it is practiced as a software development culture that integrates the following eight phases conducted in an endless cycle [71]. We will explain them briefly in our own words (for long-reads we recommend [5,63]). Additionally, we will hint at tangible activities that complement the phase with cloud native privacy engineering tactics. Therefore, we can now introduce a DevPrivOps lifecycle, that consists of the already established DevOps loop (depicted in blue) and an enveloping "ring" that illustrates the possibility to add privacy-related activities in every phase (cf. Fig. 2).

First, the lifecycle is initialized by a **planning** phase. Working with agile project management tools, this could be a scrum planning phase, in which the tasks for the next sprint are to be defined. Moreover, this phase serves as a checkpoint to plan either a new functionality or fixes and enhancements to an existing one. Changes can, e.g., be prioritized based on the developer's skill or the strategic business reason why a change is requested. In traditional software engineering, the plan phase is comparable to the requirements engineering phase, in which all functional and non-functional items are to be collected. Within the planning phase, it is convenient for the team to discuss which privacy pattern or design strategy (see Sect. 2.3) to employ. This phase may also entail the threat modelling or risk analysis to decide which technologies fit best.

Second, writing of source **code** begins. This activity is not meant be limited to programming in the general purpose languages at hand, but can also be used to write configuration files, infrastructure as code definitions [3], test cases, API specifications or database queries (non-exhaustive list). Coding is assisted by integrated development environments (IDEs), a collection of tools to assist writing code, debugging, reading documentation and so on. With regard to privacy engineering, this phase is used to employ libraries or plugging in components that feature a design goal. For the security dimension one would, e.g., choose the encryption cipher suite and library. When focusing on transparency, all personal data indicators [28] would be documented (which also streamlines auditability) or (manual or automatic) instrumentation for logging, tracing, and monitoring tools would be added. Basically, this phase is crucial for every processing activity. Some IDEs automatically hint at uncatched exceptions, possible SQL injections, non-documented function parameters, missing type checking and many possible other security flaws in the source code [42]. In addition, version control systems are used to organize multiple developers working on the same files in different development branches. These can further be used to review code changes by another team member. This enables shared responsibilities and better code quality.

Third, the application is built using **build** automation tools. These tools help to check if all external and internal dependencies can be resolved or supervise the compilation process of respective programming languages. With regard to security, outdated versions of external libraries could be identified. Taking the data minimization and purpose limitation dimensions as examples, the tools can assist in building different versions for disparate target groups. For instance, if the business model contains a paid version without targeted advertising, the build automation could exclude third party tracking functionalities. Besides, in trustless setups, for instance, zero-knowledge proofs are generated in order to keep sensitive information private [18].

After the build phase, automatic **tests** are executed. Software testing can be an exhaustive task that includes thousands of test cases. Using the testing phase

Code analysis
Tool selection
Instrumentation
Code reviews

Tooling research
Task distribution
Strategy discussion

Function placement
Compliance checks
Transparent documentation
Responsibility effects

Documentation
Communication

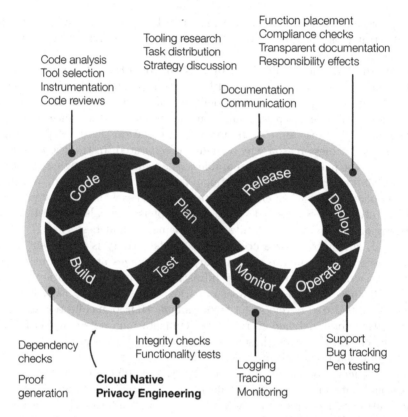

Dependency
checks

Proof
generation

Integrity checks
Functionality tests

Cloud Native
Privacy Engineering

Logging
Tracing
Monitoring

Support
Bug tracking
Pen testing

Fig. 2. Continuous DevPrivOps software development lifecycle.

for privacy-related tasks, the test suite can check several functions with different inputs if the expected accuracy or integrity are ensured. Test data sets can be used to check different behaviours or the correct calculation of obfuscation mechanisms. For instance, parts of a threat analysis and management can be automated in a CI pipeline [58]. Generally, integration tests can also be used to check the platform or infrastructure in various dimensions (esp. with security in mind) [36].

Next, the changes are **released**. Therefore, DevOps engineers automate an integration pipeline that is executed automatically. Such a pipeline may again carry out tests on different target platforms and then create a package for later delivery. Privacy engineering can play a role here again, e.g., by executing integrity checks or adding transparency-related information that can be generated out of automated analysis tasks. With this phase we leave the rather development-focused phases and enter the operation part of the loop.

Afterwards, the software is **deployed** to compute, storage, and network resources, provided by the cloud infrastructure. In automated scenarios, this may include the decision which (virtual) machine is used or at which edge device a container is placed (in a fog computing scenario). In highly distributed scenarios these decisions can have a huge impact on the regulatory obligations that apply. Thinking about services that are deployed to a data center in a third country; this has direct implications on transparency, accountability or security dimensions [12]. However, also organizational responsibilities naturally change when software is deployed to infrastructure at different locations. Advanced deployment strategies (e.g., canary releases or A/B tests) are natural candidates for reducing the risks of potentially harmful processing of personal data.

Subsequently, **operating** the software is a key task for the responsible team. This does not only include to keep running the software technically, but may also include process-related activities like internal support or bug tracking. From a privacy perspective, security-related tasks such as pen testing or research for vulnerabilities are important. Moreover, during operation potentially lots of personal data is accessed, changed, added, or deleted. These activities need to be observed and cross-checked with the prior-made assumptions about, e.g., to which degree k/k_s-anonymity [49,64], ℓ-diversity [43] or ε-differential [40] privacy can be guaranteed in real-world scenarios. In another dimension, data accuracy could be validated after each change.

Thereafter, the **monitoring** phase is entered. During this phase, cloud native architectures are watched using observability techniques. The most common tools perform logging, distributed tracing and collecting metrics [53]. These tools can also be used to achieve a higher level of privacy. First, logging helps to build an accountable system, since the controller can historically demonstrate that the system worked as intended by keeping the records of processing activity [22]. Secondly, distributed tracing can be used to observe service compositions. Thus, a data controller has full transparency over all personal data processing and can provide a summary to the data subject or supervisory authority in real-time. Moreover, all joint controllerships or de-facto processors are automatically detected independently from what was manually documented before. Additionally, purpose limitation can be guaranteed when there is a "watchdog" that detects unwanted or unlawful behaviour. Third, by the help of collected metrics we can detect adverse intrusions and therefore threats for personal data leakage. At the same time, key performance indicators allow to prove that data access or portability tasks were timely executed. As shown, this phase is exceptionally well suitable for all different kinds of cloud native privacy engineering.

In this section we showed how privacy engineering can be integrated into all phases of DevOps engineering. The term *DevPrivOps* was mentioned first in a recent position paper [57]. With this paper we want to further coin the term with regard to cloud computing environments and the chances of cloud-native tools to implement all privacy principles in practice. So far, the term DevOps was only augmented as *DevSecOps*. However, this perspective does not reflect the complexity of the privacy engineering discipline as a whole.

5 Discussion and Conclusion

Future privacy engineering tools need to be in line with the actual givens of practical information systems engineering. Without doubt, conceptual models provide us with guidelines for a better architecture of real-world systems. At the same time, a reality check is necessary to align with the environment of industry-grade cloud native computing. So far, we observed that the goal of privacy by design can then be reached when the software development lifecycle is focused on all dimensions as laid out in Sect. 3.

In this paper, malicious practices from within the corporation were not considered. It is evident that appropriate measures must also be taken in this regard. These are, however, primarily of an organizational nature. Consequently, clear processes and, above all, automated tests can also be effective protective safeguards. Manual manipulation away from the log is made significantly more difficult by DevPrivOps practices, e.g., when CI/CD pipelines alert or stop non-compliant code from running in production.

To the best of our knowledge, there have been no studies on the acceptance of privacy engineering methods that encompass all the dimensions identified above. Rather, there is the impression that priority is given to security- and data minimization related measures, while most other principles are neglected. To counteract this, further incentive models and easy-to-integrate technical options need to be developed. In this paper, we have provided first suggestions; in turn, a more comprehensive set of options for implementing privacy by design needs to be extracted from existing DevOps implementations.

In the same vein, we need evaluation methods for each of the elements in the cloud native privacy engineering matrix. For the development of these, we can first borrow ideas from both legal and technical methodology. Then, we need to carry out a cross-disciplinary discourse on the exact design of said approaches. This process is considered future work needed to be coming up next. Having these evaluation methods set up, we then can also better evaluate the "level of coverage" within each matrix element (possibly indicated by a filling level instead of binary hatching).

Finally, technological possibilities continue to grow at a rapid pace. With increasing connectivity through powerful mobile networks, the number of internet-enabled devices that will process personal data is exploding. For computing approaches such as fog computing and (I)IoT (Industrial Internet of Things), appropriate strategies need to be developed and tested to effectively implement the above privacy dimensions. However, they can also be beneficial and helpful for said principles [50].

So far, this work has presented two key models that bring privacy engineering by design and by default closer to the realities of information systems engineering. At the same time, it is intended to improve these designs in future iterations – just as suggested by the infinite loop presented above.

Acknowledgements. The work behind this paper was partially conducted within the project DaSKITA (Data sovereignty through AI-based transparency and access), supported under grant no. 28V2307A19 by funds of the Federal Ministry of Justice and Consumer Protection (BMJV) based on a decision of the Parliament of the Federal Republic of Germany via the Federal Office for Agriculture and Food (BLE) under the innovation support program.

References

1. Agarwal, A., Agarwal, A.: The security risks associated with cloud computing. Int. J. Comput. Appl. Eng. Sci. **1**, 257–259 (2011)
2. Al-Slais, Y.: Privacy engineering methodologies: a survey. In: 2020 International Conference on Innovation and Intelligence for Informatics, Computing and Technologies (3ICT), pp. 1–6 (2020). https://doi.org/10.1109/3ICT51146.2020.9311949
3. Artac, M., Borovssak, T., Di Nitto, E., Guerriero, M., Tamburri, D.A.: DevOps: introducing infrastructure-as-code. In: 2017 IEEE/ACM 39th International Conference on Software Engineering Companion (ICSE-C), pp. 497–498. IEEE (2017)
4. Balalaie, A., Heydarnoori, A., Jamshidi, P.: Microservices architecture enables DevOps: migration to a cloud-native architecture. IEEE Softw. **33**(3), 42–52 (2016)
5. Bass, L., Weber, I., Zhu, L.: DevOps: A Software Architect's Perspective. Addison-Wesley, Boston (2015)
6. Bednar, K., Spiekermann, S., Langheinrich, M.: Engineering privacy by design: are engineers ready to live up to the challenge? Inf. Soc. **35**(3), 122–142 (2019). https://doi.org/10.1080/01972243.2019.1583296
7. Cavoukian, A.: Understanding how to implement privacy by design, one step at a time. IEEE Consum. Electron. Mag. **9**(2), 78–82 (2020). https://doi.org/10.1109/MCE.2019.2953739
8. Cavoukian, A., et al.: Privacy by design: the 7 foundational principles. Inf. Priv. Comm. Ontario, Canada **5**, 12 (2009)
9. Clifford, D., Ausloos, J.: Data protection and the role of fairness. Yearbook Eur. Law **37**, 130–187 (2018). https://doi.org/10.1093/yel/yey004
10. Cloud Native Computing Foundation (CNCF): Cloud Native Definition v1.0 (2018). https://github.com/cncf/toc/blob/main/DEFINITION.md
11. California Civil Code: California consumer privacy act (CCPA) (2018)
12. Crabtree, A.: Building accountability into the Internet of Things: the IoT databox model. J. Reliable Intell. Environ. **4**(1), 39–55 (2018)
13. Cranor, L.F.: Web Privacy with P3P. O'Reilly Media Inc., Sebastopol (2002)
14. Deng, M., Wuyts, K., Scandariato, R., Preneel, B., Joosen, W.: A privacy threat analysis framework: supporting the elicitation and fulfillment of privacy requirements. Requirements Eng. **16**(1), 3–32 (2011)
15. Diker Vanberg, A., Ünver, M.B.: The right to data portability in the GDPR and EU competition law: odd couple or dynamic duo? Eur. J. Law Technol. **8**(1) (2017)
16. Dragoni, N., et al.: Microservices: yesterday, today, and tomorrow. In: Present and Ulterior Software Engineering, pp. 195–216. Springer, Cham (2017). https://doi.org/10.1007/978-3-319-67425-4_12
17. Dyck, A., Penners, R., Lichter, H.: Towards definitions for release engineering and DevOps. In: 2015 IEEE/ACM 3rd International Workshop on Release Engineering, p. 3 (2015). https://doi.org/10.1109/RELENG.2015.10

18. Eberhardt, J., Tai, S.: ZoKrates - Scalable privacy-preserving off-chain computations. In: IEEE International Conference on Blockchain, pp. 1084–1091. IEEE (2018)
19. Erich, F., Amrit, C., Daneva, M.: A qualitative study of DevOps usage in practice. J. Softw.: Evol. Process **29**(6), e1885 (2017)
20. European Parliament and Council of the European Union: Regulation (EU) 2016/679 of 27 April 2016. General Data Protection Regulation (2018)
21. Federal Trade Commission: Privacy online: Fair information practices in the electronic marketplace (2000). https://www.ftc.gov/reports/privacy-online-fair-information-practices-electronic-marketplace-federal-trade-commission
22. Felici, M., Koulouris, T., Pearson, S.: Accountability for data governance in cloud ecosystems. In: 2013 IEEE 5th International Conference on Cloud Computing Technology and Science, vol. 2, pp. 327–332. IEEE (2013)
23. Finck, M., Biega, A.J.: Reviving purpose limitation and data minimisation in data-driven systems. Technol. Regul. **2021**, 44–61 (2021). https://techreg.org/index.php/techreg/article/view/63
24. Gannon, D., Barga, R., Sundaresan, N.: Cloud-native applications. IEEE Cloud Comput. **4**(5), 16–21 (2017)
25. Gill, S.S., et al.: Transformative effects of IoT, blockchain and artificial intelligence on cloud computing: evolution, vision, trends and open challenges. Internet of Things **8**, 100118 (2019)
26. Goldberg, I., Wagner, D., Brewer, E.: Privacy-enhancing technologies for the internet. In: Proceedings IEEE COMPCON 97. Digest of Papers, pp. 103–109. IEEE (1997)
27. Grünewald, E., Pallas, F.: TILT: a GDPR-aligned transparency information language and toolkit for practical privacy engineering. In: Proceedings of the 2021 Conference on Fairness, Accountability, and Transparency. ACM, New York (2021). https://doi.org/10.1145/3442188.3445925
28. Grünewald, E., Wille, P., Pallas, F., Borges, M.C., Ulbricht, M.R.: TIRA: an OpenAPI extension and toolbox for GDPR transparency in RESTful architectures. In: 2021 International Workshop on Privacy Engineering (IWPE). IEEE Computer Society (2021)
29. Gürses, S., Del Alamo, J.M.: Privacy engineering: shaping an emerging field of research and practice. IEEE Secur. Priv. **14**(2), 40–46 (2016)
30. Gürses, S., Troncoso, C., Diaz, C.: Engineering privacy by design. Comput. Priv. Data Protect. **14**(3), 25 (2011)
31. Gürses, S., van Hoboken, J.: Privacy after the Agile Turn. In: Cambridge Law Handbooks, pp. 579–601. Cambridge University Press (2018). https://doi.org/10.1017/9781316831960.032
32. Hansen, M.: Data protection by design and by default à la European general data protection regulation. In: Lehmann, A., Whitehouse, D., Fischer-Hübner, S., Fritsch, L., Raab, C. (eds.) Privacy and Identity 2016. IAICT, vol. 498, pp. 27–38. Springer, Cham (2016). https://doi.org/10.1007/978-3-319-55783-0_3
33. Hansen, M., Berlich, P., Camenisch, J., Clauß, S., Pfitzmann, A., Waidner, M.: Privacy-enhancing identity management. Inf. Secur. Tech. Rep. **9**(1), 35–44 (2004)
34. Heurix, J., Zimmermann, P., Neubauer, T., Fenz, S.: A taxonomy for privacy enhancing technologies. Comput. Secur. **53**, 1–17 (2015). https://doi.org/10.1016/j.cose.2015.05.002
35. Hoepman, J.-H.: Privacy design strategies. In: Cuppens-Boulahia, N., Cuppens, F., Jajodia, S., Abou El Kalam, A., Sans, T. (eds.) SEC 2014. IAICT, vol. 428, pp.

446–459. Springer, Heidelberg (2014). https://doi.org/10.1007/978-3-642-55415-5_38

36. Hsu, T.H.C.: Hands-On Security in DevOps: Ensure Continuous Security, Deployment, and Delivery with DevSecOps. Packt Publishing Ltd. (2018)

37. Kostova, B., Gürses, S., Troncoso, C.: Privacy engineering meets software engineering. on the challenges of engineering privacy by design. arXiv preprint arXiv:2007.08613 (2020)

38. Kratzke, N., Quint, P.C.: Understanding cloud-native applications after 10 years of cloud computing-a systematic mapping study. J. Syst. Softw. **126**, 1–16 (2017)

39. Kuner, C., Bygrave, L.A., Docksey, C.: Background and evolution of the EU general data protection regulation (GDPR). In: The EU General Data Protection Regulation (GDPR). Oxford University Press (2020)

40. Lee, J., Clifton, C.: How much is enough? Choosing ε for differential privacy. In: Lai, X., Zhou, J., Li, H. (eds.) ISC 2011. LNCS, vol. 7001, pp. 325–340. Springer, Heidelberg (2011). https://doi.org/10.1007/978-3-642-24861-0_22

41. Lenk, A., Klems, M., Nimis, J., Tai, S., Sandholm, T.: What's inside the cloud? An architectural map of the cloud landscape. In: 2009 ICSE Workshop on Software Engineering Challenges of Cloud Computing, pp. 23–31. IEEE (2009)

42. Li, J., Beba, S., Karlsen, M.M.: Evaluation of open-source IDE plugins for detecting security vulnerabilities. In: Proceedings of the Evaluation and Assessment on Software Engineering, pp. 200–209 (2019)

43. Machanavajjhala, A., Kifer, D., Gehrke, J., Venkitasubramaniam, M.: l-diversity: privacy beyond k-anonymity. ACM Trans. Knowl. Discov. Data (TKDD) **1**(1), 3 (2007)

44. Marston, S., Li, Z., Bandyopadhyay, S., Zhang, J., Ghalsasi, A.: Cloud computing-the business perspective. Decis. Support Syst. **51**(1), 176–189 (2011)

45. Mell, P., Grance, T., et al.: The NIST definition of cloud computing (2011)

46. Mulligan, D.K., Koopman, C., Doty, N.: Privacy is an essentially contested concept: a multi-dimensional analytic for mapping privacy. Phil. Trans. R. Soc. A. **374**(2083) (2016). https://doi.org/10.1098/rsta.2016.0118

47. Nieuwenhuis, L.J., Ehrenhard, M.L., Prause, L.: The shift to cloud computing: the impact of disruptive technology on the enterprise software business ecosystem. Technol. Forecast. Soc. Chang. **129**, 308–313 (2018)

48. OECD: OECD Guidelines on the Protection of Privacy and Transborder Flows of Personal Data (1980)

49. Pallas, F., Legler, J., Amslgruber, N., Grünewald, E.: RedCASTLE: practically applicable k_s-anonymity for IoT streaming data at the edge in Node-RED. In: Proceedings of the 8th International Workshop on Middleware and Applications for the Internet of Things. Association for Computing Machinery, New York (2021). https://doi.org/10.1145/3493369.3493601

50. Pallas, F., Raschke, P., Bermbach, D.: Fog computing as privacy enabler. IEEE Internet Comput. **24**(4), 15–21 (2020). https://doi.org/10.1109/MIC.2020.2979161

51. Pallas, F., et al.: Towards application-layer purpose-based access control. In: Proceedings of the 35th Annual ACM Symposium on Applied Computing, pp. 1288–1296 (2020)

52. Pfitzmann, A., Borcea-Pfitzmann, K., Camenisch, J.: Primelife. In: Camenisch, J., Fischer-Hübner, S., Rannenberg, K. (eds.) Privacy and Identity Management for Life, pp. 5–26. Springer, Heidelberg (2011). https://doi.org/10.1007/978-3-642-20317-6_1

53. Picoreti, R., do Carmo, A.P., de Queiroz, F.M., Garcia, A.S., Vassallo, R.F., Simeonidou, D.: Multilevel observability in cloud orchestration. In: 2018 IEEE 16th International Conference on Dependable, Autonomic and Secure Computing, 16th International Conference on Pervasive Intelligence and Computing, 4th International Conference on Big Data Intelligence and Computing and Cyber Science and Technology Congress (DASC/PiCom/DataCom/CyberSciTech), pp. 776–784. IEEE (2018)

54. Rajkumar, M., Pole, A.K., Adige, V.S., Mahanta, P.: DevOps culture and its impact on cloud delivery and software development. In: 2016 International Conference on Advances in Computing, Communication, & Automation (ICACCA) (Spring), pp. 1–6. IEEE (2016)

55. Rauhofer, J.: "Privacy is dead, get over it!" information privacy and the dream of a risk-free society. Inf. Commun. Technol. Law **17**(3), 185–197 (2008). https://doi.org/10.1080/13600830802472990

56. Schwaber, K.: Agile Project Management with Scrum. Microsoft Press, Redmond (2004)

57. Sion, L., Landuyt, D.V., Joosen, W.: The never-ending story: on the need for continuous privacy impact assessment. In: 2020 IEEE European Symposium on Security and Privacy Workshops (EuroS PW), pp. 314–317. IEEE (2020). https://doi.org/10.1109/EuroSPW51379.2020.00049

58. Sion, L., Van Landuyt, D., Yskout, K., Verreydt, S., Joosen, W.: Automated threat analysis and management in a continuous integration pipeline. In: 2021 IEEE Secure Development (SecDev) (2021)

59. Spiekermann, S.: The challenges of privacy by design. Commun. ACM **55**(7), 38–40 (2012)

60. Spiekermann, S., Cranor, L.F.: Engineering privacy. IEEE Trans. Softw. Eng. **35**(1), 67–82 (2009). https://doi.org/10.1109/TSE.2008.88

61. Spiekermann, S., Korunovska, J., Langheinrich, M.: Inside the organization: why privacy and security engineering is a challenge for engineers. Proc. IEEE **107**(3), 600–615 (2019). https://doi.org/10.1109/JPROC.2018.2866769

62. Srivastava, P., Khan, R.: A review paper on cloud computing. Int. J. Adv. Res. Comput. Sci. Softw. Eng. **8**(6), 17–20 (2018)

63. Stahl, D., Martensson, T., Bosch, J.: Continuous practices and DevOps: beyond the buzz, what does it all mean? In: 2017 43rd Euromicro Conference on Software Engineering and Advanced Applications (SEAA), pp. 440–448. IEEE (2017)

64. Sweeney, L.: k-anonymity: a model for protecting privacy. Int. J. Uncertain. Fuzziness Knowl.-Based Syst. **10**(05), 557–570 (2002)

65. Tai, S.: Continuous, trustless, and fair: changing priorities in services computing. In: Lazovik, A., Schulte, S. (eds.) ESOCC 2016. CCIS, vol. 707, pp. 205–210. Springer, Cham (2018). https://doi.org/10.1007/978-3-319-72125-5_16

66. United Nations General Assembly: Universal Declaration of Human Rights (UDHR) (1948)

67. Voigt, P., von dem Bussche, A.: Enforcement and fines under the GDPR. In: The EU General Data Protection Regulation (GDPR), pp. 201–217. Springer, Cham (2017). https://doi.org/10.1007/978-3-319-57959-7_7

68. Voigt, P., Von dem Bussche, A.: The EU General Data Protection Regulation (GDPR). A Practical Guide, 1st edn. Springer, Heidelberg (2017). 10, 3152676

69. Warren, S.D., Brandeis, L.D.: The right to privacy. Harv. Law Rev. **4**(5), 193–220 (1890). https://doi.org/10.2307/1321160

70. Whitman, J.Q.: The two western cultures of privacy: dignity versus liberty. Yale LJ **113**, 1151 (2003)

71. Yarlagadda, R.T.: DevOps and its practices. Int. J. Creat. Res. Thoughts (IJCRT), ISSN, pp. 2320–2882 (2021)
72. Zhou, M., Zhang, R., Xie, W., Qian, W., Zhou, A.: Security and privacy in cloud computing: a survey. In: 2010 Sixth International Conference on Semantics, Knowledge and Grids, pp. 105–112 (2010). https://doi.org/10.1109/SKG.2010.19
73. Zimmermann, C.: Automation potentials in privacy engineering. In: Roßnagel, H., Schunck, C.H., Mödersheim, S., Hühnlein, D. (eds.) Open Identity Summit 2020, pp. 121–132. Gesellschaft für Informatik e.V., Bonn (2020). https://doi.org/10.18420/ois2020_10
74. Zuboff, S.: The Age of Surveillance Capitalism: The Fight for a Human Future at the New Frontier of Power. Profile Books, London (2019)

Gamification in mHealth - Opportunities and Privacy Risks

Ramona Schmidt$^{(\boxtimes)}$ and Ina Schiering

Institute for Information Engineering, Ostfalia University of Applied Sciences,
Wolfenbüttel, Germany
{ramo.schmidt,i.schiering}@ostfalia.de

Abstract. The use of mobile devices and wearables in healthcare is
an important trend. To increase the motivation for regular use of such
mHealth applications gamification elements have a huge potential. On
the other hand for the integration of gamification concepts in mHealth
applications personal health related data and usage data needs to be processed. Based on a categorization of gamification elements and examples
for mHealth applications an overview about the aim of the use of gamification is given. It is analysed whether the processing of personal data is
needed and if privacy is considered in the examples for the realization of
gamification elements. Based on this analysis approaches for addressing
privacy risks in gamification in mHealth are proposed.

Keywords: mHealth · Gamification · Privacy · Motivation

1 Introduction

The broad availability of mobile devices and wearables has fostered such trends
as mHealth, the increasing use of mobile devices in the health context [12]. At
first many applications addressed fitness and well-being. Due to the increasing
possibilities concerning sensors and data processing assistive technologies are
more commonly used. This allows integrating health monitoring and rehabilitation training into everyday life. But despite the potential benefits people often
stop using mHealth applications after a few times [31].

It is important to find approaches to motivate regular usage of mHealth applications and long-term commitment, to achieve the underlying health objectives
[16]. Mechanics used in games motivate users to change their health behaviors
and to stay engaged with the application [26]. Especially younger people are
used to motivational concepts used in computer games. The derived concept
of gamification tries to shape the activity itself to be motivating [25] and has a
huge potential [18]. But to integrate such elements as e.g. badges, daily goals and
leaderboards in mHealth applications personal data and usage data has to be
processed. Since security and privacy of mHealth applications are crucial [22,23],
privacy risks need to be considered also for gamification elements.

M. Friedewald et al. (Eds.): Privacy and Identity 2021, IFIP AICT 644, pp. 142–159, 2022.
https://doi.org/10.1007/978-3-030-99100-5_11

To this end typical examples are selected based on a categorization of archetypes of applications [27], motivational aim of these elements is summarized and it is explored to which extent privacy aspects are already considered. Applications focused on specific illnesses are still in the process of development. To consider a broad range of users, who will sooner or later also be part of the target group of medical programs, fitness and well-being applications are as well evaluated as mHealth applications for rehabilitation and other health-related therapies. Further the usages of the gamification elements are investigated from a privacy perspective. Approaches for a privacy-preserving realisation are proposed.

2 Gamification

Gamification is defined by Deterding as the use of design elements characteristic for games in non-game contexts [6]. A gamification concept is typically based on a variety of elements, as e.g. *points*, *leaderboards* and *daily goals*, that foster the motivation of users. The variety of game elements employed in gamification is broad. Different sources discuss and differentiate varying elements. Garett and Young identified 14 different elements [8] whereas Sardi et al. focus on only four elements and sum up "others" [26] for additional elements. Based on an investigation of literature reviews concerning gamification elements, the following ten elements are stated as the most common and most used elements which are directly visible to users [4,7,14,25,26,28]: *avatars, badges, daily goals, leaderboards, level, performance graphs, points, progress bars, storytelling* and *teams* (see Table 1 for an overview).

Typically, a combination of elements is used in a specific context. An *avatar* of a user or a *team* can be for example integrated in a narrative context and combined with *storytelling* [25]. As an example an application in which users have to run regularly could draw a narrative context by embedding this activity in a story about a zombie apocalypse. Within the storytelling multiple users could form a group of survivors doing the health-related activities together as a team.

Avatars and *storytelling* can furthermore be linked with rewards [26,28] or with *badges, level* or *daily goals* while unlocking new content. Expending the previous example in the context of running and the story of surviving, levels could be represented as different forms of survivors e.g. from "fearful newbie" to "survival artist". *Leaderboards, level, progress bars* and *performance graphs* are representations of a users performance based on defined metrics. Therefore these elements are typically combined with *points* as a basis to make metrics transparent. *Performance graphs* can also render the fulfillment's of *daily goals* over time transparent for users.

To describe the motivational aim of gamification elements, the psychological background needs to be briefly summarized. The effect of gamification is according to the self-determination theory based on basic psychological and intrinsic needs for *competence, autonomy* and *social relatedness* [16,25]. *Competence* is

Table 1. Gamification elements

		Aim		
		Autonomy	Relatedness	Competence
Elements with social focus				
Avatar	*Avatars* are visual representations (e.g. of the user). Users can design them individually or chose them out of a given collection. The visual options are manifold [25]. They can also be used as personifications of aspects of the application [28]	x		
	Personalizing, self-identification [25]			
Storytelling	The element of *storytelling* embeds activities of an application in a narrative context which can be fictive or trying to convert a complex matter in a real context [25]	x	x	
	Cooperation [25]			
Teams	A *team context* motivates multiple users to work in a cooperative way on a shared goal [25]. Enabling the option to compare multiple teams or the users performance in the team itself adds additional competitive aspects [33]		x	
	Relevance, cooperation, competition [4, 25]			
Elements for specific goals				
Daily goals	*Daily goals* are primary goals or multiple daily challenges which can change on a daily basis [7] or can simply be renewed after a specific period of time. It is additionally possible to adapt the corresponding goals according to the performance of the users [33]			x
	Randomness, curiosity [4]			
Badges	*Badges* are optional goals and rewards for achieving these goals consisting of the visual badge itself, the reward and the condition for fulfillment [13]		x	x
	Cumulative feedback [25], self-confidence, guidance [13]			
Elements for continuous monitoring				
Points	*Points* are a basic game element. Specified defined activities within the gamified environment can give the user points [26]. They can be used as a simple representation of progress or as redeemable currency or reputation points [25]			x
	Constant feedback [25], progress [4]			
Level	*Levels* are a representation of progress by depending on specific achievements (e.g. a number of points). It can be further a representation of varying difficulties [28]			x
	Progress, increasing difficulty [4]			
Progress bar	A *progress bar* displays progress for example within a level or a badge condition. It illustrates feedback over already accomplished progress and the amount of effort still to be performed to achieve the level or badge [14, 26]			x
	Progress over time [26], overview [14]			
Performance graph	*Performance graphs* represent the users performance described via metrics over time [25]			x
	Continuing feedback [25]			
Complementary element				
Leader board	*Leaderboards* foster competition between participants. They represent a ranking of participants according to their performance [26]		x	x
	Cumulative feedback, competition [25, 26]			

experienced in events with positive feedback that imply effectiveness. *Autonomy* is achieved by providing choice and acknowledging experience. *Relatedness* is combined with social acceptance and recognition. The satisfaction of these needs fosters intrinsically motivated behaviour and can be integrated in extrinsic motivations [5]. Providing feedback on a users performance is a way to evoke the feeling of competence [25]. Additionally other psychological effects like curiosity [4], self-identification [25] and self-confidence [24] can lead to the interaction with gamification elements.

Furthermore the elements can be sub-classified according to the context they are typically used in. Elements which can be seen in a *social context* drawing a narrative context and representing the users themselves as well as their role in the narrative or application are avatars, storytelling and teams. These elements create representations and frames within the application. Through different psychological effects, e.g. personalizing and cooperation, they satisfy the needs for autonomy and social relatedness. Daily goals and badges can be described as *specific goals* with clear conditions and the possibility of fulfilling. Whereas points, level, progress bars and performance graphs have a *continuous* background. They mostly provide different forms of feedback and satisfy with that the need for competence. Leaderboards are a combination of continuous goals in a social environment and for that are *complementary* to the other elements.

3   Related Work

The use of gamification in mHealth is already investigated in several contexts. For an overview of gamification research in general and an investigation of effectiveness see Koivisto and Hamari [16]. An example is *The Heart Game* [7], a prototype with daily challenges and additional gamification elements to motivate users like badges, leaderboard, levels and a point system. Other Examples are the prototypical applications *Sana* [17], *Fitrust* [29], *bant* [3], *More Stamina* [9] and *Regain* [1].

Cheng et al. [4] investigated applications of gamification for mental health and well-being. They considered which elements are most commonly applied, which domains are most commonly targeted and what reasons are given for using gamification in these applications. An overview of gamification elements employed in an healthcare context is presented by Garett and Young [8]. Especially employed gamification strategies in e-Health as well as the benefits and the most encountered challenges are analyzed by Sardi et al. [26]. There the potential of gamification for health application is broadly investigated.

Disregarding privacy and effectiveness Schmidt-Kraepelin et al. [27] investigated different archetypes of gamification approaches and their relationship to the targeted health behavior. Furthermore independent of the gamification context Pires et al. [24] constructed a classification of mobile health applications by their functionality.

Mavroeidi et al. [20,21] investigated potential conflicts of specific elements with privacy requirements like anonymity, pseudonymity, unlinkability, undetectability and unobservability and categorized different game elements in harmful and non-harmful elements but without considering the context of the application. The categorization is amongst others based on the differentiation whether users information or actions are recorded and constrained by time.

Although gamification can introduce additional privacy risks by acquiring and recording a huge amount of personal data [11], in the description of gamified applications privacy issues are often not discussed. Several examples which are investigates as *The Heart Game* [7], *Sana* [17] and *Fitrust* [29]. Sardi et al. [26] mention the importance of privacy and security in general in the context of the protection of personal health data, but do not provide a deeper analysis.

Bilbey and Sandikkaya [2] studied the effects of gamification on privacy in a gamified context. They concluded that users of gamified environments are less careful protecting their private information especially when participants are already lured into the gamified environment and enforced to disclose personal information to continue. Therefore the investigation of privacy in gamification applications is an interesting field for further investigation in the conflict between fostering the important aspect of motivation of users to enhance usage times on one hand and the consideration of privacy risks on the other hand.

4 Methodology

Mavroeidi et al. [20,21] already investigated privacy in gamification on a general basis. But in an health context especially in the area of mental health and cognitive deficiencies already the use of an app contains the risk of stigmatization. For example a person using a mobile device at work is often considered a distracted worker, although the used application actually might help the person to stay focused.

To provide a broad overview of gamification in mHealth the archetypes of Schmidt-Kraepelin et al. [27] are used and examples for mHealth apps for the considered types are provided. Using these archetypes ensures that the examples are selected from different fields of mHealth applications which pursue different objectives and use the concept of gamification in various forms. For these examples the employed gamification elements and their motivational aim is summarized and it is investigated whether in the context of the application itself and the additional gamification elements privacy is directly mentioned. In addition it is investigated whether the data needed for gamification elements is justified by the intended effect from the point of view of the users and which opportunities exist to reduce privacy risks.

5 Analysis

5.1 Selection of Examples

Based on the archetypes of Schmidt-Kraepelin et al. [27] examples of mHealth applications targeting patients were selected which employ gamification. *Archetype 7 Positive and Negative Reinforcement Without Rewards* and

Archetype 8 Progressive Gamification for Health Professionals were both disregarded since they solely target health professionals. In the following the examples and their classification according to the archetypes are described. For an overview see Table 2.

Table 2. Selection of examples of mHealth applications based on the archetypes of Schmidt-Kraepelin et al. [27]

Archetype	Application	Goal of application
1: Competition and Collaboration	Fitrust	Help to lose, maintain or gain weight
1: Competition and Collaboration	Heart game	Assist heart patients in their telerehabilitation
2: Pursuing Self-Set Goals Without Rewards	Zwift	Indoor athletic performance
3: Episodical Compliance Tracking	Sana	Imitate physiotherapy sessions for post-operative acl reconstruction patients
3: Episodical Compliance Tracking	Regain	Help stroke patients in rehabilitation at home
4: Inherent Gamification for External Goals	Let's farm	Help stroke patients in rehabilitation
5: Internal Rewards for Self-Set Goals	More stamina	Help persons with multiple sclerosis managing their energy
6: Continuous Assistance Through Positive Reinforcement	Bant	Management of type 1 diabetes in adolescents

Fitrust is an application integrating Fitbit's and Nutritionix web API to gain and analyse information like users steps and heart rate time series as well as record food and exercise calorie information to help the users to lose, maintain or gain weight [29]. This can be assigned to *Archetype 1 Competition and Collaboration* which contains competitive and collaborative gamification elements helping the users reaching externally and self-set goals while the gamification approach is independent of the underlying health activity. To the same archetype another application *The Heart Game* assisting heart patients in their telerehabilitation process can be allocated. It uses several gamification elements presenting each day exercises as daily goals for a team of two, a patient and a companion, while offering the use of a point system, badges, a leaderboard, a progress bar, level and performance graphs [7].

Archetype 2 Pursuing Self-Set Goals Without Rewards exclusively draws on goals that are set by the users themselves and does not offer any type of explicit rewards for specific health-related activities like badges. An example that can also be seen as a serious game but is still a good example to represent this archetype is *Zwift*. This application enables virtual sports while recording real-world athletic performances [32].

The *Sana* system and the *Regain* App are both developed for increasing engagement and improving rehabilitation programs. *Sana* imitates real-life physiotherapy sessions for post-operative anterior cruciate ligament reconstruction patients simplifying the exercises to the goal of reaching a green circle [17]. *Regain* helps stroke patients in rehabilitation at home by providing exercises with animated self-avatars in a familiar environment like a garden or living room [1]. Both systems belong to *Archetype 3 Episodical Compliance Tracking* targeting amongst other therapy adherence where the narrative is always episodical.

Another application concerning stroke patients is *Let's Farm* transferring and embedding recovery exercises as various farming activities [19]. This is an implementation of *Archetype 4 Inherent Gamification for External Goals* where the health-related activity is partially or fully embedded in the gamification approach and therefore it is impossible to execute this without interacting with the gamification elements.

Archetype 5 Internal Rewards for Self-Set Goals describes the use of gamification evoking users' behavior and attitude to change by experiencing positive and negative reinforcements for decisions concerning self-set goals. For that solely internal rewards like points and badges are used without any form of competition. *More Stamina* tries to help persons with multiple sclerosis to manage their energy by transferring it to a point system. The users spend these points on self-set activities and achieve badges for example for continuous usage and correct energy assessments [9].

An application consistent with *Archetype 6 Continuous Assistance Through Positive Reinforcement* is the *bant* app for the management of type 1 diabetes in adolescents [3]. This archetype targets patients requiring continuous assistance and therapy adherence not containing any competitive elements or negative reinforcements and offering no rewards like badges.

5.2   Investigation of the Examples

As a first step of the analysis it was investigated whether privacy was already addressed in the description of the examples. Table 3 shows the results. Five of the examples, *Fitrust*, *Heart Game*, *Zwift*, *Sana* and *Let's farm*, did not discussed privacy at all. For *Regain* a requirement for security was defined, but no privacy issues were addressed. *More Stamina* and *Bant* addressed some privacy considerations. However, while these considerations refer to privacy concerning the functionality of the application, the gamification elements were not considered.

Investigating possible privacy risks, all examples were analysed which data is needed or shown by the ten different elements presented in Sect. 2. The results for elements with social focus are summarised in Table 4a, for elements for continuous monitoring in Table 4b and for elements for specific goals as well as the complementary element in Table 4c.

Table 3. How privacy was addressed in the examples

Fitrust [29]	Not addressed
Heart game [7]	Not addressed
Zwift [32]	Not addressed
Sana [17]	Not addressed
Regain [1]	Only addresses security: "The design artifact has to enable healthcare professionals to have access to the stroke survivors' data remotely and in a secure way in order to assess the progress, and make adjustment to the rehabilitation program" [1]
Let's farm [19]	Not addressed
More stamina [9]	Addresses privacy concerning the functionality: "Usage statistics are gathered locally for each added activity to keep track and collect assessments; the user can choose to share these statistics to a secure server for analysis" [9] and "users will have full control as to which information to disclose and with whom, whether it is personal, clinical, or treatment-related. Additionally, they can opt in to send de-identified information for research purposes" [9]
Bant [3]	Addresses privacy concerning the functionality: Communication between peers happen "in a secure community area of the app" [3] and that "this was achieved through a private microblogging platform similar to the social network Twitter. It used the open-source alternative StatusNet (available at http://status.net/) running on a secure server at our center at Toronto General Hospital." [3] Additionally they provided the possibility of sharing "test results and diabetes-related information with parents (as well as peers and clinic staff) via secure online tools and communities for sharing results" and for that "elected to integrate the mobile app with a secure online personal health record called TELUS health space" [3]

The investigated examples needed for elements with social focus primarily to record customization choices. Only the progression of the storyline in *Let's Farm* or the individual engagement based on the users improvement in *Sana* needed additionally a small amount on user-specific performance data.

In contrast for gamification elements for continuous monitoring the choices of the users have hardly influence on the recorded data. Points were given for activities needed to use the application as intended. For example *bant* is an application for management of type 1 diabetes. To manage diabetes it is important to do blood glucose testing. Points are given and recorded for each test the users perform and for that only depend on the choice to use the application itself. In every example the points were recorded accumulated.

Table 4. Analysis which data is needed or shown

(a) Data for gamification elements with social focus

	avatar	story	team
Heart Game [7]	▬	▬	names and points per teammate ●
Regain [1]	adjustable gender and colors ●	selectable environment (garden/living room) ●	▬
Let's Farm [19]	user-picture, customizable story-avatar ●	monitoring if all available exercises were executed and storage progress approval by therapist ●	user-picture for each teammate participating in specific exercise ●
Sana [17]	▬	e.g. average pain score ●	▬
Fitrust [29]	customizable abstract picture, name and title ●	○	▬

(b) Data for gamification elements for continuous monitoring

	points	level	progress bar	performance graph
bant [3]	e.g. amount of tests per day and per different context ●	per 200 points ◐	▬	▬
More Stamina [9]	available energy to be spend user-controlled ●	▬	additional representation of energy (see points)	▬
Heart Game [7]	gained for each task in individually amount and accumulated weekly ●	for specific amount or progress until a specific amount of points ◐	depend on specific amount of points on weekly basis ◐	points per day, finished challenges and corresponding points ●
Let's Farm [19]	Accumulation of coins gained per task in individual amount ●	completion of all current tasks and approval by therapist ●	amount of executions per exercise ●	▬
Sana [17]	▬	▬	progress concerning therapy goal (specific height and last achieved/average height) ●	Accuracy and range per day ●
Fitrust [29]	Accumulated and earned per daily goal and exercise mode (different per exercise) ●	▬	progress within daily goal ◐	steps per day ●

(c) Data for gamification elements for specific goals and complementary elements

	daily goals	badges	leaderboard
Heart Game [7]	○	e.g. amount of completed challenges ●	team names and points per team ◐
Let's Farm [19]	▬	▬	user-picture and points ◐
Fitrust [29]	amount of steps and glasses of water drunk ●	e.g. rank in leaderboard or number of exercises executed ●	points, badges and avatar ◐

▬ element not used, ○ no data needed, ◐ no additional data needed, ● data needed

For the implementation of level two of three applications did not need any other data and could calculate the level based on the points. Similarly four of five applications used the progress bar only as additional display and reuse the data already recorded by other elements. All examples using a performance graph recorded the shown data per day.

The gamification elements for specific goals were mostly described exemplarily. Especially the badges could have needed far more data than shown. However the daily goals were significantly simpler than the badges. In *The Heart Game* they were solely used as daily suggestion and therefore did not need any personal data at all. Further in *Fitrust* only simple data like steps and glasses drunk were needed. The leaderboard as complementary element did not need specific data itself but rather combined other gamification elements and thus needed the data they record.

When multiple users are linked together as in case of teams and leaderboards a centralized component for data processing is needed. If the teammates share the usage data locally as for example in *The Heart Game*, since they both use the same device, this is not necessary. The actual connection of users within a leaderboard can be avoided by using virtual opponents which in addition can be adapted to the users performance. The other elements like points, level, progress, performance graphs, badges, daily goals, avatars and storytelling could be processed locally.

In summary the elements with social focus needed some customization choices but recorded only a small amount of performance data. Elements for continuous monitoring on the contrary did not need customization choices, instead constant performance data had to be collected. Points were always accumulated and the performance graphs displayed data per day. Level and progress bars were mostly solely used as additional displays. The elements for specific goals were only described exemplary. However the daily goals were simpler than badges. Finally the leaderboard does not record data itself but needs other elements (e.g. points) which record data. The privacy issues concerning the used gamification elements were not discussed in the investigated examples and should be evaluated further.

6   Addressing Privacy Risks of Gamification Elements

Since gamification is an important mean to foster motivation for continuous use of mHealth apps [18], it is not the main aim of the mHealth app but nevertheless supports the corresponding goals. Therefore, these additional elements should not include additional privacy risks. Hence the principle of data minimisation should be a central design criteria and since in some cases (e.g. mental health) already the use of an mHealth app may result in stigmatization of patients, anonymization or at least a strong pseudonymization of patient data and the privacy protection goal of unlinkability [15] are important. To realize these central goals beside data minimization, decentralization [30] as a guiding principle is important. Data for gamification elements should be processed only on the device of the user where possible. In the following it is analyzed how these principles could be applied in the context of the gamification elements employed in the context of the examples for mHealth applications.

Based on the classification of the gamification elements in Sect. 2 in the following the privacy risks are further investigated. *Regain*, *More Stamina* and *bant* used in each case only two gamification elements while in addition for *More Stamina* and *bant* the level and progress bar was only a further representation. The Heart Game and Fitrust are both applications of the archetype 1 (see Sect. 5.1). Because of this as leading examples the applications *Fitrust*, *Sana* and *Let's Farm* are used. None of these already addressed privacy risks (see Sect. 5.2). All three applications use elements with *social focus* and will be compared for the investigation. The elements with a focus on *continuous monitoring* will be further described by the examples *Let's Farm* for points and level as well as *Sana* for the progress bar and the performance graph. The elements for *specific goals* and the leaderboard as example for *complementary elements* are investigated based on the example *Fitrust*.

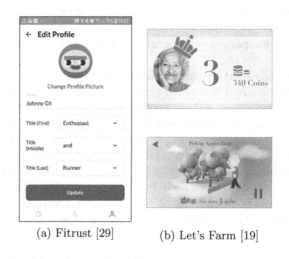

(a) Fitrust [29]   (b) Let's Farm [19]

Fig. 1. Avatars

6.1 Elements with Social Focus

Elements with *social focus* offer many opportunities for personalization. The more options are available, the more information about the user might be revealed. In *Let's Farm* the users can upload an individual user picture (see Fig. 1b). These pictures can reveal a lot about a person especially when interconnected with other users like in a leaderboard or in a team context. For example a user could upload a picture that shows the person itself in the living room. This reveals on the one hand the person behind this user. On the other hand the background shows how this person lives and for example possibly the wealth

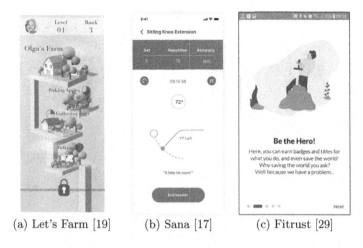

(a) Let's Farm [19]   (b) Sana [17]   (c) Fitrust [29]

Fig. 2. Storytelling

status or some clues about the location. In contrast in *Fitrust* users can choose from a given selection of abstract pictures. Additionally the users can choose and arrange different titles describing themselves and provide a freely choosable name (see Fig. 1a). Although the options of pictures and titles are limited, the same issue of revealing personal aspects might occur. Since this privacy issue is mostly based on users choices, it is advisable to use a privacy awareness panel. In such a panel the users can be warned about the consequences of specific shared data and which data are visible to others and to whom [10].

The more adapted a story is to a specific user the more information about the person is needed. *Fitrust* only provides a short story at the beginning independent of the users interests (see Fig. 2c) creating a frame the users can draw further in their minds while using the application. This implementation does not lead to privacy issues. However personalization can be desirable because a story is particularly inspiring and motivating if it is in line with the personal interests of the user [25]. For that *Sana* simulates a physiotherapist encouraging the user to create a familiar environment. Only expressing encouragement by cheering up users during an exercise with motivational messages like "A little bit more" (see Fig. 2b) does not need permanent storage of data, only the current progress within the exercise. To personalize this encouragement without recording data over a longer period, it is possible to solely store the performance of the last time. Saying that the user have done better than yesterday as an additional motivation factor. Furthermore *Sana* additionally encourages users outside the exercises by messages which for example address the decrease of users average pain score. For this feedback the recording of the pain score is needed. Personalized feedback like that is based on processing of personal data. Even though the adjustment of feedback appropriate to the level of the patient is crucial [26], it is important to investigate for each context which amount of personalization and data is needed for a meaningful feedback.

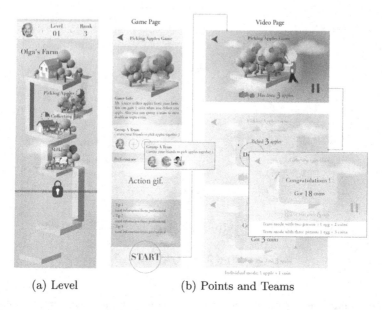

| (a) Level | (b) Points and Teams |

Fig. 3. Elements for continuous monitoring and teams in Let's Farm [19]

As noted before gamification elements should not include additional privacy risks. However to effectively simplify a complex matter within a story, it is often necessary to process additional data. As example in *Sana* the users have to train their knee. The application wraps this activity in the simple goal of reaching a green circle instead of only specifying a specific angle the knee shall reach (see Fig. 2b). This can be implemented in two ways. On the one hand the users can be provided with this goal but still have to monitor the position of their knee themselves. On the other hand, if the users should get specific feedback so that they do not have to monitor the angle themselves, it is necessary to measure the performance of the users leg. How much the user is embedded in the wrapping story and for that is motivated by simplification depends on the implementation. To this end it is important to discuss for each context what level of personalization and simplification is actually needed.

6.2   Elements for Continuous Monitoring

Gamification elements for *continuous monitoring* often need to record data for longer periods. Points based on a reward system like in *Let's Farm* (see Fig. 3b) and level persist, though the raw data needed to earn a level or a specific amount of points does not have to be stored permanently when aggregation is applied and data storage is limited. *Let's Farm* rewards the users after an exercise with coins per execution. After each exercise the earned coins can be aggregated and added to coins a user already earned so far such that only the sum of coins and the actual level needs to be stored.

(a) Progressbar   (b) Performance graph

Fig. 4. Elements for continuous monitoring in Sana [17]

However, the direct conversion from one execution of an activity to a specific amount of coins might lead to the issue of deriving additional information, like how many activities were executed. To avoid this issue differing amounts of points per specific activity can be chosen or the data can be perturbed by adding random points. Nevertheless these principles depend on the attacker model and which information is available to the attacker. Even if aggregation is always recommendable an attacker who can observe the changes could reveal which kind of activities a user did or reduce the possibilities if different amount of points per activity were chosen.

A progress bar is another typical element for visualizing progress. As mentioned in Sect. 5 most of the applications use the progress bar as additional visual element and use data already needed by other elements like for example points. As of that aggregation and storage limitation shall be applied in this case as well. Two data points are needed for each progress bar, the current status and the intended goal (see Fig. 4a). Recorded data can be aggregated to one current progress point. After reaching the goal, all information about the progress and the specific goal can be deleted and at most the information about the completed goal needs to be saved.

In a performance graph the data is time-related and aggregation is limited. These graphs provide information about the users performance compared to their preceding performance over a fixed period. The users focus on improvements by evaluating their own performance over time [25]. The recorded data can still be minimized by recording and saving only relations between data points and not

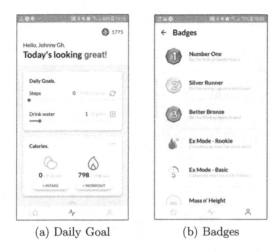

(a) Daily Goal   (b) Badges

Fig. 5. Elements for specific goals in Fitrust [29]

time-stamps. In *Sana* for example the users can check their accuracy over the days using the application without any precise dates (see Fig. 4b).

6.3   Elements for Specific Goals

A relatively comprehensive set of data is needed in case of defining specific goals. The more goals are provided and the more complex and diverse these goals are, the more corresponding specific progress data is needed and has to be captured. To render it more difficult to combine or correlate this data it might be useful to separate it by isolating the data in different databases. In *Fitrust* for example all data needed for badges concerning the exercise mode could be stored in a different database than data referring to the monitoring of intake (see Fig. 5).

A badge consists of its visualisation, the achievement and the condition for fulfillment (see as example Fig. 5b). The condition defines which data and what amount of data is needed. The achievement of a badge can be recorded via a single data point. After completing the condition of a specific badge, the related data is not necessary anymore and can be deleted. Only the information about the achieved badges has to be stored.

6.4   Leaderboard as Complementary Element

The main issue concerning a *complementary element* like a leaderboard, that shares information with other users, is the possibility of deducing additional information. In *Fitrust* the leaderboard shows to other users generally the picture and the name of the avatar and the earned points of a user. By clicking on a specific user the chosen titles as well as all earned badges of this user are revealed. In Fig. 6 for an explanatory example, the leading place in the leaderboard is

Fig. 6. Complementary element (Leaderboard) in Fitrust [29]

actually a user with an avatar name "Johnny Gh". Furthermore this user has earned all badges regarding the leaderboard as well as two badges for using the exercise mode. As title the user has chosen "Enthusiast and Runner". With this information it can be assumed that this user is male and actively involved in sports, mainly in running activities. He is not monitoring his intake since he has not got any badges regarding the option of recording intake (see Fig. 5, 6). Since the badges suggest that he is using the application only for doing workout but still got a lot of points, this user is doing a lot of workout and is probably using *Fitrust* for a longer period than most of the others.

Because of this issue of deduced information, it is important to inform users about potential risks and to be careful with the decision to connect multiple users and elements. An important factor is that the more elements are visible to other users the more information about a specific user can be deduced. Furthermore it should be possible to hide personal data by for example restricting the access to this information.

7 Conclusion

The investigation of privacy risks of gamification elements in mHealth applications is often not considered. Especially in an healthcare context motivational aspects are important but should be integrated in a privacy aware manner. Privacy risks should be taken into account for developing a gamification strategy in the context of a privacy by design process. Gamification elements could be clustered according to their focus. As central goals data minimization, unlinkability and decentralization should be considered as central principles.

References

1. Aljaroodi, H.M., Adam, M.T.P., Chiong, R., Cornforth, D.J., Minichiello, M.: Empathic avatars in stroke rehabilitation: a co-designed mHealth artifact for stroke survivors. In: Maedche, A., vom Brocke, J., Hevner, A. (eds.) DESRIST 2017. LNCS, vol. 10243, pp. 73–89. Springer, Cham (2017). https://doi.org/10.1007/978-3-319-59144-5_5

2. Bilbey, T., Sandikkaya, M.T.: Effects of gamification to private data collection. J. Comput. Des. **1**(3), 131–152 (2020)

3. Cafazzo, J.A., Casselman, M., Hamming, N., Katzman, D.K., Palmert, M.R.: Design of an mHealth app for the self-management of adolescent type 1 diabetes: a pilot study. J. Med. Internet Res. **14**(3), e70 (2012)

4. Cheng, V.W.S., Davenport, T., Johnson, D., Vella, K., Hickie, I.B.: Gamification in apps and technologies for improving mental health and well-being: systematic review. JMIR Mental Health **6**(6), e13717 (2019)

5. Deci, E.L., Ryan, R.M.: The "what" and "why" of goal pursuits: human needs and the self-determination of behavior. Psychol. Inquiry **11**(4), 227–268 (2000)

6. Deterding, S., Dixon, D., Khaled, R., Nacke, L.: From game design elements to gamefulness: defining "gamification". In: Proceedings of the 15th International Academic MindTrek Conference: Envisioning Future Media Environments, pp. 9–15 (2011)

7. Dithmer, M., et al.: "The heart game": using gamification as part of a telerehabilitation program for heart patients. Games Health J. **5**(1), 27–33 (2016)

8. Garett, R., Young, S.D.: Health care gamification: a study of game mechanics and elements. Technol. Knowl. Learn. **24**(3), 341–353 (2019)

9. Giunti, G., Mylonopoulou, V., Romero, O.R.: More stamina, a gamified mHealth solution for persons with multiple sclerosis: research through design. JMIR mHealth uHealth **6**(3), e51 (2018)

10. Graf, C., Wolkerstorfer, P., Geven, A., Tscheligi, M.: A pattern collection for privacy enhancing technology. In: The 2nd International Conference on Pervasive Patterns and Applications (PATTERNS 2010), pp. 21–26 (2010)

11. Groh, F.: Gamification: state of the art definition and utilization. Institute of Media Informatics Ulm University (2012)

12. Guo, X., Han, X., Zhang, X., Dang, Y., Chen, C.: Investigating m-Health acceptance from a protection motivation theory perspective: gender and age differences. Telemed. e-Health **21**(8), 661–669 (2015)

13. Hamari, J.: Do badges increase user activity? A field experiment on the effects of gamification. Comput. Hum. Behav. **71**, 469–478 (2017)

14. Hamari, J., Hassan, L., Dias, A.: Gamification, quantified-self or social networking? Matching users' goals with motivational technology. User Model. User-Adap. Inter. **28**, 35–74 (2018)

15. Hansen, M., Jensen, M., Rost, M.: Protection goals for privacy engineering. In: 2015 IEEE Security and Privacy Workshops, pp. 159–166 (2015)

16. Koivisto, J., Hamari, J.: The rise of motivational information systems: a review of gamification research. Int. J. Inf. Manag. **45**, 191–210 (2019)

17. Kungwengwe, T., Evans, R.: Sana: a gamified rehabilitation management system for anterior cruciate ligament reconstruction recovery. Appl. Sci. **10**(14), 4868 (2020)

18. Lee, C., Lee, K., Lee, D.: Mobile healthcare applications and gamification for sustained health maintenance. Sustainability **9**(5), 772 (2017)

19. Li, C.: Gamified rehabilitation service designed for stroke patient. Master's thesis, Høgskolen i Oslo og Akershus. Institutt for Produktdesign (2017)
20. Mavroeidi, A.G., Kitsiou, A., Kalloniatis, C.: The role of gamification in privacy protection and user engagement. In: Security and Privacy From a Legal, Ethical, and Technical Perspective. IntechOpen (2020)
21. Mavroeidi, A.G., Kitsiou, A., Kalloniatis, C., Gritzalis, S.: Gamification vs. privacy: identifying and analysing the major concerns. Future Internet **11**(3), 67 (2019)
22. Nurgalieva, L., O'Callaghan, D., Doherty, G.: Security and privacy of mHealth applications: a scoping review. IEEE Access **8**, 104247–104268 (2020). https://doi.org/10.1109/ACCESS.2020.2999934
23. Papageorgiou, A., Strigkos, M., Politou, E., Alepis, E., Solanas, A., Patsakis, C.: Security and privacy analysis of mobile health applications: the alarming state of practice. IEEE Access **6**, 9390–9403 (2018). https://doi.org/10.1109/ACCESS.2018.2799522
24. Pires, I.M., Marques, G., Garcia, N.M., Flórez-Revuelta, F., Ponciano, V., Oniani, S.: A research on the classification and applicability of the mobile health applications. J. Personalized Med. **10**(1), 11 (2020)
25. Sailer, M., Hense, J.U., Mayr, S.K., Mandl, H.: How gamification motivates: an experimental study of the effects of specific game design elements on psychological need satisfaction. Comput. Hum. Behav. **69**, 371–380 (2017). https://doi.org/10.1016/j.chb.2016.12.033
26. Sardi, L., Idri, A., Fernández-Alemán, J.L.: A systematic review of gamification in e-Health. J. Biomed. Inform. **71**, 31–48 (2017). https://doi.org/10.1016/j.jbi.2017.05.011
27. Schmidt-Kraepelin, M., Toussaint, P.A., Thiebes, S., Hamari, J., Sunyaev, A.: Archetypes of gamification: analysis of mHealth apps. JMIR mHealth uHealth **8**(10), e19280 (2020)
28. Seaborn, K., Fels, D.I.: Gamification in theory and action: a survey. Int. J. Hum. Comput. Stud. **74**, 14–31 (2015). https://doi.org/10.1016/j.ijhcs.2014.09.006
29. Setiawan, S.S., Suryadibrata, A.: Fitrust: promoting healthy lifestyle through gamified mobile health application. In: 2019 5th International Conference on New Media Studies (CONMEDIA), pp. 26–30 (2019)
30. Troncoso, C., Isaakidis, M., Danezis, G., Halpin, H.: Systematizing decentralization and privacy: lessons from 15 years of research and deployments. Proc. Priv. Enhancing Technol. **4**, 307–329 (2017)
31. Vaghefi, I., Tulu, B.: The continued use of mobile health apps: insights from a longitudinal study. JMIR mHealth uHealth **7**(8), e12983 (2019). https://doi.org/10.2196/12983
32. Westmattelmann, D., Grotenhermen, J.G., Stoffers, B., Schewe, G.: Exploring the adoption of mixed-reality sport platforms: a qualitative study on Zwift. ECIS 2021 Research Papers (2021)
33. Zuckerman, O., Gal-Oz, A.: Deconstructing gamification: evaluating the effectiveness of continuous measurement, virtual rewards, and social comparison for promoting physical activity. Pers. Ubiquit. Comput. **18**(7), 1705–1719 (2014). https://doi.org/10.1007/s00779-014-0783-2

Exploration of Factors that Can Impact the Willingness of Employees to Share Smart Watch Data with Their Employers

Alexander Richter[1(✉)], Patrick Kühtreiber[1], and Delphine Reinhardt[1,2]

[1] Computer Security and Privacy, University of Göttingen,
Goldschmidtstr. 7, 37073 Göttingen, Germany
{richter,kuehtreiber,reinhardt}@cs.uni-goettingen.de
[2] Campus Institute Data Science, Goldschmidtstr. 1, 37073 Göttingen, Germany

Abstract. Companies increasingly equip employees with smart watches to, e.g., support them in carrying out their work. Smart watches can however collect data about them and reveal sensitive information. This may result in limiting the acceptance of these devices by employees, despite their potential helpfulness. In this paper, we therefore analyze factors that influence employees' willingness to share smart watch captured private data. In more detail, we investigate employees' technological knowledge about data collection and processing and the associated risks, their technical affinity, their smart watch ownership and usage, and their legislation knowledge about respective laws. To this end, we have conducted an online survey with more than 1,000 full-time employees. Our findings suggest that employees are aware of the risk associated with smart watches but partially have incorrect knowledge about legal frameworks. Moreover, more than one-third of the participants own a personal smart watch and have a certain technological affinity. However, our results reveal different impacts from these factors on employees' willingness to share data with their employers.

Keywords: Privacy · Employees · Willingness · Knowledge · Smart watch

1 Introduction

An increasing number of smart wearables are sold worldwide and this trend is expected to continue in the next years [3]. Smart wearables are not only deployed for personal uses, but also in so-called smart workplaces. For example, companies seek to enhance their manufacturing processes and thus increase their productivity by using such devices [25,29]. Among these smart wearables, smart watches can help support workers while they have their hands free for other tasks [16,29,37]. Similarly, they can lead to improvements in employees' health, if they encourage them to walk more [11]. For example, smart watches are

M. Friedewald et al. (Eds.): Privacy and Identity 2021, IFIP AICT 644, pp. 160–177, 2022.
https://doi.org/10.1007/978-3-030-99100-5_12

already deployed in the BMW group. Employees in the production process wear smart watches which alert them when the next vehicle on the assembly chain has unusual requirements to remind them about the specifics of the next tasks to execute [2]. Other examples include Amazon and Tesco warehouses, in which such devices support employees in finding and collecting goods [6,19]. While smart watches may offer several benefits, the collection and processing of data collected using their embedded sensors pose several risks to the wearers' privacy, as information about themselves and their environment can be obtained [1,20]. Especially in this context, the devices have been used to monitor employees' movement potentially, heart rate, daily number of steps, or their compliance to work process [1,17]. This not only poses new challenges for employees' privacy, but can also be seen as a surveillance tool deployed by employers [17]. The resulting concerns may be amplified through the power imbalance between employees and employers, as employees usually cannot opt-out. However, they would likely choose to opt-out if they could [17]. In general, technical and legislation knowledge can be expected to influence users' privacy concerns or behaviors. For example, prior work suggest that knowledge about the collection and use of private data leads people to tend to be less concerned about their privacy [12,22]. Likewise, legislation knowledge could help to reduce users' privacy concerns [23,34]. Consequently, the lack of knowledge about technology and legislation would increase users' privacy concerns, thus negatively influence users' intention to disclose private data. This affect of privacy concerns on users' intentions was shown in different areas [9,14,32,36]. However, other research also indicated that privacy awareness could lead to more privacy concerns [21,24]. In this paper, our ultimate goal is the understanding of employees' willingness to share data with their employers by examining various factors that may impact it. Our contributions can be summarized as follows. We (1) investigate employees' understanding of data collection and processing, (2) their legislation knowledge, and finally, (3) the impact of both factors on employees' willingness to share smart watch data with their employers. To this end, we have conducted an online questionnaire answered by 1,214 participants. Our results show that employees are aware of smart watch risks. Moreover, their knowledge, especially about company agreements, is limited and even partially incorrect. Hence, both may cause additional privacy concerns and may lead to employees' rejection to share smart watch data with their employers. Our last contribution is to propose recommendations for employers when planning to introduce smart watches to their work processes.

In the remaining sections, we discuss related work in Sect. 2. We introduce our research goals in Sect. 3 and applied methodology in Sect. 4. We present our results in Sect. 5 with a focus on our hypotheses and discuss our results in Sect. 6. We further discuss our findings and recommendations in Sect. 7, before making concluding remarks in Sect. 8.

2   Related Work

Existing studies focus on factors that may influence employees' acceptance to use smart wearables for various use cases [4,13]. In [4], the focus is on construction workers' acceptance to use two different wearable technologies (smart vest, wristband) for occupational safety and health, while the focus is on use cases and work environments predicting employees' acceptance of wearables in [13]. As a result, both differ from our work, which focuses on smart watches and privacy-relevant aspects investigating employees' intention to disclose data to their employer rather than determine factors that influence the acceptance of wearable use. In both existing works, it is shown that the acceptance of smart wearables at work can be influenced by perceived privacy risks, or experiences with such devices, social influence and use cases. Consequently, both serve as an additional motivation for our work. In addition to these works, privacy concerns related to wearable devices in general have been discussed based on a literature review in [7], while multiple works, such as [8,18,26], show the feasibility of recognizing the wearer's current activity based on the collected sensor data. Recommendations for employee performance monitoring systems have been further proposed in [31].

To the best of our knowledge, there exists no previous work investigating the impact of employees' knowledge about legislation and smart watches' data practices on their willingness to share these data with their employers.

3   Research Goals

In our study, we aim at testing the following hypotheses:

- **H1:** Employees are more willing to share smart watch data with their employers depending on their smart watch ownership and usage.
- **H2:** Employees' willingness to share smart watch data with their employer is influenced by their knowledge about the capability of smart watches in terms of data collection and processing.
- **H3:** Employees' willingness to share smart watch data with their employer is influenced by their knowledge about legal frameworks.
- **H4:** Employees' willingness to share smart watch data with their employer is influenced by their technical affinity.

4   Methodology

4.1   Survey Design

To test our hypotheses, we have conducted a user study based on an online questionnaire. In addition to the participants' usage of smart watches, we have especially investigated their awareness about smart watches' capability regarding data collection and processing and their knowledge about legislation frameworks.

To this end, we have provided a scenario to the participants (see Fig. 1), in which a deployment of smart watch was planned by their employer, after having collected their demographics to ensure a representative distribution across age and gender. In this scenario, we have detailed potential benefits along with information regarding data storage and a particular collected data type among activity, health, or location data.

Your employer wants to conduct a study to test the use of smart watches in your company. Therefore, you have to wear this smart watch while performing your work.

The smart watch has an application that helps you perform your daily tasks. Through the smartwatch, you can, for example:
o   Access information faster and
o   Request assistance if necessary.

o   The smart watch does not have any applications other than that of your employer.
o   To support you, different [**activity/health/location**] data needs to be collected.
o   This information is stored centrally on the company's servers.

Fig. 1. Provided scenario

We have then asked the participants about their intention to disclose this particular data type to their employer on a 5-point Likert scale from "strongly disagree" to "strongly agree" using three different questions derived from [30, 33, 35] (see Table 3 in Appendix A).

Next, we have asked the participants whether they own a smart watch and to respectively provide information about their usage (see Table 4 in Appendix A). Besides, we have asked them different questions about (1) smart watches' capability regarding data collection and processing (see Table 5 in Appendix A) and (2) legislation frameworks (see Table 6 and 7 in Appendix A) in order to quantify their knowledge and understanding about both matters. We have finally evaluated their technical affinity using questions from [10] (see Table 8 in Appendix A).

4.2   Survey Distribution

Our study has been approved by the Data Protection Officer and the Ethic Committee of our university. Afterwards, it has been distributed by a panel certified ISO 26362. In total, 1,214 participants from Germany have answered our questionnaire in German. The participants have been evenly distributed among the three different data types, i.e., activity (395 participants), health (406), or location data (413). Using a confirmatory factory analysis, we have tested the measurement invariance that confirms a strong measurement invariance, meaning that the factors measure the same construct across all groups [15]. All our participants should be full-time employees working in Germany and over 18. Note that we have monetarily rewarded the participants' contributions.

4.3   Survey Limitations

The questionnaire first included additional aspects that we do not consider in this paper. Since the questions were disjoint and grouped in dedicated sections, their potential influence however remains limited. Second, our questionnaire is based on a hypothetical scenario that participants needed to imagine. As a result, they may not have fully connected the given scenario with their own work. This limitation is, however, shared with all other online questionnaire. Third, we focus on employees in Germany and over 18. The obtained results may be different for other cultures and employees younger than 18. We consider a cross-cultural study as a promising future work.

5   Results

In this section, we detail the obtained results, while we specifically test our hypotheses formulated in Sect. 6.

5.1   Demographics

As shown in Table 1, our sample is evenly distributed between gender. The participants' age is between 18 and 67 years. Both distributions in terms of age and gender are representative for the German population [28]. The majority are employees or workers (77.3%) working in industry (15.6%), the health/social sector (13.8%), or commerce (10.5%).

5.2   Ownership and Usage

In our sample, 35% use a smart watch in a private context. According to [27], 26% of Germans own smart watches, whereas our sample shows a slightly higher percentage of smart watch owners. Hence, those participants could be more ready to accept smart watches in other contexts than others, thus impacting their answers. We have considered this aspect in Sect. 6 in more detail. Many of them use it daily (73.4%). Although slightly more women (36.8%) than men (33.3%) stated that they own a smart watch, a Mann-Whitney U test shows that the gender does not significantly influence the smart watch ownership ($p = 0.209$). Among the participants younger than 55, the majority own a smart watch (66%). In comparison, only 38% of older participants own one. A Kruskal-Wallis test reveals a significant correlation between participants' age and smart watch ownership ($p < 0.05$). However, a pairwise comparison (Bonferroni corrected) shows significant differences between the age categories 18-24 and 55-67 ($p = 0.019$), 25–34 and 45–54, ($p = 0.010$), as well as 25–34 and 55–67 ($p = 0.005$).

Table 1. Sample characteristics (N = 1,214).

Levels		Count	Percentage
Gender	Female	590	48.6%
	Male	624	51.4%
Age	18–24	179	14.7%
	25–34	262	21.6%
	35–44	299	24.6%
	45–54	361	29.7%
	55–67	113	9.3%
Sector	Industry	189	15.6%
	Insurance	19	1.6%
	Business	57	4.7%
	IT	65	5.4%
	Health/social sector	168	13.8%
	Energy	19	1.6%
	Construction	70	5.8%
	Commerce	128	10.5%
	Traffic	69	5.7%
	Education, research, culture	93	7.7%
	Advertisement	17	1.4%
	Print	9	0.7%
	Social insurance	24	2.0%
	Bank/fiance	53	4.4%
	Not specified	234	19.3%
Occupational function	Worker	110	9.1%
	Employee	828	68.2%
	Team leader	92	7.6%
	Head of department	68	5.6%
	Division manager	33	2.7%
	Area manager	7	0.6%
	Manager	60	4.9%
	Not specified	16	1.3%

5.3 Technical Knowledge About Smart Watch Capabilities

Our results show that many of our participants are aware of the technical capabilities of smart watches and the resulting threats to their privacy. Indeed, the participants are aware that a wide variety of profiles can be generated by combining individual personal data, such as a health profile (79.9%, Q_{TK1} in Table 5), and that these data can be used to draw inferences about their health (70.1%, Q_{TK2}

in Table 5). In addition, a majority of the participants (61.6%, Q_{TK3} in Table 5) believe that the data collected with the help of a smart watch can be used to uniquely identify them. The same picture emerges for the total score of technical knowledge about smart watch capabilities whose results are displayed in Fig. 2. To evaluate the participants' knowledge, we have attributed a point for each correct answer to the questions Q_{TK1} to Q_{TK3}. A maximum of three points could be reached. For comparison purposes, we provide the results in percent. In the mean, participants' reached 71% of all points ($M = 2.12, SD = 1.00$). A Mann-Whitney U test shows that the results between women ($M = 2.03$ (67.7%), $SD = 1.00$) and men ($M = 2.20$ (73.3%), $SD = 1.00$) are significantly different ($p = 0.001$). No significant differences can however be identified between the different age categories.

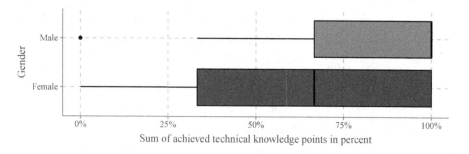

Fig. 2. Participants' technical knowledge score about smart watch capabilities per gender

5.4   Legislation Knowledge

The participants' answers to the questions related to data protection regulations and laws in Germany and in a professional context shows that over half of the participants (55.8%) either do not know the General Data Protection Regulation (GDPR) purpose (23.8%) or have incorrect knowledge about it (31.8%, Q_{LK1} in Table 6). Note that our objective is not to blame our participants about it but to understand the current state to be able to improve it in the future. The other questions regarding GDPR reveal similar results. A half of the participants (52.1%) know what personal data are, while still some answered wrong (24.8%) or stated not to know (23.2%, Q_{LK2} in Table 6). Positively, the majority know when the processing of personal data is lawful (61.8%, Q_{LK3} in Table 6) or whereby consent to the collection of personal data occurs (60.7%, Q_{LK4} in Table 6). However, some respondents stated that they do not know (17.9%, Q_{LK3}/22.1%, Q_{LK4} in Table 6). A different picture emerges about the participants' knowledge of laws concerning the deletion of personal data. 35% indicated that deletion is required when the processing purpose and the legal retention period no longer apply. In contrast, 36.2% answered the opposite and 28.7% did not know (Q_{LK5} in Table 7).

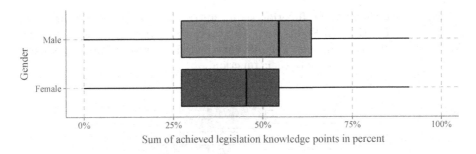

Fig. 3. Participants' legislation knowledge score per gender

The lack of knowledge becomes particularly clear when it comes to collective agreements between employees and the employer. The majority of the participants (43.5%) indicated that collective agreements are not a permissible form of agreement to collect and use employees' data (Q_{LK6} in Table 7). In addition, some participants are not able to answer this question (31.9%). Similar results are obtained for the question of whether a collective agreement can replace the consent of a person (Q_{LK7} in Table 7). Here, only 21.1% know that a collective agreement can replace the consent of individuals. Only a few participants (38.4%) are even aware that employers are allowed to make collective agreements (Q_{LK8} in Table 7). 45.1% said they did not know. However, the majority (60.1%) knows that signing the employment contract does not create consent for collecting personal data for present and future purposes (Q_{LK9} in Table 7). In contrast, only 22.7% thought the opposite. Interestingly, however, most participants are aware that employers are allowed to measure employee performance (56.2%, Q_{LK10} in Table 7) and that at least the works council must be involved in the introduction and use of technical equipment designed to monitor employee behavior or performance (73.1%, Q_{LK11} in Table 7). When looking at the aggregated results displayed in Fig. 3 over the 11 questions (each correct answer corresponding to one point), an average of 44.6% of correct answers were achieved across all participants ($M = 4.91, SD = 2.23$). The results further indicate, that males reach significantly higher scores ($M = 5.05$ (45.9%), $SD = 2.26$) than females ($M = 4.76$ (43.3%), $SD = 2.19$) ($p = 0.019$, Mann-Whitney U test). Interestingly, overall females ($M = 3.24, SD = 3.04$) chose the option "I do not know" more frequently than males ($M = 2.48, SD = 2.96$, $p < 0.001$, Mann-Whitney U test). Significant differences are however not observed between age categories for both statements. In the following, we investigate differences in the legislation knowledge across occupational functions and sectors. Figure 4 shows differences in achieved legislation knowledge points between the specified functions, while Fig. 5 presents results between the sectors. A comparison of the means shows that workers ($M = 4.33$ (39.4%), $SD = 2.33$) achieved the lowest scores, while area managers achieved the highest ($M = 6.86$ (62.4%), $SD = 1.07$). The other positions achieved means between $M = 4.88$ (44.4%) to 5.25 (47.7%). Participants who did not specify their job function reached $M = 3.56$ (32.4%). Their answers reveal that the job function significantly impacts the legislation knowledge ($p = 0.006$, Kruskal-Wallis test). However, a pairwise comparison (Bonferroni corrected) indicates only a significant difference between "area managers" and those who did not specify their function.

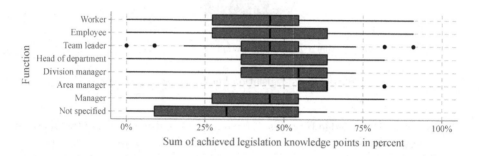

Fig. 4. Participants' legislation knowledge score per function

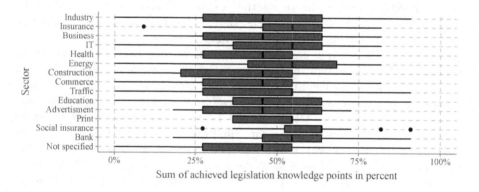

Fig. 5. Participants' legislation knowledge score per sector

Regarding the sector, participants working in construction achieved the lowest mean with 4.30 (39.1%). While participants working in social insurance achieved the highest scores ($M = 5.94$ (54%), $SD = 1.75$). A Kruskal-Wallis test reveals that the sector impacts the legislation knowledge significantly ($p = 0.006$). However, a pairwise comparison (Bonferroni corrected) indicates significant differences only between the sectors construction to social insurance ($p = 0.003$) and bank ($p = 0.006$), between commerce and social insurance ($p = 0.037$), and between not specified and social insurance ($p = 0.002$) and bank ($p = 0.001$).

5.5   Technical Affinity

We apply the technical affinity scale proposed in [10] to classify our participants based on their technology affinity in order to understand its impact on the willingness to share private data with an employer. This scale contains nine questions. The affinity is determined based on the average of all answers indicated on a 6-point Likert scale. Hence, a total of six points can be achieved. The higher the value, the higher the participant's technical affinity. Overall, the mean score for all participants is 3.97 ($SD = 0.94$). The data displayed in Fig. 6 reveal that females ($M = 3.75, SD = 0.92$) reach significantly ($p = 0.001$) lower scores than males ($M = 4.17, SD = 0.91$). However, this effect is small ($r = 0.22$) [5]. When considering the different age categories, we observe a significant difference ($p = 0.028$). In detail, however, a pairwise comparison with Bonferoni correction shows that none of the groups significantly differ after correction.

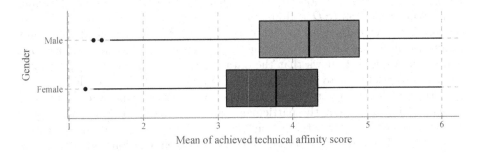

Fig. 6. Participants' technical affinity score per gender

5.6   Intention to Disclose

We finally analyze the participants' intention to disclose the particular data type, i.e., activity, health, and location included in their respective scenario description, to their employer measured using the three questions presented in Table 3 in Appendix A.

A reliability analysis indicates excellent internal consistency across the answers provided to these three dedicated questions (Cronbach's $\alpha = 0.97$) [15]. As the participants are separated into three distinct groups based on the considered data type (activity, health, and location), we have further tested these groups for strict measurement invariance using a confirmatory factor analysis [15]. A strict measurement invariance requires equal latent factor loadings, item intercepts, and residual and allows comparisons across groups as factors measure the same construct [15]. The test indicates no violation, meaning that the factors are measured identically across all groups, which allows meaningful comparisons.

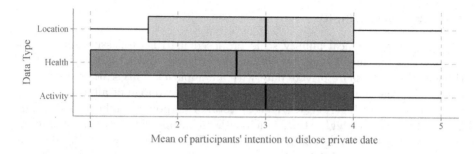

Fig. 7. Means of participants' intention to disclose for each data type

Next, we have associated each item of the Likert scale to the corresponding point, i.e., 1 for "strongly disagree" and 5 for "strongly agree" and computed the mean over all three questions (Q_{ID1} to Q_{ID3} in Table 3) for each participant. With a mean of 2.82 ($SD = 1.36$), our participants are rather not willing to disclose the three data types to their employer. Neither age nor gender have any significant influence on their willingness. Concerning the different data types, a Kruskal-Wallis test shows that the data type has an impact on participants' intention to disclose it to their employer. Figure 7 presents and Table 2 summarizes the different results for each data type. A pairwise comparison (Bonferroni corrected) indicates that the participants are less willing to share their health data with their employer than their activity ($p = 0.001$) and their location ($p = 0.026$). There is no significant difference between location and activity.

Table 2. Data type mean overview

Type	N	M	SD	MIN	MAX	$\Delta Activity$	$\Delta Health$
Activity	395	2.95	1.28	1	5	–	0.33
Health	406	2.63	1.37	1	5	−0.33	–
Location	413	2.88	1.39	1	5	−0.08	0.25
Total	1214	2.82	1.36	1	5		

6 Testing the Hypotheses

In the following, we test our hypotheses defined in Sect. 3 and discuss them with potential recommendations for employers.

H1: Employees are more willing to share smart watch data with their employers depending on their smart watch ownership and usage. As indicated in Sect. 5.2, more than one-third of the participants own a personal smart watch and many of them use it on a daily basis. Our aforementioned results further confirm that especially younger people own a smart watch. In our hypothesis, we assume that employees who own and use their personal smart watch may be more willing to share the data with their employer due to their private experience and potential benefits drawn from it. The participants' answers confirm that participants who own a smart watch differ significantly from those who do not have a smart watch on their willingness to disclose the respective data type to their employers ($p < 0.001$, Mann-Whitney U test). In contrast, the differences regarding smart watch usage can be neglected, as a significant change cannot be observed. Thus, H1 is partially supported, as only participants who own a smart watch significantly differ in their willingness to share smart watch data with their employer compared to those who do not own a smartwatch.

In summary, the results in Sect. 5.2 reveal that one-third of participants from our sample own a smart watch, many of whom are younger participants. Furthermore, we found that participants who own a smart watch differ from those without a smart watch in their intention to disclose smart watch data to their employer, while no significant differences based on smart watch usage can be observed. Reasons for this may be that employees who own a smart watch tend to be more positive about data sharing, as they may be more tech-savvy and therefore better understand smart watch potentials, regardless of how often they ultimately use their smart watch. Based on this insight, employers could develop strategies. For example, they could provide employees a smart watch for private use before their introduction at the workplace. However, the professional and private usage should be strictly separated. Employers should not collect employees' data outside the company when it is not work-related [31]. This must be ensured as no legitimate reasons for such data collection exists unless employees have agreed. Beyond the implementation of such strategy, more and more people are buying smart watches for private use. This may lead to an increasing number of individuals becoming familiar with smart watches, thus resulting in more individuals willing to also use them in a corporate context. This trend is certainly related to the advantages that a smart watch can offer compared to the associated threats including to their privacy.

H2: Employees' willingness to share smart watch data with their employer is influenced by their knowledge about the capability of smart watches in terms of data collection and processing. The obtained results for $Q_{TK1} - Q_{TK3}$ (Table 5 in Appendix A) indicate good awareness about the technical capabilities of smart watches. Overall, most participants reach high scores. In particular, the results for Q_{TK1} and Q_{TK2} indicate that our participants are aware of smart watches being able to create health profiles, which allow deriving conclusions about the wearer. We hypothesize that the participants' technical knowledge about the capability of smart watches in terms of data collection and processing may influence their willingness to share those data with their employers. However, based on our data, neither significant positive nor negative influence is found between employees' technical knowledge about smart watches capabilities and employees' willingness to disclose data to their employers. Consequently, H2 is not supported.

172 A. Richter et al.

However, to sum up, considering our findings in Sect. 5.3, our participants are
already aware of the technical possibilities offered by a smart watch. We assume
that this technological knowledge may negatively influence employees' decisions
to accept a smart watch at work, even if we could not prove it in our study.
Technical knowledge may lead employees to negatively perceive the smart watch
and the associated data collection, even if employers do not have bad intentions.
In this case, providing transparency to the employees by explaining which data
is being gathered, for which purpose, and how the data is protected is necessary.
Besides, technical solutions to minimize potential risks for the employees should
be implemented.

*H3: Employees' willingness to share smart watch data with their employer is
influenced by their knowledge about legal frameworks.* Although some participants already have partial knowledge about the GDPR, the lack of knowledge
about collective agreements is shown in Sect. 5.4. At the same time, some participants are aware that employers are allowed to monitor employees' performance if
the works council is involved. As a result, they may decide not to share their data
with the employer. Therefore, we test our third hypothesis. The results reveal
a significant positive relationship between employees' legislation knowledge and
their willingness to share data with their employer ($p = 0.002$). The employees'
disclosure intention increases by 0.053-unit ($+/-0.02$) for every increase in a
unit of legislation knowledge. Thus, H3 is supported: The legislation knowledge
influence employees' decision about smart watch data disclosure.

In summary, some of our participants have either no or even incorrect knowledge about the GDPR. Similarly, our participants are not aware of collective
agreements that employers can negotiate and that those collective agreements
can replace individual agreements. Interestingly, few participants are aware that
employers are allowed to measure the employees' performance and that at least
the works council has to be involved if technical equipment is used for such measurements. Overall, our participants thus achieved only low legislation knowledge
scores. On top of that, we found that the influence from legislative knowledge on
employees' willingness to share smart watch data with employers is positive, even
if this influence is small. This positive influence may be explained by the fact
that employees, who are aware that collective agreements are possible and that
the works council should be included, feel more comfortable sharing data because
the works council represents employees' interests and not those of the employer.
Thus, employers should be aware that not every employee is aware of the collective agreements. Therefore, employers should clarify in advance the exact process
from planning to integrating smart watches in their processes as well as which
and where related information are available to employees. In addition, employers
should generally agree on a code of conduct when dealing with employees' data
to improve their trustworthiness and redress the prevailing imbalance between
employers and employees. Furthermore, works councils should be sensitized to
the issue so that they can fill potential knowledge gaps.

H4: Employees' willingness to share smart watch data with their employer is influenced by their technical affinity. The results in Sect. 5.5 indicate that our participants have a certain technological affinity. It can be assumed that participants with an affinity for technology are more willing to use a smart watch in a company, as they enjoy the use of new technologies. This may imply that it also applies to share their data with their employer. Based on the results derived from the regression model, employees' technical affinity impacts employees' willingness significantly $(p < 0.001)$. This influence is positive, as for each increase unit in employees' technical affinity employees' willingness to share smart watch data with their employer increase by 0.27-unit $(+/-0.04)$. As a result, H4 is supported.

In short, in our sample, our participants exhibit a certain technological affinity, which positively influences employees' willingness to share smart watch data with employers. This impact may be positive as tech-savvy people tend to enjoy new technologies, which possibly implies the same in a corporate context and ultimately could foster data sharing. Nonetheless, employers could identify particularly tech-savvy employees to conduct prior studies with them to jointly identify potential barriers to later implementation and establish solutions.

In summary, our hypotheses H3 and H4 are confirmed, while H1 is partly confirmed and H2 is rejected.

7   Discussion

Derived from our results presented in Sects. 5 and 6, we highlight our following key insights and potential recommendations for employers. First, we found differences between participants who own a smart watch and those without a smart watch concerning their willingness to share data with the employer. With this in mind, employers could provide employees with smart watches for their private use before introducing them to workplace processes. A separation between private and corporate usage is beyond question and mandatory. Second, we found that our participants' knowledge about the GDPR is vague and partly incorrect. Moreover, there is a small positive influence on the willingness to share data with the employer when legislation knowledge increases. Employers should be aware of this and provide information, especially about collective agreements. They should also provide information in advance about the process of future implementation. More importantly, however, works councils should be sensitized to the issue to close any gaps in employees' knowledge when they exist.

In general, employers who decide to use smart watches in their processes should further analyze what data exactly needs to be collected. This is necessary for the employees' agreement allowing them to collect private data with a smart watch while working, which depends on the data type asked for. Our results show significant differences between the three considered types of data. Our participants were less willing to share health data with employers when compared to location and activity data. The difference between activity and health data is particularly interesting. They differ in the data collected due to the different sensors used. However, inferences about a wearer's health can be made even based on the wearer's activity. The participants might not be aware of this connection or might estimate that they are less likely. Employers should, therefore, analyze in advance exactly what data is relevant and why it should be collected. In principle, employers should always communicate with employees openly and transparently. This means that employers should provide clear information about what data is being collected and for what purpose. Implementing smart watches in workplaces requires careful planning and realization. The works council should always be included in this process if one exists. In the absence of a works council, employees should be actively involved in the implementation process. Moreover, companies should transparently report on the planned actions and provide suitable solutions for reducing employees' risks. In addition, technical solutions should be implemented to help employees enforce their rights. However, if there is strong opposition among the workforce towards smart watch implementation and the associated data collection, employers should not exploit their position of power and refrain from using smart watches, even if all previous suggestions were considered.

8   Conclusions

In our study, we have explored factors that may influence employees' willingness to share data from smart watches with their employers. More precisely, we explored the impacts of employees' legislation knowledge, technical knowledge about smart watch capabilities, and technical affinity on their willingness to share such information. Moreover, we investigated whether the smart watch ownership and usage correlate with this willingness. A majority of our participants is aware of what can be processed and used with the data collected by a smart watch. Employees have, however, partially incorrect knowledge about legal frameworks, especially about collective agreements and the GDPR purpose. Moreover, our results reveal that the ownership of a personal smart watch leads to differences in their willingness to share data, as does the employees' technical affinity. Among the different data types considered, the participants were more reluctant to share health data. Thus, we recommend employers to consider employees' knowledge about smart watches and legislation frameworks when implementing smart watches to reduce potential misunderstandings about the data to be collected. Likewise, they should provide transparency about the collected data and apply adequate privacy-preserving mechanisms. While our results provide insights about factors, which impact employees' willingness to share data with their employer, the adopted scenarios remain general. As a result, we plan as a next step to conduct studies, such as interviews, which will take into account the specifics of the participants' work. Here, we will consider activity data more concretely. In addition, we will explore employees' trust in the GDPR in the future. Based on that, we further plan to develop methods to bridge potential employees' knowledge gaps and provide them both transparency and control over such data collection in the future.

Acknowledgments. The authors would like to thank the anonymous participants who participated in the survey and our colleagues for their feedback on the survey.

References

1. Applin, S.A., Fischer, M.D.: Watching me, watching you. (Process surveillance and agency in the workplace). In: Proceedings of the 2013 IEEE International Symposium on Technology and Society (ISTAS): Social Implications of Wearable Computing and Augmediated Reality in Everyday Life, pp. 268–275 (2013)
2. BMW Group: Produktionsstart der neuen BMW 7er Limousine (2019). https://www.press.bmwgroup.com/austria/article/detail/T0292928DE
3. CCS Insight: Healthy Outlook for Wearables As Users Focus on Fitness and Well-Being (2021). https://www.ccsinsight.com/press/company-news/healthy-outlook-for-wearables-as-users-focus-on-fitness-and-well-being/
4. Choi, B., Hwang, S., Lee, S.H.: What drives construction workers' acceptance of wearable technologies in the workplace?: Indoor localization and wearable health devices for occupational safety and health. Autom. Constr. **84**(1), 31–41 (2017)
5. Cohen, J.: Statistical Power Analysis for the Behavioral Sciences. Academic Press, Cambridge (1988)
6. Collins, P.M., Marassi, S.: Is that lawful?: data privacy and fitness trackers in the workplace. Int. J. Comp. Labour Law **37**(1), 65–94 (2021)
7. Datta, P., Namin, A.S., Chatterjee, M.: A survey of privacy concerns in wearable devices. In: Proceedings of the IEEE International Conference on Big Data (Big Data), pp. 4549–4553 (2018)
8. Davoudi, A., et al.: Accuracy of Samsung gear S smartwatch for activity recognition: validation study. JMIR Mhealth Uhealth **7**(2), e11270 (2019)
9. Dinev, T., Hart, P.J.: An extended privacy calculus model for e-commerce transactions. Inf. Syst. Res. **17**(1), 61–80 (2006)
10. Franke, T., Attig, C., Wessel, D.: A personal resource for technology interaction: development and validation of the affinity for technology interaction (ATI) scale. Int. J. Human-Comput. Interact. **35**(6), 456–467 (2019)
11. Gorm, N., Shklovski, I.: Sharing steps in the workplace. In: Proceedings of the 34th ACM Conference on Human Factors in Computing Systems (CHI), pp. 4315–4319 (2016)
12. Isaak, J., Hanna, M.J.: User data privacy: Facebook, Cambridge analytica, and privacy protection. Computer **51**(8), 56–59 (2018)
13. Jacobs, J.V., et al.: Employee acceptance of wearable technology in the workplace. Appl. Ergon. **78**(1), 148–156 (2019)
14. Kehr, F., Kowatsch, T., Wentzel, D., Fleisch, E.: Blissfully ignorant: the effects of general privacy concerns, general institutional trust, and affect in the privacy calculus. Inf. Syst. J. **25**(6), 607–635 (2015)
15. Kline, R.B.: Principles and Practice of Structural Equation Modeling, 4th edn. Methodology in the Social Sciences, New York (2016)
16. Kovacs, K., Ansari, F., Geisert, C., Uhlmann, E., Glawar, R., Sihn, W.: A process model for enhancing digital assistance in knowledge-based maintenance. In: Machine Learning for Cyber Physical Systems. TA, vol. 9, pp. 87–96. Springer, Heidelberg (2019). https://doi.org/10.1007/978-3-662-58485-9_10
17. Kritzler, M., Bäckman, M., Tenfält, A., Michahelles, F.: Wearable technology as a solution for workplace safety. In: Proceedings of the 14th ACM International Conference on Mobile and Ubiquitous Multimedia (MUM), pp. 213–217. ACM (2015)

18. Mekruksavanich, S., Hnoohom, N., Jitpattanakul, A.: Smartwatch-based sitting detection with human activity recognition for office workers syndrome. In: 2018 IEEE International ECTI Northern Section Conference on Electrical, Electronics, Computer and Telecommunications Engineering (ECTI-NCON), pp. 160–164 (2018)

19. Moore, P.V.: The Quantified Self in Precarity: Work, Technology and What Counts (2017)

20. Motti, V.G., Caine, K.: Users' privacy concerns about wearables. In: Brenner, M., Christin, N., Johnson, B., Rohloff, K. (eds.) FC 2015. LNCS, vol. 8976, pp. 231–244. Springer, Heidelberg (2015). https://doi.org/10.1007/978-3-662-48051-9_17

21. Ozdemir, Z.D., Smith, H.J., Benamati, J.H.: Antecedents and outcomes of information privacy concerns in a peer context: an exploratory study. Eur. J. Inf. Syst. **26**(6), 642–660 (2017)

22. Prince, C.: Do consumers want to control their personal data? Empirical evidence. Int. J. Hum. Comput. Stud. **110**, 21–32 (2018)

23. Prince, C., Omrani, N., Maalaoui, A., Dabic, M., Kraus, S.: Are we living in surveillance societies and is privacy an illusion? An empirical study on privacy literacy and privacy concerns. IEEE Trans. Eng. Manag. (2021)

24. Schaub, F., et al.: Watching them watching me: browser extensions' impact on user privacy awareness and concern. In: Proceedings of the 2016 Workshop on Usable Security (USEC), pp. 1–10 (2016)

25. Schellewald, V., Weber, B., Ellegast, R., Friemert, D., Hartmann, U.: Einsatz von Wearables zur Erfassung der körperlichen Aktivität am Arbeitsplatz. DGUV Forum **11**(1), 36–37 (2016)

26. Shoaib, M., Bosch, S., Scholten, H., Havinga, P.J., Incel, O.D.: Towards detection of bad habits by fusing smartphone and smartwatch sensors. In: Proceedings of the 13th IEEE International Conference on Pervasive Computing and Communication Workshops (PerCom Workshops), pp. 591–596 (2015)

27. Statista Inc.: Do you personally use wearables (e.g. smart watch, health / fitness tracker)? [Graph] (2021). https://www.statista.com/forecasts/1101110/wearables-devices-usage-in-selected-countries

28. Statistisches Bundesamt (Destatis): 12111–0004: Bevölkerung (Zensus): Deutschland, Stichtag, Geschlecht, Altersgruppen (2021). https://www-genesis.destatis.de/genesis/online

29. Stocker, A., Brandl, P., Michalczuk, R., Rosenberger, M.: Mensch-zentrierte IKT-Lösungen in einer Smart Factory. e & i Elektrotechnik und Informationstechnik **131**(7), 207–211 (2014)

30. Sun, Y., Wang, N., X., S.: Perceived benefits, privacy risks, and perceived justice in location information disclosure: a moderated mediation analysis. In: Proceedings of the 2014 Pacific Asia Conference on Information Systems (PACIS) (2014)

31. Tomczak, D.L., Lanzo, L.A., Aguinis, H.: Evidence-based recommendations for employee performance monitoring. Bus. Horiz. **61**(2), 251–259 (2018)

32. Trang, S., Weiger, W.H.: The perils of gamification: does engaging with gamified services increase users' willingness to disclose personal information? Comput. Hum. Behav. **116**, 106644 (2021)

33. Wang, T., Duong, T.D., Chen, C.C.: Intention to disclose personal information via mobile applications: a privacy calculus perspective. Int. J. Inf. Manag. **36**(4), 531–542 (2016)

34. Wirtz, J., Lwin, M.O., Williams, J.D.: Causes and consequences of consumer online privacy concern. Int. J. Serv. Ind. Manag. **18**(4), 326–348 (2007)

35. Xu, H., Teo, H.H., Tan, B.C., Agarwal, R.: The role of push-pull technology in privacy calculus: the case of location-based services. J. Manag. Inf. Syst. **26**(3), 135–174 (2009)
36. Zhang, X., Liu, S., Chen, X., Wang, L., Gao, B., Zhu, Q.: Health information privacy concerns, antecedents, and information disclosure intention in online health communities. Inf. Manag. **55**(4), 482–493 (2018)
37. Ziegler, J., Heinze, S., Urbas, L.: The potential of smartwatches to support mobile industrial maintenance tasks. In: Proceedings of the 20th IEEE Conference on Emerging Technologies Factory Automation (ETFA), pp. 1–7 (2015)

A Questions

Table 3. Intention to disclosure

ID	Questions
Q_{ID1}	I am likely to share my information collected by the smart watch with my employer
Q_{ID2}	I am probably going to be willing to share my information captured by the smart watch with my employer
Q_{ID3}	I am certainly ready to be willing to share my information captured by the smart watch with my employer

Possible answers: *5-point Likert scale from strongly disagree to strongly agree*

Table 4. Smart watch ownership and usage

ID	Questions
Q_{S1}	Do you own a smart watch that you use?

Possible answers: *Yes/No*

Q_{S2}	How often do you use your smart watch?

Possible answers: *Daily/Several times a week/Once a week/Less frequently*

Table 5. Technical knowledge about smart watch capabilities

ID	Questions
Q_{TK1}	Do you think that by combining individual personal data, it is possible to create a wide variety of profiles of you, such as a health profile or an activity profile?
Q_{TK2}	By capturing data collected with the help of a smart watch, for example, it is possible to identify them uniquely
Q_{TK3}	The data collected with the help of a smart watch allows conclusions to be drawn about your state of health

Possible answers: *Yes/No/I do not know*

Table 6. Legislation knowledge - part 1

ID	Questions
Q_{LK1}	What is the purpose of the General Data Protection Regulation (GDPR)?
A_{LK1}	*The GDPR regulates how any data collected exclusively via the Internet may be collected by companies*
A_{LK2}	*The GDPR regulates how European citizens must provide their personal data to companies*
A_{LK3}	*The GDPR regulates how companies may maintain and use the integrity of personal data*
A_{LK4}	*The GDPR regulates how companies from non-EU countries may contact you*
A_{LK5}	*I do not know*
Q_{LK2}	According to the GDPR, personal data are...
A_{LK1}	*... any information relating to an identified or identifiable natural person*
A_{LK2}	*... all online information relating to an identified or identifiable natural person*
A_{LK3}	*... all online information that relates to an identified or identifiable legal entity*
A_{LK4}	*... all information relating to an identified or identifiable legal entity*
A_{LK5}	*I do not know*
Q_{LK3}	The processing of personal data is lawful if...
A_{LK1}	*... a company clearly explains and demonstrates the purpose of the collection*
A_{LK2}	*... the processing is absolutely necessary for the purpose of using a service*
A_{LK3}	*... the data subject has given consent to processing for a specific purpose*
A_{LK4}	*... the data subject is granted the right to erasure*
A_{LK5}	*I do not know*
Q_{LK4}	Consent to the collection of personal data takes place,...
A_{LK1}	*... already when the person concerned is inactive or silent*
A_{LK2}	*... even if a company does not ask you directly, but a service is used*
A_{LK3}	*... if the consent is given by a clear confirming action for a specific purpose*
A_{LK4}	*... already when you call up a company website*
A_{LK5}	*I do not know*

Table 7. Legislation knowledge - part 2

ID	Questions
Q_{LK5}	According to the GDPR, personal data must be deleted if...
A_{LK1}	... the data subject changes to another provider of a service
A_{LK2}	... the purpose of the processing as well as the legal retention period ceases to apply
A_{LK3}	... the purpose of the processing, regardless of the legal retention period, no longer applies
A_{LK4}	... the data subject has requested information about the data, the data will subsequently be deleted
A_{LK5}	I do not know
Q_{LK6}	A collective agreement between employees and the employer can replace the consent of an individual
Q_{LK7}	Collective agreements between employers and employees, constitute a permissible form of agreement to collect and use personal data of employees
Q_{LK8}	Employers are permitted to conclude collective agreements (e.g., collective bargaining agreements) within the meaning of the German Federal Data Protection Act (BDSG)
Q_{LK9}	Signing your employment contract creates consent for any purposes of collecting personal data for present and future
Q_{LK10}	Companies are generally prohibited from measuring employee performance
Q_{LK11}	The works council must be involved in the introduction and use of technical equipment designed to monitor the behavior or performance of employees

Possible answers: *True/Not true/I do not know*

Table 8. Affinity for technology interaction [10]

ID	Questions
Q_{ATI1}	I like to occupy myself in greater detail with technical systems
Q_{ATI2}	I like testing the functions of new technical systems
Q_{ATI3}	I predominantly deal with technical systems because I have to
Q_{ATI4}	When I have a new technical system in front of me, I try it out intensively
Q_{ATI5}	I enjoy spending time becoming acquainted with a new technical system
Q_{ATI6}	It is enough for me that a technical system works; I don't care how or why
Q_{ATI7}	I try to understand how a technical system exactly works
Q_{ATI8}	It is enough for me to know the basic functions of a technical system
Q_{ATI9}	I try to make full use of the capabilities of a technical system

Possible answers: *6-point Likert scale from completely disagree to completely agree*

Public Education, Platformization and Cooperative Responsibility: The Case of the Privacy Covenant in the Netherlands

Marco Houben[1]([⊠]) [iD] and Jo Pierson[2] [iD]

[1] imec-SMIT-Vrije Universiteit Brussel, Pleinlaan 9, 1050 Brussels, Belgium
marco.houben@vub.be
[2] imec-SMIT-Vrije Universiteit Brussel, Brussels, Belgium

Abstract. Platformization increasingly changes educational pedagogies, policies, governance, financing, and the role of teachers in public education. As such, platforms start to play a vital role in the realization of the values and societal goals of public education. Platform governance typically focuses on the responsibility of one actor. Cooperative responsibility argues that instead, platform governance should be the result of the dynamic interaction and allocation of responsibilities between platforms and users, supported by a legal and policy framework created by state institutions. Qualitative interviews into the construction of the Privacy Covenant for public education in the Netherlands are used as a case to investigate cooperative responsibility 'on the ground'. The findings show that the Privacy Covenant has functioned as a driving force for strengthening data protection. The public education sector organizes themselves, and extensively cooperates with both state institutions and platform companies in order to improve data protection. Many of these stakeholders take more responsibility in protecting the privacy of children and keep on collaborating for the ongoing improvement of data protection. In this collaboration, schools should take into account an observed diversity in platforms which influences the distribution of responsibilities between them.

Keywords: Cooperative responsibility · Data protection · Platformization · Public education

1 Introduction

1.1 Platformization of Public Education

Platformization is defined as "the penetration of infrastructures, economic processes, and governmental frameworks of digital platforms, in different economic sectors and spheres of life (Poell et al. 2019, pp. 5–6)". It is a process that we have seen earlier in sectors like taxi services (e.g. Uber), hotel accommodation (e.g. Airbnb) (van Dijck and Poell 2015) and the media landscape (e.g. Netflix) (van Dijck and Poell 2013). In public education, platformization emerges through 'educational technology' (EdTech) platforms that offer

M. Friedewald et al. (Eds.): Privacy and Identity 2021, IFIP AICT 644, pp. 180–194, 2022.
https://doi.org/10.1007/978-3-030-99100-5_13

technologies that combine IT and educational practices and facilitate learning. A global industry of EdTech platforms and services is growing and increasingly encompassing every aspect of education including enrolment; online program management; learning analytics; digital libraries; alumni relation management; exam proctoring; plagiarism detection and so on (HolonIQ 2020; Wiley 2018 in Williamson 2020). An example of how platformization works is the integration between public education and digital infrastructures of companies like Alphabet/Google and Microsoft. Kerssens and Dijck (2021) show how this works through corporate strategies of intra-operability and public sector strategies of interoperability. Interoperability is a strategy aimed at promoting transparency and openness between a variety of educational technology systems and data flows under public oversight and control. Intra-operability is a strategy that aims at the connection of educational technologies to their central platforms under private control, fostering lock-in effects.

1.2   Impact of Platformization on Public Education

Platformization increasingly changes educational pedagogies, policies, governance, financing and the role of teachers in public education (Cf. Williamson 2017). It challenges the interests and values of public education, and impacts the governance and control of schools over the pedagogy and organization of public education (Kerssens and Dijck 2021). The impact on governance indirectly affects the right to privacy and to data protection of children (who are a special category of data subjects in the GDPR that needs strict protection[1]), for example by raising questions about controllership and challenging the implementation of data protection in schools regarding purpose limitation, transparency, as well as extra EU data transfers (Angiolini et al. 2020). Whether schools operate ethically and protect their children's data according to data protection law is questionable (Botta 2020; Ducato et al. 2020).

The impact on governance and data protection manifests itself in, amongst others, the construction of data processing agreements (DPA) in which the relationship between schools as data controllers and data processors like Alphabet/Google, Microsoft, Magister or Squla is formally settled according to Art. 28 (3) (EU 2016). This can be exemplified through the obligation for schools to only contract data processors who provide sufficient guarantees to implement appropriate technical and organizational measures for protecting personal data (EU 2016, art. 28 (1)), and the obligation to impose detailed instructions on the processing and protection of personal data by data processors, as expressed in Article 28 (3) of the General Data Protection Regulation (GDPR) (EU 2016). But are schools able to comply to these obligations? Initial drafts of data processing agreements often lay the foundation for negotiating and stipulating guarantees and instructions. However, who drafts the contract may depend on varying power (im)balances which includes market position, technical expertise, and access to legal services. Platforms tend to set up standard terms and conditions that include data processing agreements, often from a 'take it or leave it' perspective, leaving schools uncertain about GDPR compliance. This imbalance in power, however, doesn't absolve schools from their responsibility as data controllers (Olbrechts 2020).

---

[1] See for example Art. 6 (1f), Art. 8, and Art. 12 (1) of the GDPR (EU 2016).

1.3   Remedying the Power Imbalance

The platformization of public sectors increasingly comes with debate around public values, platform governance, and questions about how to remedy the power imbalance between schools and platforms. Some proposals from academia are to critically assess the integration of technologies in education through strategies of intra-operability, the promotion and securing of interoperability, and an inclusive approach to governance: on, and between, national and supranational levels (Kerssens and Dijck 2021). Also the promotion of the embedding of data protection principles in the design and development of technologies, more scrutiny by data protection authorities, critical procurement, collective negotiations with platforms and the development of 'public infrastructures' that serve the common good are proposed (Angiolini et al. 2020). GAIA-X is an example in which partners from business, science and politics work since 2019 towards a European Cloud Infrastructure based on European values (Energy 2020; Funk 2021). On the national level, the Dutch government's Digital Strategy (Ministerie van Algemene Zaken 2021) pays attention to public values. Another Dutch example is 'Public Spaces'[2]: an initiative in which a coalition of public organizations in public media, cultural heritage, festivals, museums and education works together 'to reclaim the internet as a force for the common good' and advocates 'a new internet that strengthens the public domain', including for education (Public Spaces 2021). A similar, European, initiative is recently launched under the name 'Shared Digital European Public Sphere' (SDEPS)[3].

The Dutch public education sector is also actively working to secure public values like equality, privacy, and accessibility. It has initiated several collective initiatives, like a number of Data Protection Impact Assessments (DPIA) into Google Workspace for Education[4] and the biggest Learning Management System (LMS) providers (ESIS, ParnasSys, Magister, Somtoday and SchoolOAS)[5], who serve a huge majority of schools with their products and services (Kerssens and Dijck 2021), and constructed a 'value framework'[6] for the use of ICTs. The sector has also constructed the (legally obliged) 'ECK-iD'[7], a technical standard and a privacy-friendly way to exchange personal data between different systems that allows schools to control data flows (ECK-iD 2021). Such a standard helps "the sector to jointly exercise public control over digitization by designing interoperability as a collective principle (Kerssens and Dijck 2021, p. 10)". The sector now also calls for a European interoperable system in which public education can profit from technology innovation, but keeps the data in public hands (SURF 2021).

---

[2] https://publicspaces.net/.

[3] https://sdeps.eu/.

[4] https://www.privacycompany.eu/blogpost-en/privacy-assessment-google-workspace-g-suite-enterprise-dutch-government-consults-dutch-data-protection-authority-on-high-privacy-risks.

[5] https://www.kennisnet.nl/artikel/12377/dpias-op-leerlingadministratiesystemen/.

[6] https://www.kennisnet.nl/artikel/12352/waardenwijzer-in-gesprek-over-onderwijswaarden-en-digitalisering/.

[7] https://www.eck-id.nl.

1.4 Cooperative Responsibility

We propose 'cooperative responsibility' as a participatory approach to remedy the power imbalance between schools and platforms. Inspired by the work of technology philosopher Andrew Feenberg and social constructivist perspectives of Science & Technology Studies (Cf. Pinch and Bijker 1984), we believe that powerful (Big Tech) platforms and subordinate groups like schools (which we call stakeholders) 'fight' over the future of public education. Feenberg's Critical Theory of Technology (Feenberg 1999) argues that technologies are not neutral but have values and interests of people inscribed through its design and development. These 'formally biased' technologies usually embody and reproduce the values and interests of dominant forces, like those of EdTech platforms. However, sometimes also subordinate groups involved in the design and development can influence the construction of technologies. Feenberg calls this 'democratic rationalization'. Thus, schools are able to influence the design and development of platforms in education and preserve public values like protection the privacy of school children.

Platforms have become so important in public sectors that they have started to play a vital role in the realization of public values. But how, and to what extent, do platforms take up responsibility for this? Platforms operate relatively independent of public governance and distance themselves often from their responsibility. Discussions around platform governance, then, often depart from the standpoint that platforms have to be held accountable, focusing to a large extent on the responsibility of one actor (e.g., data controller, data processor, editor, host, gatekeeper). But platforms are by their very architectures only partly able to exercise such control (Helberger et al. 2018, p. 2). Users are responsible as well.

Scholars have approached the power of online platforms from different perspectives (De Gregorio 2021, p. 42). One of these perspectives is 'cooperative responsibility' (Helberger et al. 2018). This theory argues, contrary to the 'one actor' approach, that unilateral governance of platforms for the realization of public values doesn't work. Instead, it should be the result of a dynamic interaction and allocation of responsibilities between platforms and users, supported by a legal and policy framework created by state institutions (government). These responsibilities should be both backward-looking (retrospective, such as who is responsible for occurred data breaches or bad security) and forward-looking (prevention, like creating awareness and data literacy, privacy by design and critically assessing cookie notices by users). How these responsibilities are distributed depends on specific contexts of power, expertise, capacities, resources, values, and interests of stakeholders. Here, cooperative responsibility follows Fahlquist's argument (2009, pp. 115–116) that "power and capacity entails responsibility": users don't have the same power as companies and the government, and users are not always able to take responsibility, unless they collaborate (which is not always the case). For this reason platforms and government have strong forward-looking responsibilities to empower users so they can take their responsibilities (Pierson 2012). For example, platforms should encourage users to meaningfully assess the consequences of cookie consent, and restrain from designing dark patterns, while the government should stimulate and facilitate cooperation between stakeholders.

To operationalize cooperative responsibility, Helberger et al. (2018) developed a framework including four key steps: 1) the context-specific, collective identification of public values; 2) the distribution and acceptance of responsibility between actors in a value network; 3) a multi-stakeholder process of public deliberation to advance the identified public values; and 3) the translation of public deliberation into regulations, codes of conduct, terms of use, and the design of technologies. Our research question is therefore: How is cooperative responsibility operationalized in an 'on the ground' setting in public education, where data controllers and data processors actually have to enter into data processing agreements with each other?

1.5   The Case of the Privacy Covenant

As discussed, drafts of data processing agreements can be drawn up by the data controller or the data processor. 'Models' of data processing agreements are often provided to groups of data controllers and data processors by organizations that represent their (public) sectors and stakeholders. These models can be used by data controllers as a draft for negotiating and stipulating detailed instructions with data processors. When we look at the construction of these models in the public sector in the Netherlands, we see different forms, covering at least the main requirements as expressed in Article 28 of the GDPR. Some can be used and be adjusted freely, others are stricter. Some standards are mandatory for data controllers like the one of the Dutch Association of Municipalities (VNG 2021), some are voluntary such as the standard made for Housing Associations in the Netherlands (Aedes 2018). The standard data processing agreement of the Dutch Healthcare organizations (Brancheorganisaties Zorg 2017) is required by some data controllers in the sector. In public education in the Netherlands, SURF, a cooperative association of Dutch educational and research institutions provides the 'SURF Framework of Legal Standards for Cloud Services' including a "Model Processing Agreements" and accompanying documents like a Safety Measures Guide (SURF 2019). Sector organizations that represent schools in primary (PO-Raad) and secondary education (VO-raad), as well as vocational secondary education (MBO-Raad), and three trade organizations that represent publishers that develop and supply learning material, tests and educational services to public education ('GEU')[8], distributors of textbooks for public education ('KBb-Educatief')[9] and digital education suppliers (VDOD)[10] also drafted a model data processing agreement. This model is part of the broader 'Convenant Digitale Onderwijsmiddelen en Privacy', or in short 'Privacy Covenant'[11] (PO-Raad et al. 2018). A covenant is a form of an umbrella agreement in which all stakeholders agree upon the protection of personal data of school children in general. To answer the research question, we have conducted a case study into the construction, meaning and relevance of the Privacy Covenant. The objective of our research is to empower data controllers in data protection by giving insights into how this can be done through an example of cooperative responsibility. Where we speak of the Privacy Covenant, this includes the accompanying model data processing agreement.

---

[8] https://geu.nl/english/.
[9] https://www.boekbond.nl/kbb-educatief/.
[10] https://vdod.nl/.
[11] https://www.privacyconvenant.nl/.

2 Methodology

This research reports on a qualitative case-study (Yin 2014) conducted in public education in the Netherlands in which we analyze the construction of the 'Privacy Covenant' through the lens of the framework for cooperative responsibility. We analyzed both the process of constructing the Privacy Covenant, as well as its issues, pros and cons while used in practice. We conducted 6 semi-structured interviews with stakeholders (representatives from schools, from a privacy consultancy, from SURF and SIVON - a cooperative procurement organization for education -, and from one of the trade organizations) that have participated in the construction of the Privacy Covenant, and 8 semi-structured interviews with school employees (university of applied sciences, secondary- and secondary vocational education) for whom drawing-up and checking data processing agreements before they are signed by the schoolboard is part of their job. We choose this 'on the ground' setting to investigate how stakeholders actually manage agreements between them and what motivates them (Bamberger and Mulligan 2018). We selected the interviewees based on purposeful sampling, and on the following background criteria: business, legal and ICT, to guarantee a variety of insights from different perspectives (Table 1).

Table 1. Selection of interviewees and backgrounds

#	Interviewee from	Background
i1	Universities	ICT
i2	Universities	Legal
i3	SURF	Business/ICT
i4	Universities	ICT
i5	Secondary education	ICT
i6	Secondary education	ICT
i7	Secondary education	Business
i8	Secondary vocational education	ICT
i9	Secondary vocational education	Legal
i10	Secondary education	Business
i11	EDU-K	Legal
i12	SIVON	Legal
i13	Privacy consultancy	Business
i14	Trade organization	Legal

Interviews were transcribed with a combination of the transcription functionality in MS Word as well as through the qualitative research software MAXQDA, which has also been used to analyze the results.

3 Results

3.1 Defining Public Values for Public Education

The construction of the 'Privacy Covenant' started in 2013 when the Dutch Government initiated the 'Breakthru projects ICT', aimed at stimulating ICT innovation and its potential for economic growth, as well as tackling societal challenges. One of the projects was the 'Breakthru project Education & ICT', a partnership between the Dutch government and the public education sector. The main (societal) goal of the project was stimulating personalized learning so that justice is done to the diversity in learning capacity and needs of children, and to optimally support them in developing their talent. This goal, then, supports the Dutch position in a globalizing economy and economic growth. The importance of privacy as a public value has been acknowledged as a precondition for realizing the potential of personalized learning already from the start of the project, when, initiated by the government, stakeholders from both schools as well as companies started talks about data protection.

3.2 Allocating Responsibility in Data Protection

The different stakeholders (companies, users, and state institutions) have taken a diversity of responsibilities.

Companies
We focus on national and international EdTech companies whose products and services are being used in Dutch public education. Our research shows that there are huge differences between companies that affect the power imbalance between schools and companies. Indicators that we used to categorize companies are: the ability of schools to impose detailed instructions and to get sufficient guarantees by the data processor; who drafts the data processing agreements; represented by trade organization or not; and usage of the model data processing agreement (Table 2). The categories are: 1) the 'Chain Partners': a diverse, often powerful group of Dutch companies like Topicus, Iddink, ThiemeMeulenhoff and VanDijk that are to a great extent represented by the three private trade organizations GEU, KBb-Educatief and VDOD and/or have huge market shares with their software products; 2) Big Tech (which often refers to US companies Alphabet/Google, Microsoft, Apple, Meta Platforms/Facebook and Amazon, and in public education in the Netherlands predominantly to Alphabet/Google and Microsoft): a very powerful group of companies that due to their technical expertise, financial means and infrastructural power plays a very dominant role in public education in the Netherlands; 3) all other, (assumed) less powerful, companies (mostly referred to as 'small' companies or examples of start-ups); and 4) 'independent apps' (those companies that have entered into contract with children/students themselves like TikTok and Duolingo). See Table 2 for an overview and summary of the categories and the power distribution between different groups of companies and schools, where it should be emphasized that each company is unique, and that this categorization has only been made for the clarity of our analysis.

In the first category (Chain Partners), a group of publishers (e.g. Noordhoff and ThiemeMeulenhoff) and distributors (e.g. VanDijk and Iddink) has a long powerful history in public education as book suppliers that have expanded their portfolio with digital learning material. Digital education suppliers such as Heuitink.ict and CITO are also part of the group of Chain Partners. The trade organizations GEU, KBb-Educatief and VDOD, of which the Chain Partners are members, are at the center of how digital education is being shaped: they participated in the construction of the Privacy Covenant and are also members of EDU-K, a platform in which the private trade organizations and public sector organizations talk about, and work together for a better functioning, educative ICT chain, and create the conditions for the successful application of ICT in learning through e.g. privacy, security, standardization and accessibility of digital learning material (EDU-K 2021). When looking at the allocation of responsibilities between the Chain Partners and schools, the main issue in the early discussions of the Privacy Covenant was the interpretation of 'data controllership'. The publishers, that amongst others also process personal data and provide learning analytics based on this data, maintained the view that they were data controller, a position that would enable them to commercially exploit personal data. On the contrary, the standpoint of the schools was that not the publishers, but they themselves were data controllers and that the publishers were data processors and thus processed the data under responsibility of the schools. This dispute was only settled after a lot of media attention and critique around the processing of personal data of minors by publishers[12] as well as the involvement of the Dutch Data Protection Authority through the 'Snappet'-case[13]. From that moment, schools are in principle appointed as data controllers and all companies that process data on behalf of schools as data processors. Only if companies have a direct relationship with children or their parents, and not via the school, they are the data controller themselves. This is for example the case of many apps like TikTok, YouTube or Duolingo that are being used by teachers and students, often out of sight of the schools (category 4 in Table 2). The settlement of this discussion might look like just a legal interpretation of the GDPR, but it was, in line with the second step of cooperative responsibility (the distribution and acceptance of responsibility between actors in a value network), an important milestone for 'data protection-maturing' schools in the discussions around the growing and unregulated use of personal data by a plethora of companies in Dutch public education. Apart from the discussion about data controllership, the Chain Partners take responsibility by helping schools to fulfill their GDPR requirements by providing assistance in filling in the data processing agreement. This form of forward-looking responsibility is very useful as these companies have more expertise and are more familiar with the data processing and the organizational and technical measures they apply. It also stimulates the actual and correct use of the model. This correct use is, however, still not a given: the model data processing agreement is not always used and if it is, it is sometimes changed unilaterally (e.g. liability) by companies. Besides taking these responsibilities, the DPIA into some of the Chain Partners has shown that they should take even more forward-looking responsibility by: empowering schools regarding access control; privacy by design/default (e.g. deleting certain fields); security measures (e.g. multifactor authentication); handling data retention periods; and data transfers to third parties.

---

[12] https://www.rtlnieuws.nl/nieuws/bundel/1497271/privacyschending-basisscholen.

[13] https://autoriteitpersoonsgegevens.nl/nl/nieuws/cbp-constateert-overtreding-wet-bij-snappet.

The second to the fourth category of companies are not represented by one of the private trade organizations[14]. Companies in the second category, 'Big Tech' companies like Google and Microsoft, are also not a participant in the Privacy Covenant. Big Tech mostly dictates the rules of the game as expressed in their own data processing agreements where they take a 'take it or leave it' approach. Schools (must) have a lot of confidence in the expertise of Big Tech and rely to a great extent on the (discourse related to) data protection efforts made by these companies. However, Big Tech companies pose many risks for data protection as is again and extensively shown through the aforementioned DPIA's conducted on Google Workspace for Education and on Microsoft Office tools. In the 'power struggle' between schools and Big Tech, both SURF and SIVON are well equipped to help, as they have shown in the agreement with Alphabet/Google on the mitigation of 11 high risks for data protection in Google Workspace for Education[15]. Or as one interviewee said: "the discussion should not be only about Big Tech, but with Big Tech" (i3, SURF, business/ICT), which can result in improvements in data protection.

The third category of companies consist of all other, (assumed) less powerful, platform companies. Examples are start-ups, 'small' companies, and photographers. Schools are worried about their ability to sufficiently protect personal data and say that questions about data controllership are possible again.

The fourth and last category consists of 'independent apps'. These companies have not entered into contract with the school, but with minors, their parents or teachers themselves. Examples of independent apps are TikTok, Kahoot, Duolingo and YouTube. The apps are frequently used by teachers and minors for learning purposes: "(…) and then they [children during classes] are going to dance and shoot short videos etc...." (i5, secondary education/ICT). However, the use of these apps could clash with the responsibility of schools for data protection. Of course, as data controllers, the companies behind the apps have their own responsibilities towards data protection, but they are no stakeholder in the Privacy Covenant and have not entered into a data processing agreement with the school at all. Independent apps come and go and as such continuously reconfigure and complicate discussions around data protection by these apps.

Users

The second group of stakeholders are the users (schools, minors/parents, and representatives of these groups). In cooperative responsibility, it is this group that has to be empowered by companies and the government (as respectively has been and will be discussed in the former and next paragraph).

In schools, we discern people working at schools (e.g. schoolboard, teachers and other employees). There are differences between schools in their ability to take responsibility in data protection, mainly because of differences in size, expertise, and financial means available. Not all schools (are able to) take their responsibility as a data controller. Data processing agreements provided by platform companies are for example sometimes approved and signed by schools based on gut feelings. Or as one interviewee said: "it's just signing or also looking at the content […] it depends on the school or who the

---

[14] However, Microsoft is member of trade organization VDOD and participated in some of the earliest meetings of the construction of the Privacy Covenant.

[15] https://www.sivon.nl/actueel/akkoord-onderwijs-met-google-over-privacyrisicos/.

Table 2. Distribution of power between different groups of platform companies and the school

	Category	Detailed instructions/guarantees	Usage model DPA
Data processors represented by trade organizations	1 - Chain partners (powerful) like Topicus, Iddink, VanDijk and ThiemeMeulenhoff	Detailed instructions dependent on data processor; sufficiency of guarantees given by companies are unchecked by schools	Chain Partners participate in the privacy covenant, have to use of the model, but do often derogate from it; data processing agreement provided by the company; data processing agreement is not periodically checked and updated
Data processors (mostly) not represented by trade organizations	2 - Big Tech (powerful) in Dutch education predominantly Alphabet/Google and Microsoft	Detailed instructions dependent on data processor; schools have confidence in sufficiency of guarantees given by companies	No subscriber privacy covenant; data processing agreement provided and updated by the company (take it or leave it approach); data processing agreement is not periodically checked and updated
	3 - All other platform companies (less powerful data processors) like (some) start-ups and 'small' companies	Detailed instructions dependent on data controller or data processor; schools have worries about the sufficiency of guarantees given by companies	Companies can be a participant in, or a supporter of the privacy covenant; they mainly use the model as provided schools; schools more critical towards small parties; data processing agreement is not periodically checked and updated
	4 - Independent apps (can be powerful) like TikTok and Duolingo	N.A.	N.A.

schoolboard is (i14, trade organization, legal)". It looks like that the bigger the school, the more 'professional' the school can operate, and the more resources and expertise are available for data protection. In this regard, MBO-schools are better positioned to tackle these problems and take the responsibility needed, as these schools are much more consolidated and have more means for data protection: "they [MBO-schools] are really professional organizations, they do really look at the data processing agreement (i14, trade organization, legal)". Further research must show to what extent this claim can be substantiated. Interesting is how the education sector is empowering itself via numerous ad hoc and (more) formal collaborations through which schools are being represented in data protection. Examples of these collaborations are: Kennisnet (the ICT support organization for primary, secondary and vocational secondary education which is subsidized by the government); SURF, SIVON, EDU-K, and SAMBO-ICT (an IT network in MBO), which are all cooperatively organized; the 'Information Security and Privacy Networks' in which data protection and security experts from schools participate, facilitated by Kennisnet; 'SCIPR' (a community for privacy and security in higher education that is facilitated by SURF); and the sector organizations PO-Raad, VO-raad, and MBO-Raad that represent schools in the construction of the Privacy Covenant.

The second group of users are minors/parents. This group depends to a great extent on the data protection efforts made by schools and the aforementioned collaborations. 'Ouders & Onderwijs' is an organization for parents that was consulted during the early discussions around the Privacy Covenant but did not participate because they trusted the parties in constructing an adequate covenant. In the group of parents, we see an emerging tendency of democratic rationalization (Feenberg 1999), with parents that increasingly criticize data protection of schools and in that way contribute to its improvement: "We more and more get critical questions of parents because they are increasingly aware of GDPR, with which they have to deal with in their work as well. Schools that don't mature in this and don't involve parents, will face critical parents (i12, SIVON, legal)".

Government

The government, the third and last group of stakeholders involved, includes the Ministries of Education, Culture and Science (OCW)[16] and Economic Affairs (EZ)[17], Kennisnet[18] and the Dutch Data Protection Authority[19]. The government takes its responsibility by for example implementing data protection law. It also supports schools directly through facilitating and stimulating the Privacy Covenant and data protection in general via Kennisnet that is publicly funded by the government. The government also cooperates with the education sector in conducting DPIAs like the one on Microsoft products, and through the publicly funded Rathenau Institute[20] which cooperates for example with the education sector in the construction of the 'value framework'.

3.3   Public Deliberation and the Translation of Data Protection into an Agreement: The Privacy Covenant in Practice

The construction of a 'Privacy Covenant' started in 2013 and the first version was finally agreed upon in 2015. The Covenant, now in its' version 3.0, is formally positioned under the responsibility of EDU-K. The "Ketenadviesgroep Privacy", part of EDU-K, maintains and develops the Privacy Covenant, and also handles complaints from stakeholders. All schools and all companies that are represented by one of the sector/trade organizations have to become a participant of the Privacy Covenant. But where schools are most of the time automatically participant of the Privacy Covenant, different rules

---

[16] https://www.rijksoverheid.nl/ministeries/ministerie-van-onderwijs-cultuur-en-wetenschap.

[17] https://www.rijksoverheid.nl/ministeries/ministerie-van-economische-zaken-en-klimaat.

[18] https://www.kennisnet.nl/.

[19] https://www.autoriteitpersoonsgegevens.nl/.

[20] https://www.rathenau.nl/en.

apply for companies that process data on behalf of schools. Companies can only sign up to the Privacy Covenant if they have a contract with one or more school(s), process personal data, and provide (digital) education systems and services. The latter provision is a source for much debate around the definition of '(digital) education systems and services' and the wish of many companies that process data, from photographers to printers, to participate in the Privacy Covenant. These companies en masse subscribed themselves because they saw it as a certificate of 'good practices in data processing'. However, the Privacy Covenant is tailored to suppliers of digital learning materials and as such the Privacy Covenant and its model data processing agreement have no added value for other companies. The solution is now that these companies can become a 'supporter' and can make use of another model data processing agreement. If the requirements for becoming a participant are met, companies can become participant of the Privacy Covenant by signing a letter of intent and thereby commit themselves to its rules. It should be emphasized that signing up to the Privacy Covenant as well as the use of the model is not mandatory *by law*, and schools can always decide to do otherwise. Even if stakeholders are signed up to the Privacy Covenant, they are not legally bound to obey its rules and use the model. However, signing up to the Privacy Covenant implies the mandatory and correct use of the model data processing agreement. In practice, this is not a given as for example sometimes the model is used, but adapted by one of the parties, and sometimes a data processing agreement is signed 'right by the X', without being reviewed, or eventually not signed at all. In other cases, different models are being used. To tackle this, trade organizations now check their members for the correct use of the model by assessing participants and to let them sign a declaration. Clearly, the process of actually drawing up data processing agreements in public education is far from straightforward and the stakeholders are still in the process of improving this process.

4 Discussion

The Privacy Covenant is an example of how the public education sector, (platform) companies and state institutions cooperatively shape data protection. Privacy is an important value in education, not least because it concerns the privacy of children and is a special category of data subjects in the GDPR, and the massive collection of personal data needed for personalized learning can seriously harm the future of young people as a child's data profile can be used for many purposes such as credit checks, assessments of insurance rates, and hiring processes. We have seen strong commitment to data protection of all stakeholders.

We found a distinction of categories of companies which influences the way responsibilities between schools and platforms are being distributed. The first category of companies, represented by trade organizations, is intensively involved in the construction of the Privacy Covenant and beyond (like in the example of EDU-K). This is not only beneficial regarding for example providing (legal) clarity and efficiency to their members, it also benefits their commercial and political interests as participating in the construction of the Privacy Covenant enables them to influence the rules of the game. According to Fahlquist (2009) this power comes with responsibilities, something which the representing trade organizations take in various forms. However, the Chain Partners only represent about 20% of the participants and supporters of the Privacy Covenant. For example, an important and dominant company in education in the Netherlands like Alphabet/Google, start-ups as well as children and parents have not actively been involved in the construction of the Privacy Covenant. From a cooperative responsibility perspective these stakeholders should also be involved. The second category of companies (Big Tech) in general has a great responsibility due to their omnipresence and power in education. They have the responsibility to be transparent and make their systems privacy by design. However they also have responsibilities towards many other platform companies that supply software to the education sector, as Big Tech companies are often the providers of the infrastructures (e.g. cloud-, analytics- and security facilities) on which many of these companies build their software (Poell 2018). Schools should take more forward-looking responsibility towards the third ('small' companies) and the fourth category (the broadly used 'independent apps' like TikTok and Duolingo that have no contract with the school) of companies, for example by determining data controllership in the relation with new companies, and by initiating, drawing up and following up data processing agreements. Schools can also restrict the use of apps that have not entered into contract with them, and/or conduct DPIA's on them.

Schools often lack the expertise and means to take full responsibility for data protection. Schools could empower themselves by cooperating with other schools regarding data protection (e.g. joint DPO, privacy officer, joint policy etc.), by facilitating more financial means, awareness and data literacy (e.g. of teachers) in schools, by cooperating with SURF and SIVON in taking more responsibility towards companies like TikTok and other Big Tech companies, and by seeking the view of children and parents. Regarding the latter, Article 35 of GDPR even "explicitly demands to 'where appropriate, [...] seek the views of data subjects or their representatives on the intended processing' in so-called Data Protection Impact Assessments (DPIA) (Breuer and Pierson 2020)". Finally, schools that lack expertise and means could also be empowered by the government, e.g. through the support of Kennisnet.

In our analysis we focused on three main types of stakeholders: platform companies, users, and state institutions. In further research we aim to broaden and refine the value network with additional stakeholders, as proposed by Helberger et al (2018, p. 12). The four categories of companies we identified (see Table 2) can thereby be the focus to further enrich our understanding. Next, we also found that deploying the high level four steps of the cooperative responsibility for our analysis was not always straightforward. Our future research aims at further operationalizing this framework, foremost based on comparative analyses of different case studies.

5   Conclusion

Processes of platformization increasingly impact the governance of public education. This manifests itself in the construction of data processing agreements in which the relationship between schools and (platform) companies that process data on behalf of schools, is formally settled according to Art. 28 (EU 2016). Through a qualitative analysis of the construction of the Privacy Covenant, an umbrella agreement in which both schools and companies agree upon the protection of personal data of school children in general, we investigated 'cooperative responsibility' as a participatory approach to platform governance in schools. The results show that the Privacy Covenant has functioned as a driving force for strengthening data protection and as a remedy for power imbalances between platforms and schools. Collaborations like the Privacy Covenant can be successful as now all stakeholders take more responsibility in protecting the privacy of children. The results also show that the public education sector organizes themselves very well for data protection, and in this regard extensively cooperates with both platform companies and state institutions on the ongoing improvement of data protection. In the collaboration with platform companies, schools should take into account an observed diversity in platforms (Chain Partners, Big Tech, all other platforms, and independent apps).

References

Aedes. Gegevensbescherming Verwerkt in Nieuw Model Inkoopvoorwaarden. Aedes (2018). https://www.aedes.nl/artikelen/bedrijfsvoering/inkoopsamenwerking/gegevensbescherming-verwerkt-in-nieuw-model-inkoopvoorwaarden.html

Angiolini, C., Ducato, R., Giannopoulou, A., Schneider, G.: Remote Teaching during the Emergency and Beyond: Four Open Privacy and Data Protection Issues of 'Platformised' Education (SSRN Scholarly Paper ID 3779238). Social Science Research Network (2020). https://papers.ssrn.com/abstract=3779238

Bamberger, K.A., Mulligan, D.K.: Privacy law – on the books and on the ground. In: van der Sloot, B., de Groot, A. (eds.) The Handbook of Privacy Studies, pp. 349–354. Amsterdam University Press, JSTOR (2018). https://doi.org/10.2307/j.ctvcmxpmp.19

Botta, J.: The Dark Side of the MOOC? The Rise of EdTech in Times of COVID-19: A Data Protection Challenge for Universities. Brussels Privacy Hub (2020)

Brancheorganisaties Zorg. Modelverwerkersovereenkomst voor de zorgsector. Brancheorganisaties Zorg (2017). https://www.brancheorganisatieszorg.nl/nieuws_list/modelverwerkersovereenkomst-voor-de-zorgsector/

Breuer, J., Pierson, J.: The right to the city and data protection for developing citizen centric digital cities. AoIR Select. Pap. Internet Res. (2020). https://doi.org/10.5210/spir.v2020i0.11178

De Gregorio, G.: The rise of digital constitutionalism in the European Union. Int. J. Constit. Law 19(1), 41–70 (2021). https://doi.org/10.1093/icon/moab001

Ducato, R., et al.: Emergency Remote Teaching: A Study of Copyright and Data Protection Policies of Popular Online Services (Part II), 4 June 2020. Kluwer Copyright Blog (2020). http://copyrightblog.kluweriplaw.com/2020/06/04/emergency-remote-teaching-a-study-of-copyright-and-data-protection-policies-of-popular-online-services-part-ii/

ECK-iD. Veilig digitaal leren: ECK iD. ECK (2021). https://www.eck-id.nl

EDU-K. Edu-K. Edu-K (2021). https://www.edu-k.nl

Energy, F.M.: GAIA-X - the European project kicks off the next phase (2020). https://www.bmwi.de/Redaktion/EN/Publikationen/gaia-x-the-european-project-kicks-of-the-next-phase.html

EU. Regulation (EU) 2016/679 of the European parliament and of the council on the protection of natural persons with regard to the processing of personal data and on the free movement of such data (2016). https://eur-lex.europa.eu/eli/reg/2016/679/oj

Fahlquist, J.N.: Moral responsibility for environmental problems—individual or institutional? J. Agric. Environ. Ethics 22(2), 109–124 (2009). https://doi.org/10.1007/s10806-008-9134-5

Feenberg, A.: Questioning Technology. Routledge, London (1999)

Funk, M.: The European Strategy on Data—Analysing GAIA-X's influence strategy in light of the EU Commission's digital strategy from a Multi-level Governance perspective (2021). http://lup.lub.lu.se/student-papers/record/9045107

Helberger, N., Pierson, J., Poell, T.: Governing online platforms: from contested to cooperative responsibility. Inf. Soc. **34**(1), 1–14 (2018). https://doi.org/10.1080/01972243.2017.1391913

HolonIQ. 2021 Global Learning Landscape (2020). https://globallearninglandscape.org/index.html

Kerssens, N., van Dijck, J.: The platformization of primary education in The Netherlands. Learn. Media Technol. (2021). https://doi.org/10.1080/17439884.2021.1876725

Ministerie van Algemene Zaken. Nederlandse Digitaliseringsstrategie 2021—Kamerstuk—Rijksoverheid.nl [Kamerstuk], 26 April 2021. Ministerie van Algemene Zaken (2021). https://www.rijksoverheid.nl/documenten/kamerstukken/2021/04/26/nederlandse-digitaliseringsstrategie-2021

Olbrechts, A.: Guidelines 07/2020 on the concepts of controller and processor in the GDPR [Text], 7 September 2020. European Data Protection Board - European Data Protection Board (2020). https://edpb.europa.eu/our-work-tools/public-consultations-art-704/2020/guidelines-072020-concepts-controller-and-processor_en

Pierson, J.: Online Privacy in Social Media: A Conceptual Exploration of Empowerment and Vulnerability (SSRN Scholarly Paper ID 2374376). Social Science Research Network (2012). https://papers.ssrn.com/abstract=2374376

Pinch, T.J., Bijker, W.E.: The social construction of facts and artefacts: or how the sociology of science and the sociology of technology might benefit each other. Soc. Stud. Sci. **14**(3), 399–441 (1984). https://doi.org/10.1177/030631284014003004

PO Raad et al.: Verwerkersovereenkomsten. Aanpak informatiebeveiliging en privacy in het onderwijs (2018). https://aanpakibp.kennisnet.nl/verwerkersovereenkomsten/

Poell, T.: Boekpresentatie: The Platform Society 4 December 2018 (2018). https://www.youtube.com/watch?v=w13dL2QNbzg

Poell, T., Nieborg, D., van Dijck, J.: Platformisation. Internet Policy Rev. **8**(4) (2019). https://policyreview.info/concepts/platformisation

Public Spaces. What is Public Spaces? PublicSpaces (2021). https://publicspaces.net/english-section/

SURF. SURF Framework of Legal Standards for (Cloud) Services I SURF.nl (2019). https://www.surf.nl/en/surf-framework-of-legal-standards-for-cloud-services

SURF. Terugblik seminarreeks publieke waarden—Deel II I SURF.nl (2021). https://www.surf.nl/surf-magazine/surf-magazine-in-gesprek-met-bestuurders-over-publieke-waarden/terugblik-0

van Dijck, J., Poell, T.: Understanding Social Media Logic (SSRN Scholarly Paper ID 2309065). Social Science Research Network (2013). https://papers.ssrn.com/abstract=2309065

van Dijck, J., Poell, T.: Higher Education in a Networked World: European Responses to U.S. MOOCs (SSRN Scholarly Paper ID 2645629). Social Science Research Network (2015). https://papers.ssrn.com/abstract=2645629

VNG. Handreiking Standaard Verwerkersovereenkomst Gemeenten (VWO). Informatiebeveiligingsdienst (2021). https://beheer.informatiebeveiligingsdienst.nl/product/handreiking-standaard-verwerkersovereenkomst-gemeenten/

Williamson, B.: Big Data in Education: The Digital Future of Learning, Policy and Practice. SAGE (2017)

Williamson, B.: Making markets through digital platforms: Pearson, edu-business, and the (e)valuation of higher education. Crit. Stud. Educ. (2020). https://doi.org/10.1080/17508487.2020.1737556

Yin, R.K.: Case study research: Design and methods (2014)

Observing Road Freight Traffic from Mobile Network Signalling Data While Respecting Privacy and Business Confidentiality

Rémy Scholler[1,2]([✉]), Oumaïma Alaoui-Ismaïli[1], Jean-François Couchot[2],
Eric Ballot[3], and Denis Renaud[1]

[1] Orange Labs, 92320 Châtillon, France
remy.scholler@orange.com
[2] Femto-ST Institute, DISC Department, UMR 6174 CNRS,
University of Bourgogne, 25000 Besançon, Franche-Comté, France
[3] Mines ParisTech, CGS—Centre de Gestion Scientifique,
75272 Paris Cedex 06, France

Abstract. Nowadays, there is no tool that provides a global, permanent and "real time" view of road freight transport flows. However, this type of mapping is already available for air and sea traffic and could be useful to transport companies, e.g., setting up logistics hubs in strategic locations, and to public authorities, e.g., quickly knowing the impact of regulations, the contribution to congestion, or the impact of emissions. This kind of tool could obviously make information about road freight traffic more accessible, and allow for the consolidation of flows at both the interurban and urban levels to help decarbonize freight transport and logistics. The main contribution of this paper aims to provide a design sketch of an observatory of road freight transport flows based on signalling data from mobile network, which is accurate enough for that type of study and which does not require any supplementary installation of application on mobile devices. This kind of observatory is therefore related to the concept of Physical Internet through its objectives. This observatory will have to ensure privacy and business confidentiality by respecting the constraints set by the General Data Protection Regulation (GDPR) and the ePrivacy directive, i.e., a short-term anonymization in the French case. Thus, the second contribution of this paper is a literature review on the methods that could be useful to solve these questions.

Keywords: Privacy · Anonymization · Business confidentiality · Mobile network data · Road freight transport

1 Introduction

Roads are currently the most common freight transport mode in France. Indeed, in 2020, the ton.kilometer share of road transport represented 89.1% of land

M. Friedewald et al. (Eds.): Privacy and Identity 2021, IFIP AICT 644, pp. 195–205, 2022.
https://doi.org/10.1007/978-3-030-99100-5_14

transport excluding pipelines, while rail transport represented 9.0% and inland waterway transport 1.9% [11]. However, there is less public data and global models for road freight transport compared to other sectors (air or maritime transport). This limits the action of public actors, potentially represents a limit for road freight transport actors and restricts academic research to a fragmented vision.

This work aims to provide a design sketch of a dynamic observatory of road freight transport in France. The goal of such an observatory is to obtain a near-real-time inventory of freight transport flows across the country and an end-to-end vision of these flows. This observatory will initially focus on interurban transport, and then on urban transport, as most urban deliveries are made by light commercial vehicles, which are harder to identify because they can be related to a wider variety of behaviours and uses (hence the less strict regulations for the latter). It is based on signalling data from Orange's mobile network collected by observation probes on a regular basis. The signalling data of a device, also called mobile trace, is a time-stamped sequence of events (usually calls, SMS, data connection, network re-selection) occurring on a network antenna whose position is known. It is basically trajectory micro-data as defined in [17], i.e., information about single individuals that describe their spatiotemporal trajectories. These trajectories are sequences of geographical positions of the monitored individuals over time except that here we do not have access to precise positions but to network cells positions, i.e., the positions of the network cells (defined by an antenna of the network and its coverage area) which the user connects to through time.

Signalling data have already proven their great potential in different fields [6], especially in the study of human mobility [28] and road traffic [7]. In particular, some works using signalling data have tried to classify vehicle types [20], to study congestion and traffic states [15,19] or even to estimate vehicle speeds [10]. However, these kind of studies are often very local, e.g., they focus on a highway segment or on one city center and to the best of our knowledge there is no work targeting a business sector and the vehicle uses related to this sector as we are trying to do with the road freight transport sector.

The observatory sketched here aims to improve the accessibility and quality of information on transport flows across all the country. In the long run, it could help to promote the best behaviours (reduction of empty trips, pooling, logistics networks interconnection) and thus increase the efficiency and sustainability of freight transport. These objectives match those of the Physical Internet concept [3], which is, in logistics, an open global logistics system founded on physical, digital, and operational interconnectivity, through encapsulation, interfaces and protocols, intended to replace current logistical models. The aim of the sketched observatory is not to model [25] or simulate freight transport on a national scale [12], but to observe it, by collecting a large amount of quality data and generate statistical indicators while respecting privacy and business confidentiality. This objective can be divided into two parts:

- Provide global statistics at the finest possible spatial-temporal granularity while respecting the anonymization constraints imposed by the GDPR, the ePrivacy directive and their respective versions in France, Spain and Belgium to ensure privacy and business confidentiality. This is the main objective and would constitute a dynamic real-time observatory of road freight transport flows nationwide.
- Provide more specific statistics with consent of the interested industrial actors. This would allow specific marketing analyses in comparison with the global data of the observatory (carbon footprint estimation, estimated market share, etc.) and would lead to partnership optimizations between economic actors.

The main objective of the observatory of freight transport flows is to show counting of trucks on various origin-destinations, zones of interest or road segments, augmented with various statistical indicators such as counts or density in a logistic zone or on a specific road, pollution estimations, or some points of interests. To achieve this goal an interesting way is to compute origin-destination matrices [8] for road freight traffic that ensure privacy, using probabilistic data structures for example [1]. In order to produce useful estimates for the transport sector, it is necessary to propose a methodology for classifying objects and their behaviours. We have to propose an algorithm that can both predict the class (e.g., truck, Light Commercial Vehicle) of a new object while assigning it to a group of objects of the same class with similar spatial-temporal behaviours [26]. This methodology would be based on supervised and unsupervised incremental clustering techniques [4].

Particular attention will be paid to compliance with the requirements of the European GDPR and the new ePrivacy directive [16]. Especially in France, attention will be paid to compliance with the "Loi Informatique et Libertés" and the "Code des Postes et Télécommunications Electroniques". In particular, all the algorithms must be applicable to a history of events whose retention period is limited by a legal constraint. The legal constraints due to the GDPR and more specifically by the ePrivacy directive in Europe could be different from one country to another but in France, mobile signalling events can be processed only if an irreversible short-term anonymization is carried out. The short-term anonymization terminology refers to a French legal constraint imposed by the "Commission Nationale de l'Informatique et des Libertés" (CNIL). In our case, we have a "short" time to do all the necessary treatments to go from raw signalling data to the publication of aggregate statistics that respects privacy and business confidentiality, and then delete raw data (which is personal). This "short" time is a result of a negotiation with the CNIL, and for works about human mobility that could be useful for cities, public organizations they usually give a time of 15 min. Moreover, in the case of signalling data, when users appears in the dataset we only have access to a "short" history of their personal data (usually around 15 min too). This short-term anonymization constraint does not exists in other European countries as Spain and Belgium, so when we will reach our goal in France it will be easier to adapt our work to other countries.

This rest of this paper is organized as follows. Section 2 describes some related work concerning privacy and business confidentiality in our case, Sect. 3 presents our methodology to solve the problem, and Sect. 4 draws conclusions and outline areas of future work.

2   State of the Art

Signalling data concerns all types of connected objects such as connected watches or industrial production equipment but we do not use signalling data from drivers' devices or transport management systems (TMS) data. In fact, we use in-vehicle IoT modems (2G/3G/4G) which are devices that receive wireless data from remote sensors and forward these data to a different communications format. However, using signalling data corresponding to road freight vehicles remains a privacy issue, even if this is not the data from the vehicle driver's phone. For example, if an attacker knows the location of a freight vehicle, he knows indirectly the location of its driver. The common practice of pseudonymization approach which consists of removing identifiers and replacing them with dummy identifiers is not sufficient. More precisely it has been shown that a small number of locations can be used to identify individuals with a high probability [14]. A difference can be made between two ideas of privacy protection: the protection of business confidentiality and the protection of personal information. To understand the problem of business confidentiality it is important to know that the trips and routes of freight vehicles are essential in the business model of freight companies. For example, well known homogeneity issues can occur if multiple trucks of the same company are counted on a road segment. As another example, we could consider a warehouse, and the freight flows flowing in. If an attacker deduces all the business partners of this warehouse thanks to the origins of these freight flows, there is a confidentiality issue. All the statistics published from signalling data have to be anonymized [13] and in France the methods used for creating the observatory of freight flows have to satisfy the short-term anonymization constraint defined in Sect. 1, be applied in real time and be adapted to streaming data.

We are close to a situation of privacy-preserving data publishing (PPDP) of trajectory micro-data databases which recommends that databases should be transformed prior to publication in potentially hostile environments, so as to grant that the published data remains useful while individual privacy is preserved [17]. Therefore literature in this domain is a good start for our work. Fiore et al. in [17] explains that in the case of trajectory micro-data publishing, databases of millions of records are mined offline, and the challenge is ensuring that their circulation does not pose a threat to user privacy, but retains data utility. In the case of Location Based Systems (LBS), single (geo-referenced and time-stamped) queries generated by mobile devices must be processed in real-time, and the objective is location privacy, i.e., ensuring that such a process preserves users privacy by preventing the service provider from locating users. This difference leads to very diverse attacker models and anonymization techniques for the two scenarios. Indeed, Xiao and Xiong [29] and Bindschaedler et al. [5] have shown that individual spatiotemporal points anonymized via solutions for location privacy are still vulnerable to attacks when their time-ordered sequence is considered, i.e., when they are treated as a spatiotemporal trajectory. Fiore et al. propose in [17] the first survey that provides a literature overview that comprehensively addresses trajectory micro-data privacy. They explored the attacks against trajectory micro-data that allow re-identifying users, the anonymization of trajectory micro-data, i.e., the counter measures against privacy threats, and discuss open issues and research opportunities.

However, we may not try to publish anonymized trajectory databases but databases containing origin-destinations, statistical indicators and aggregate statistics about the original trajectory micro-data databases instead. Moreover, our techniques must satisfy a short-term anonymization constraint and will have to be applied in real-time to streaming data. Therefore, the main problem we are trying to address is the privacy preserving data publication of aggregate statistics from trajectory micro-data taking in account spatial and temporal dimensions, adapted to the case of streaming data (in real time) and respecting short-term anonymization constraints. We could add to this problem statement that the trajectories should be constrained by a road network.

To the best of our knowledge, the two main methods that could be adapted to achieve our goal are differentially private synthetic trajectory datasets preserving the statistics of originals datasets [18,23] and differential privacy methods adapted to streaming data [9,21,27]. In what follows, we develop some ideas used to generate some differentially private trajectory datasets.

As explained in [17], differential privacy can be ensured by a different process where some representation of the original trajectory micro-data is randomized so as to meet differential privacy constraints, and synthetic trajectories are derived from such representations. Then, databases of synthetic trajectories can be distributed with strong privacy guarantees. The two main approaches here are representing trajectory datasets as trees [18] or as probability distributions [23].

The first idea is to model the original database as a prefix tree, i.e., a hierarchical structure where trajectories are grouped based on matching location subsequences whose length grows with tree depth. A privacy-preserving version of the prefix tree is then obtained by considering multiple levels of spatial generalization, and adding noise to the nodes. Following an iterative process nodes are created for all locations at the highest level of generalization, as children of each leaf from the previous iteration. Then, Laplacian noise is added to the count of trajectories associated to each generalized node at the current prefix tree layer. Finally, nodes with a noisy count below a tunable threshold are not expanded further, while nodes with noisy counts above threshold generate children nodes for all locations at the following level of generalization. The process is repeated from the second step above until a user-defined tree height is reached with Laplacian noises set so that the total privacy budget is equally divided across all tree and nodes. The tree is then pruned so that only nodes at the lowest level of generalization are preserved. The noisy counts associated to such nodes are made consistent across levels, ensuring that the count of each node is not less than the sum of counts of its children nodes. Finally, the synthetic trajectories are generated by visiting the resulting prefix tree. He et al. in [18] demonstrate that the approaches above work well with coarse trajectories defined on small location domains, but fail to scale to realistic database with large geographical span. Therefore, the authors propose to generate multiple prefix trees, each referring to a different spatial resolution. Each transition in a trajectory contributes to one specific tree, based on the travelled distance (i.e., low-resolution trees for long distances, and high-resolution trees for short distances). This results in multiple trees with a very small branching factor each, and in a significant reduction of the overall number of counts maintained. Then, the usual procedure of adding Laplace noise to counts, pruning the prefix trees, and extracting the synthetic trajectories is followed. In this last step, the authors also adopt an original sampling technique that allow preserving the correct directionality in the output trajectories. The proposed solution, named Differentially Private Trajectories (DPT), is evaluated with both real and synthetic datasets that are queried for distributions of diameters and trips, and for frequent sequential patterns.

The second idea is to create a differentially private synthetic trajectory generator that does not rely on a tree model of the original trajectory micro-data. Instead, DP-WHERE [23] performs the following steps: derives a number of distributions that describe different statistical features of the movements in the original trajectory database, such as the spatial distribution of home and work locations, or the number of spatiotemporal points in a trajectory; adds Laplacian noise to such distributions; extracts realizations from the noisy distributions to generate synthetic trajectories. The synthetic movement data produced by DP-WHERE is proven to preserve population density distributions over time, as well as daily ranges of commutes in the reference area.

Orange already uses methods that satisfy a short term anonymization constraint to calculate aggregate statistics of mobility from signalling data. These methods are mainly based on structures of probabilistic sets and k-anonymity [24], and satisfy a short term anonymization constraint at every steps of the process (e.g., during the creation of probabilistic sets that respects k-anonymity and when publishing aggregated statistics). The limits of these methods could be usual attacks to break k-anonymity by using extended knowledge or by combining some of the probabilistic sets created. However, the data used to create statistics is often not precise spatial-temporal location but is blurred in time (due to short-term anonymization constraint) and space (a certain area size) so even if an attack is successful, the utility of this data that leaks seems not very high. Moreover, raw data and created data are secure at every step of the process. It could be very useful to dig into these methods and try to create probabilistic sets such as in [1,2] in order to calculate aggregate statistics with union, intersection of these sets, or tests of membership in them.

3   Methodology

In the following section, we sketch an approach to create an observatory of road freight transport flows which respects privacy and business confidentiality. First, we describe globally the areas of interest, then we present the different phases and technical steps of our project work, and finally we discuss how we intent to solve the short-term anonymization problem in our case.

3.1   Areas of Interest

We study in parallel the different areas listed below.

The quality of the raw material, i.e., the IoT modems traces: spatio-temporal uncertainties, sample characteristics, perspectives of evolution, pros and cons compared to other data sources.

The legal framework of signalling data processing and its evolution: GDPR, ePrivacy directive, and their respective versions in France, then in Spain and Belgium. The differences in practice depending on the context, research or operational. The feasibility of real-time processing for short-term anonymization.

Modelling steps needed to increase the data source's utility: increase in spatiotemporal accuracy, dynamic correction of sample biases, data science compatible with "On Line" and "Off Line" processing.

Software processing tools: finding a suitable software stack (big data and data science), defining target infrastructures to provide the service.

Business Exploration: be able to make demos, prototypes to target B2B, B2G or B2R, carry out discussions on various business plans.

3.2   Phases and Technical Steps

There are two main phases of technical work which are presented below.

Research Phase: This is the design of the processing of pseudonymised data awaiting for anonymization. The aim is to define the main operations that will serve as specifications for the transition to operations. The use of pseudonymised data is allowed only in the research phase, because this method of privacy protection is weaker than the anonymization process (irreversible by definition).

Operational Transition Phase: This is the design of the real-time data processing for short-time anonymization. Here, we seek to satisfy the specifications of the first phase under a constraint of short time anonymization.

Our methodology for estimate and visualise freight traffic is summarised in Fig. 1. Then, we detail the six different steps.

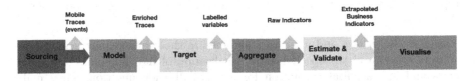

Fig. 1. Technical steps of the sketched approach.

Source: Design of a dataset capture and processing architecture. Adapt this architecture for the operational transition phase. The output of this part is a dataset containing IoT modems traces (events).

Model: Modelling on longitudinal data with the aim of reducing spatial uncertainties, estimating mobility conditions, and creating more reliable trajectories from mobile network data. The work carried out in this step uses simulations of signal propagation and probabilistic mapping of devices' pick-up by network antennas. GPS tracks from fleets of consenting partners can be used as validation data. We then obtain enriched IoT modems traces (more precise position, more precise speed, in particular). This part has been the main area of interest for this first year of work, and two patents have been filed. However, we do not detail this work here because it is not related to privacy and business confidentiality.

Target: Creation of trips, mapping, prediction of vehicles types and identification of behaviours and uses. In this part, we can use supervised incremental clustering methods. We thus obtain groups of traces associated with an origin, a destination, places and times of breaks, a use, a type of vehicle, and possibly other behavioural variables. We can obtain business variables (which will characterise uses) and useful variables for the estimation of indicators by group (for example, travel speed or intensity of signalling on the network). We could also use GPS data from willing partners to validate this part (trip creation, spatiotemporal mapping). This part has been the second mail area of interest for this first year of work, and we are now able to detect some typical behaviors for vehicles and we will link these behaviors with vehicle types (heavy trucks, light freight vehicles) thanks to labelled data from partners.

Aggregate: Use clustering methods to generate new groups of traces that satisfy anonymization constraints. Compute indicators corresponding to the different aggregates, maximise the aggregates' meaning, and construct specific aggregates for subsequent correction. This aggregation allows us to obtain raw indicators, i.e., statistics representative of certain types of vehicles and uses.

Estimate and Validate: Creation of reference spatio-temporal data, development of a model for the transition from the sample studied to the total population, errors estimations and validation, feedback on the parameters of the "Aggregate" and "Target" parts. The additional data useful for the transition from the sample studied to the total population, for the validation and for the errors estimation would be, for example, ticketing data or usual traffic measurement data [22] as magnetic counting loops. Through statistical indicators and a database of aggregates associated with origins, destinations, locations and break times, uses, type of vehicles, etc., we obtain an estimate of the overall freight traffic across the country.

Visualise: Show data and indicators obtained in the previous part, carry out a state of the art on the specific data visualisation of moving connected object flows and find a suitable solution for our visualisation question. Then make adjustments in contact with potential users (e.g. economic actors, cities, freight transport companies) in order to make sure that the tool developed is useful for them. Finally, find additional data sources that may be useful for the analysis and the calculation of new indicators such as pollution or congestion.

3.3 Short-Term Anonymization Considerations

The database obtained at the end of the "Estimate and Validate" part and the method to create it must respect privacy and business confidentiality. It is possible to integrate anonymization constraints into several steps, e.g., adding noise in an origin-destination matrix (with uses and other behavioural variables) created in the "Target" part, adding noise in the clusters of uses in the "Target" or "Aggregate" part, adding noise within each aggregate in the "Aggregate" part, adding or leaving noise in the enriched IoT modems traces resulting from the "Model" part. Privacy constraints are easier to apply in the "Aggregate" part. We could use aggregates based on k-anonymity, methods based on differential privacy or any other method based on those cited in Sect. 2 such as [18,23] because our datasets are quite similar to the ones used in these approaches. The main adaptations to these two methods could be to take in account the temporal dimension in trees or distribution approaches and to constrain all trajectories in a road network. However, because of the research experience at Orange in probabilistic sets that respect privacy, we will probably concentrate on approaches mixing probabilistic sets and differential privacy, as in [1,2]. The kind of attacker we will consider is one with nearly unlimited computing power, and we want to prevent reconstruction attacks, i.e., if an attacker have some side knowledge (for example he knows that a user is in the raw data and have some of his locations), can he reconstruct his trajectory with the aggregate statistics that we publish? Concerning the evaluation of our approach, the private counts of trucks should be "not too far" from the real counts, at every time slot (temporal granularity still to be defined), and we have multiple choices of metrics to measure a distance between those counts and define an appropriate threshold. Unfortunately, we cannot make clear the time we can retain data legally because it depends on the CNIL decision. However, we can consider the time granted usually for this type of applications, which is around 15 min.

4 Summary and Future Research

In this paper we proposed an approach to create an observatory of road freight transport flows based on traces on the cellular network of IoT modems in vehicles. This observatory has to respect anonymization constraints to protect privacy and business confidentiality. The work is divided in two parts: a research phase and an operational phase. We proposed a methodology in six steps (Source, Model, Target, Aggregate, Estimate and Validate, Visualise) to create such an observatory during the research phase. For the moment, we have made good progress in speed, direction and mobility state estimations from signalling data (in the "Model" step), in identifying typical behaviours of vehicles in our datasets (in the "Target" step), in identifying and studying various data sources that could be useful to correct and validate our estimations on freight traffic (in the "Estimate and Validate" step), in visualisation of moving objects' flows (not associated to freight transport for the moment) and in the calculation of some basic indicators about these flows.

This work will continue during at least two years at Orange Labs and in the future we will continue to explore in depth the "Target", "Aggregate" which are essential to obtain a functional observatory. It is also essential to implement an approach that will be compliant with the anonymization constraints we need to respect in order to ensure privacy and business confidentiality. Anonymization is one of the main focuses of our work for the next two years and we already participated in the DARC hackathon at the workshop APVP 2021, where we had to protect and attack trajectory datasets, in order to improve our knowledge in this domain.

Acknowledgements. This work is carried out at Orange Labs, in collaboration with the Internet Physics Chair (Mines ParisTech - PSL University). This work is supported by the Île de France region as part of the "Territorial Support" call for interest (launched in 2020) which aimed at promoting collaboration between local authorities and logistics professionals, to develop a virtuous logistics system that will enhance the attractiveness of the Ile-de-France region and reduce environmental pollution. The project was selected in the "new methods for collecting and processing logistics data for companies and local authorities" category. This work is (partially) supported by the EIPHI Graduate School (contract ANR-17-EURE-0002).

References

1. Alaggan, M., Gambs, S., Matwin, S., Tuhin, M.: Sanitization of call detail records via differentially-private bloom filters. In: Samarati, P. (ed.) DBSec 2015. LNCS, vol. 9149, pp. 223–230. Springer, Cham (2015). https://doi.org/10.1007/978-3-319-20810-7_15. Part 5: Privacy and Trust
2. Alaggan, M., Gambs, S., Kermarrec, A.-M.: BLIP: non-interactive differentially-private similarity computation on bloom filters. In: Richa, A.W., Scheideler, C. (eds.) SSS 2012. LNCS, vol. 7596, pp. 202–216. Springer, Heidelberg (2012). https://doi.org/10.1007/978-3-642-33536-5_20
3. Ballot, E., Montreuil, B., Meller, R.: The physical internet, September 2014
4. Bhattacharjee, P., Mitra, P.: BISDBx: towards batch-incremental clustering for dynamic datasets using SNN-DBSCAN. Pattern Anal. Appl. **23**(2), 975–1009 (2020)
5. Bindschaedler, V., Shokri, R.: Synthesizing plausible privacy-preserving location traces. In: 2016 IEEE Symposium on Security and Privacy (SP), pp. 546–563 (2016)
6. Blondel, V.D., Decuyper, A., Krings, G.: A survey of results on mobile phone datasets analysis. EPJ Data Sci. **4**(1), 1–55 (2015). https://doi.org/10.1140/epjds/s13688-015-0046-0
7. Caceres, N., Wideberg, J., Benitez, F.: Review of traffic data estimations extracted from cellular networks. Intell. Transp. Syst. IET **2**, 179–192 (2008)
8. Calabrese, F., Di Lorenzo, G., Liu, L., Ratti, C.: Estimating origin-destination flows using mobile phone location data. IEEE Pervasive Comput. **10**(4), 36–44 (2011)

9. Cao, Y., Yoshikawa, M.: Differentially private real-time data release over infinite trajectory streams. **2**, 68–73 (2015)
10. Chen, C.-H.: A cell probe-based method for vehicle speed estimation. IEICE Trans. Fundam. Electron. Commun. Comput. Sci. **E103.A**, 265–267 (2020)
11. DataLab. Chiffres clés du transport (2020)
12. de Jong, G., et al.: The issues in modelling freight transport at the national level. Case Stud. Transp. Policy **4**, 13–21 (2015)
13. de Montjoye, Y.-A., et al.: On the privacy-conscientious use of mobile phone data. Sci. Data **5**, 180286 (2018)
14. de Montjoye, Y.-A., Hidalgo, C., Verleysen, M., Blondel, V.: Unique in the crowd: the privacy bounds of human mobility. Sci. Rep. **3**, 1376 (2013)
15. Derrmann, T., Frank, R., Viti, F., Engel, T.: Estimating urban road traffic states using mobile network signaling data, pp. 1–7 (2017)
16. Council EU. Proposal for a regulation of the European parliament and of the council concerning the respect for private life and the protection of personal data in electronic communications and repealing Directive 2002/58/EC (Regulation on Privacy and Electronic Communications) (2021)
17. Fiore, M., et al.: Privacy in trajectory micro-data publishing: a survey, August 2020
18. He, X., Cormode, G., Machanavajjhala, A., Procopiuc, C.M., Srivastava, D.: DPT: differentially private trajectory synthesis using hierarchical reference systems. Proc. VLDB Endow. **8**(11), 1154–1165 (2015)
19. Janecek, A., Valerio, D., Hummel, K.A., Ricciato, F., Hlavacs, H.: The cellular network as a sensor: from mobile phone data to real-time road traffic monitoring. IEEE Trans. Intell. Transp. Syst. **16**(5), 2551–2572 (2015)
20. Ji, Q., Jin, B., Cui, Y., Zhang, F.: Using mobile signaling data to classify vehicles on highways in real time, pp. 174–179 (2017)
21. Kellaris, G., Papadopoulos, S., Xiao, X., Papadias, D.: Differentially private event sequences over infinite streams. Proc. VLDB Endow. **7**(12), 1155–1166 (2014)
22. Leduc, G.: Road traffic data: collection methods and applications, January 2008
23. Mir, D., Isaacman, S., Caceres, R., Martonosi, M., Wright, R.: DP-where: differentially private modeling of human mobility. In: Proceedings - 2013 IEEE International Conference on Big Data, Big Data 2013, pp. 580–588, October 2013
24. Sweeney, L.: K-anonymity: a model for protecting privacy. Int. J. Uncertain. Fuzziness Knowl. Based Syst. **10**(5), 557–570 (2002)
25. Toilier, F., Gardrat, M., Routhier, J.-L., Bonnafous, A.: Freight transport modelling in urban areas: the French case of the FRETURB model. Case Stud. Transp. Policy **6**, 753–764 (2018)
26. Wang, H., Calabrese, F., Di Lorenzo, G., Ratti, C.: Transportation mode inference from anonymized and aggregated mobile phone call detail records. In: 13th International IEEE Conference on Intelligent Transportation Systems, Funchal, Madeira, Portugal, 19–22 September 2010, pp. 318–323. IEEE (2010)
27. Wang, S., Sinnott, R., Nepal, S.: Privacy-protected statistics publication over social media user trajectory streams. Futur. Gener. Comput. Syst. **87**, 792–802 (2017)
28. Wang, Z., He, S., Leung, Y.: Applying mobile phone data to travel behaviour research: a literature review. Travel Behav. Soc. **11**, 141–155 (2017)
29. Xiao, Y., Xiong, L.: Protecting locations with differential privacy under temporal correlations. In: Proceedings of the 22nd ACM SIGSAC Conference on Computer and Communications Security, CCS 2015, pp. 1298–1309. Association for Computing Machinery, New York (2015)

Author Index

Printed in the United States
by Baker & Taylor Publisher Services